The Christ-Centered Exposition series has been a steady help to me in pastoral ministry. This new volume from Phillip Bethancourt is written with careful exegesis and a rich grasp of biblical theology. I warmly commend this commentary to pastors, theologians, or anyone wanting to grow in their understanding of Genesis in the unfolding story of Scripture.

Matthew Boswell, hymnwriter, and pastor of The Trails Church in Celina, TX

It is hard to overestimate the importance of Genesis. This first book of Holy Scripture is the foundation of everything that follows. As we reflect on origins, the problem of sin, hope for a deliverer, and covenantal promises, we must engage the book of Genesis, and we must understand it. I'm thankful for Phillip Bethancourt's accessible, clear, and edifying commentary. Preachers and students will find it to be a faithful guide from start to finish.

Mitch Chase, associate professor of biblical studies, The Southern Baptist Theological Seminary

Understanding Genesis is essential to understanding the rest of God's revelation and to understanding the beauty and fallenness of our present world. This commentary is an essential resource for pastors who are seeking to preach this glorious book to their congregations. Bethancourt's thorough and in-depth insights help readers see Jesus in Genesis and connect the first pages of the Bible with the rest of the scriptural canon. You'll want to add *Exalting Jesus in Genesis* to your library.

Daniel Darling, director of the Land Center for Cultural Engagement and author of several books, including *The Characters of Creation*.

Well worth reading, rereading, and referencing. Bethancourt has a knack for keeping the larger Story of Scripture in view as he proceeds through the first volume of that Story. And he shows deftly and carefully how the contours in the outline of Jesus Christ sketched in Genesis are not an artificial imposition but arise naturally from it. Plenty of insights here as well as plenty of application and stimulating questions for study at the end of each chapter. Great for pastors and ministers as well as students of the Word.

Stephen Dempster, emeritus professor of religious studies, Crandall University

Exalting Jesus in Genesis brings together solid biblical exposition, thoughtful biblical theology, and pastoral application, with special attention along the way to contemporary issues related to ethics, culture, and worldview. Through the window of biographical and life-shaping accounts, the author seeks to walk us through the fifty chapters of Genesis by emphasizing the topics of creation, fall, flood, faith, faithfulness, family, struggle, and failure. Consistent with the overarching theme of the commentary series, this volume highlights, develops, and guides readers in insightful ways to think deeply about the Christ-centered themes of promise, hope, and redemption. Many will join me in offering gratitude to Phillip Bethancourt for providing this fresh look at the book of Genesis.

David S. Dockery, president and distinguished professor of theology, Southwestern Baptist Theological Seminary; president, International Alliance for Christian Education

This might be the most important volume to date in the Christ-Centered Exposition Commentary series. Phillip Bethancourt serves pastors and Bible teachers well through this volume, showing them that not only can Genesis be taught with clarity, but there is no better time than now for it to be taught. I am thankful for the heart behind this book and for the care it gives to guide church members to the important truths of Scripture and, most of all, point them to the Savior.

Jason G. Duesing, provost and professor of historical theology, Midwestern Baptist Theological Seminary

The great Bible teachers have often said that every single thing you need to know about God's Word and his plan for humanity is in Genesis, and the rest of the Bible merely expands on the themes introduced there. That's what you'll sense as you delve into Phillip Bethancourt's Christ-Centered Exposition Commentary: *Exalting Jesus in Genesis*. Insightful, faithful, practical, and inspiring, this is a resource you'll want to use for study, read devotionally, and share with others.

J. D. Greear, pastor, The Summit Church, Raleigh-Durham, NC

I was absolutely thrilled when I found out that the commentary for Genesis in the Christ-Centered Exposition series would be written by Phillip Bethancourt. What I appreciate about Phillip as a pastor and teacher of the Bible is his commitment to preaching Christ in all of Scripture, while simultaneously helping others to live practically the content being preached. He is both a pastor/theologian and a practitioner.

I know that when I preach through Genesis, Phillip's work will be the first commentary I consult. This will be a great resource for the church and for those of us who want to rightly understand, teach, and apply the first book of the Bible.

Dean Inserra, pastor, City Church, Tallahassee, FL

I am very pleased to recommend Phillip Bethancourt's wonderful commentary on the book of Genesis. Genesis is a book about "beginnings" and tells the story of the beginning of the cosmos, humanity, the people of God, and more. Bethancourt's pastoral and Christ-centered interpretation brings insight and understanding to this important book. His commentary not only informs our minds but also shapes our hearts.

Tremper Longman III, distinguished scholar and professor emeritus of biblical studies, Westmont College

Exalting Jesus in Genesis shows readers that Genesis is ever looking forward beyond itself to the glories of our Lord Jesus Christ. Genesis is not a history book, not even a history of Israel's religion, but a life-giving proclamation taken up by Jesus and the apostles to declare the salvation of creation and creature. Phillip Bethancourt has produced a biblical theology of Genesis drawing on both Testaments by tracing the theme of divine blessing fulfilled in Christ and his gospel. He gives readers insights that are spiritually enriching and intellectually stimulating. The study is written with clarity and understanding, available to all those seeking to better grasp the breadth and depth of this foundational story. Pastors and teachers of God's Word will be helped in their holy tasks by this informative study.

Kenneth Mathews, professor of divinity emeritus, Beeson Divinity School

Phillip Bethancourt's Christ-centered exposition of Genesis reflects the natural gifts that Phillip has to conceptually organize large amounts of information into organized systems. That's the very best of what biblical theology has to offer—understanding the text of Scripture within a unified horizon that tells one major story: the reign of Christ. Bethancourt tells this story masterfully by beginning literally "in the beginning." This commentary will benefit preacher and teacher alike as they understand the text and narratives of Genesis as a foreshadowing and typology of Christ's coming, his sufficiency, and ultimately, his victory.

Andrew T. Walker, associate professor of Christian ethics and public theology, The Southern Baptist Theological Seminary

CHRIST-CENTERED

Exposition

OT / COMMENTARY FEATURING CSB

AUTHOR **Phillip Bethancourt**

SERIES EDITORS **David Platt, Daniel L. Akin, and Tony Merida**

CHRIST-CENTERED

Exposition

EXALTING JESUS IN

GENESIS

HOLMAN®
REFERENCE
NASHVILLE, TENNESSEE

Christ-Centered Exposition Commentary: Exalting Jesus in Genesis
© Copyright 2024 by Phillip Bethancourt

B&H Publishing Group
Brentwood, Tennessee
All rights reserved.

ISBN: 978-0-8054-9655-0

Dewey Decimal Classification: 220.7
Subject Heading: BIBLE. O.T. GENESIS—
COMMENTARIES\JESUS CHRIST

Printed in the United States of America
1 2 3 4 5 6 7 8 9 10 • 29 28 27 26 25 24
BP

SERIES DEDICATION

Dedicated to Adrian Rogers and John Piper. They have taught us to love the gospel of Jesus Christ, to preach the Bible as the inerrant Word of God, to pastor the church for which our Savior died, and to have a passion to see all nations gladly worship the Lamb.

—David Platt, Tony Merida, and Danny Akin
March 2013

AUTHOR'S DEDICATION

To John Powell (1982–2020). Loving husband, devoted father, beloved pastor, and faithful friend. In sacrificing his life to rescue others from a burning car, John embodied the words of Jesus: "No one has greater love than this: to lay down his life for his friends" (John 15:13). Even in his death, John was showing us how to live.

—Phillip Bethancourt
February 2023

TABLE OF CONTENTS

ACKNOWLEDGMENTS

The book of Genesis tells a story of the fulfillment of a promise involving many people over many years. This book, too, was a labor of love involving many people over much time. Originally, this volume was intended to be cowritten with Russell Moore. I still remember being a young Southern Seminary student and soaking up the Christ-centered teaching series on Genesis that Moore offered the Dean's Class at Ninth & O Baptist Church in Louisville, Kentucky. That material laid a foundation for the earliest iteration of this manuscript. Though the volume shifted to being a solo project, the influence of Moore's thinking still shapes it. I am grateful for his willingness to allow me to adapt the research and content from our original efforts. Despite not being involved in the final version of the project, Moore mirrored Joseph, one of the key figures in Genesis, as he "gave instructions concerning [its] bones" (Heb 11:22).

The support of a number of other people also made this book possible. I am grateful for Daniel Patterson's steadying hand and keen eye, both during the early days of this project while we were together at the Ethics and Religious Liberty Commission and now as he serves as our executive pastor at Central Church. I also appreciate the aid and support of these team members: Patrick McGinty, Jenn Kintner, Andrew Walker, Dan Darling, Brent Leatherwood, Alex Ward, Jordan Cramer, Matt Herriman, Megan Shelburne, Sam Dahl, and others. I am particularly thankful for the efforts of Central Church's Matthew Emery, who played a key role in helping me get this project across the finish line. The opportunity to partner with all of them, not just on this effort but in all our gospel ministry, has made leadership over the last decade a true joy.

This effort would not have been possible without the encouragement of many family and friends either. First, I must recognize my wife, Cami. When Abraham's servant found Rebekah to be Isaac's wife, he rejoiced that God had "not withheld his kindness and faithfulness" (Gen 24:27). That's the way I feel toward God about you, Cami. You are a loving wife and faithful mother to our four incredible sons: Nathan, Lawson, Weston, and Hudson. Boys, I am grateful to have a front-row seat in watching God shape you into the men he has designed you to be. Keep seeking Jesus above anything this world has to offer! Also, I am grateful for my parents, John and Debbie, who modeled what it looks like to combine deep love for Jesus with a strong work ethic.

Gratitude to our amazing congregation at Central Church in College Station, Texas, must be expressed as well. I started there as a pandemic pastor, having been called to the church in April 2020 through a virtual voting process during the COVID-19 shutdown. It has been the greatest joy to return to lead this amazing church that deeply shaped me while I was a student at Texas A&M University. Our sermon series through the book of Genesis that began in 2021 profoundly influenced the heart of this volume. There is nothing I enjoy more than partnering with such an amazing group of ministers and lay leaders as we seek to be a church where every generation is reaching the next generation.

I am also grateful for my time serving in previous churches. First, alongside Ben Dockery at Vine Street Baptist Church in Louisville, Kentucky. Then alongside Jed Coppenger at Redemption City Church in Franklin, Tennessee. The two of you have worked on me like iron sharpening iron.

Finally, I am grateful for all those who partnered with me to make this book possible. I appreciate the initial vision of Jed Coppenger, who conceptualized this commentary series while working at Lifeway. I am thankful for the series leadership of Danny Akin, Tony Merida, and David Platt and their willingness to entrust this important volume to my efforts. I appreciate Andrew Wolgemuth's role as a friend and Sherpa throughout the book writing process. I am also grateful for Dave Stabnow and the team at B&H for their efforts in publishing this work.

One of the key themes in Genesis is that the story of redemption is not about us. From the first pages of Genesis, the storyline of Scripture centers on King Jesus. How thankful I am that God has used this current book's writing process to better conform me to the image of his Son, my King.

SERIES INTRODUCTION

Augustine said, "Where Scripture speaks, God speaks." The editors of the Christ-Centered Exposition Commentary series believe that where God speaks, the pastor must speak. God speaks through His written Word. We must speak from that Word. We believe the Bible is God breathed, authoritative, inerrant, sufficient, understandable, necessary, and timeless. We also affirm that the Bible is a Christ-centered book; that is, it contains a unified story of redemptive history of which Jesus is the hero. Because of this Christ-centered trajectory that runs from Genesis 1 through Revelation 22, we believe the Bible has a corresponding global-missions thrust. From beginning to end, we see God's mission as one of making worshipers of Christ from every tribe and tongue worked out through this redemptive drama in Scripture. To that end we must preach the Word.

In addition to these distinct convictions, the Christ-Centered Exposition Commentary series has some distinguishing characteristics. First, this series seeks to display exegetical accuracy. What the Bible says is what we want to say. While not every volume in the series will be a verse-by-verse commentary, we nevertheless desire to handle the text carefully and explain it rightly. Those who teach and preach bear the heavy responsibility of saying what God has said in His Word and declaring what God has done in Christ. We desire to handle God's Word faithfully, knowing that we must give an account for how we have fulfilled this holy calling (Jas 3:1).

Second, the Christ-Centered Exposition Commentary series has pastors in view. While we hope others will read this series, such as parents, teachers, small-group leaders, and student ministers, we desire to provide a commentary busy pastors will use for weekly preparation of biblically faithful and gospel-saturated sermons. This series is not academic in nature. Our aim is to present a readable and pastoral style of commentaries. We believe this aim will serve the church of the Lord Jesus Christ.

Third, we want the Christ-Centered Exposition Commentary series to be known for the inclusion of helpful illustrations and theologically driven applications. Many commentaries offer no help in illustrations, and few offer any kind of help in application. Often those that do offer illustrative material and application unfortunately give little serious attention to the text. While giving ourselves primarily to explanation, we also hope to serve readers by providing inspiring and illuminating illustrations coupled with timely and timeless application.

Finally, as the name suggests, the editors seek to exalt Jesus from every book of the Bible. In saying this, we are not commending wild allegory or fanciful typology. We certainly believe we must be constrained to the meaning intended by the divine Author Himself, the Holy Spirit of God. However, we also believe the Bible has a messianic focus, and our hope is that the individual authors will exalt Christ from particular texts. Luke 24:25-27,44-47 and John 5:39,46 inform both our hermeneutics and our homiletics. Not every author will do this the same way or have the same degree of Christ-centered emphasis. That is fine with us. We believe faithful exposition that is Christ centered is not monolithic. We do believe, however, that we must read the whole Bible as Christian Scripture. Therefore, our aim is both to honor the historical particularity of each biblical passage and to highlight its intrinsic connection to the Redeemer.

The editors are indebted to the contributors of each volume. The reader will detect a unique style from each writer, and we celebrate these unique gifts and traits. While distinctive in their approaches, the authors share a common characteristic in that they are pastoral theologians. They love the church, and they regularly preach and teach God's Word to God's people. Further, many of these contributors are younger voices. We think these new, fresh voices can serve the church well, especially among a rising generation that has the task of proclaiming the Word of Christ and the Christ of the Word to the lost world.

We hope and pray this series will serve the body of Christ well in these ways until our Savior returns in glory. If it does, we will have succeeded in our assignment.

David Platt
Daniel L. Akin
Tony Merida
Series Editors
February 2013

Genesis

Introduction

Genesis is the story of our spiritual family. To know who we are, we must know not only from where we came but also from whom. Genesis provides us necessary insight. The story of Adam and Eve is the story of us all. Abraham, the man of faith, is the spiritual grandfather of every Christ follower. The accounts of his life, as well as those of his descendants—Ishmael, Isaac, Jacob, Esau, and the twelve tribes—reveal much about what God is like and how he works to create a people for himself.

This commentary will introduce you to these individuals. But more importantly, it will show you how our elder brother Jesus is present from the beginning of the biblical story. This commentary will not focus on questions on which Christians of goodwill can disagree (such as the age of the earth). Instead, it will focus on the redemptive arc of Genesis and its connections to the larger story of salvation and redemptive history.

Genesis is all about a promise. The story of redemption begins in Genesis as God creates and humanity rebels. But the fall does not thwart God's plans. He promises to bring about an "offspring," a seed who will conquer sin and death (Gen 3:15). This promise becomes the plumb line of Genesis, indeed of all of Scripture.

Genesis is one of the most read yet least understood books of the Bible. Our familiarity with it can blunt its effect in our lives. But as the text unfolds, it addresses issue after issue that shows up today as a cultural flashpoint: creation versus evolution, gender identity, marriage, sexuality, race, capital punishment, abuse. That's all there in the ancient text. Yet the book of Genesis is not primarily about those things. It is not even primarily about the complicated characters at the center of the narrative or about the rules that guide their lives. It is not primarily about the historical stories captured there, either. Genesis—like the whole storyline of Scripture—is primarily about one thing: the kingdom of Christ.

Although a book full of human failure, Genesis is also one full of God's faithfulness. It is a book full of our pain, but it is also one full of God's providence. Throughout this commentary, I will highlight God's work in the lives of many individuals. His work is done to preserve the line of the promised seed who would redeem his people. Noah, for instance, is preserved from the destruction of the flood. Abraham is called from the nations. Joseph saves his family from a famine in Canaan. In all of this, God is working to accomplish his plan to redeem his people through his Son.

Importantly, Genesis is not a story about perfect people. Abraham is a paragon of faith but a cowardly husband. Jacob is a deceitful trickster. Joseph, at least in his teen years, is arrogant. Yet the story of redemption is one of God working through sinful people. He bestows blessing because of his grace, not because it is deserved. Yes, in the storyline of Genesis, God is continually at work through and in spite of the sinfulness of our spiritual ancestors.

Family history is often related with reference to genealogy. "Well, of course he's like that. Don't you remember his father?" "Well, her mother was the same way." "That whole family has always been a bit strange." We should not find it surprising, then, to see the story of the faith family begin with a couple in a garden walking in the presence of God before they and their offspring all tumble into sin. Nor should we be surprised to see it narrowing down to a humble couple in a stable swaddling the presence of God. He would bring both Jews and Gentiles into his family because of the work of Christ, who came as a human baby. Eventually, this family will find itself in the kingdom of God gathered around a risen King. All of that begins in Genesis.

The genealogies of Genesis, which highlight human faith but more so the faithfulness of God, point to his promise to multiply his people. Even the story of Lot's incestuous relationship with his daughters gives rise to the people of Moab, from whom would come Ruth, the great-grandmother of King David and ancestress of Jesus. The faith of Jacob concerning his burial points toward the hope of all the patriarchs: a "city" whose "builder is God" (Heb 11:10). The key to Genesis is the story of redemption. Creation. Fall. Promised Messiah. Hopeful expectation.

Christians should find in Genesis both hope and warning. We can be hopeful because in the book we see the faithfulness of God toward his Son and his people. We are warned about the danger of besetting sin. Nevertheless, we have a Father and elder Brother who are faithful to us even amid our sin.

The story of Genesis provides both the record of our shared beginning and the sign identifying where believers are headed. Humanity started in a garden walking with God. Redeemed humanity will end in a kingdom as coheirs with Jesus. Genesis does not just give us believers a picture of our past but a preview of our future. A glimpse into a coming kingdom. The book sets the stage for the entirety of Scripture to show us how God is faithful to his promises and preserves a kingdom for his Messiah.

In the Beginning, God

GENESIS 1:1–2:3

Main Idea: God establishes his kingdom by speaking the universe into existence. He designs creation to reflect his glory and goodness as humanity takes leadership over it.

I.   God Forms the Created Kingdom (1:1-2).
II.   God Frames the Created Kingdom (1:3-13).
   A.   The first day of creation (1:3-5)
   B.   The second day of creation (1:6-8)
   C.   The third day of creation (1:9-13)
III. God Fills the Created Kingdom (1:14-31).
   A.   The fourth day of creation (1:14-19)
   B.   The fifth day of creation (1:20-23)
   C.   The sixth day of creation (1:24-31)
IV.   God Finishes the Created Kingdom (2:1-3).

Genesis 1 tells how God created the world. It provides the setting for the unfolding narrative of Scripture. Chapter 1 shows who the main character of the Bible is—namely, God—and reveals his goodness.

The Bible's opening, in fact, is more concerned about the *who* of creation than the *how*. In contrast to the creation accounts of other ancient Near Eastern religions, Genesis 1 demonstrates the authority and sovereignty of Yahweh over creation. While many resources on Genesis consider complicated questions about the age of the earth and God's method of creating, this volume does not go into great detail. Instead, it recognizes there are numerous approaches to the specific details of the creation account in Genesis and that Christians can disagree on the mechanics of that account while still remaining in gospel fellowship.

Even so, three nonnegotiables are central to a Christian doctrine of creation. First, sound doctrine must recognize the virgin birth of creation, acknowledging that God creates *ex nihilo*. Before he speaks the universe into being, there is nothing in existence other than God. Second, such a doctrine must affirm the virtuous birth of creation, that

6

is, the goodness of all creation before the fall. Genesis 1 repeatedly declares that what God makes is "good." Third, sound doctrine must affirm the verified "birth" of a historical, literal Adam. As Jesus affirms in the Gospels, there is one man, created by God, from whom the entire human race descends (see Acts 17:26).

With the sentence, "In the beginning God created the heavens and the earth," the Bible begins in a manner both simple and profound. It gives a summary of the account ahead by portraying the timing of creation, the author of creation, and the scope of creation. Genesis 1, like each of the Bible's creation accounts (cf. Ps 8; John 1; etc.), affirms the centrality of the Creator. It also provides insight concerning the purpose of both humanity and the universe.

Chapter 1 of Genesis repeatedly declares how "good" God deems creation to be. But many readers miss this point. Indeed, it is not uncommon for pastors to overlook the goodness of creation in their teaching. Due to the spiritual nature of the Christian faith, their focus is often drawn toward the goodness of our immaterial souls instead of our bodies or the creation around us. But Genesis speaks a different story. It teaches us the goodness of God's creation expands beyond the spiritual realm into the physical world.

In Genesis, author Moses provides an overview of the earliest history of earth to his people. This helps them make sense of the world and understand their origins. Where we come from, after all, shapes the way we see the rest of the world and helps form our perspective of our purpose and future. That's precisely what Moses is seeking to aid in writing this passage. The land in which the ancient Israelites lived, after all, had many competing stories about how the world was created. Many of these myths involved cosmic warfare between divine beings. Most "creation" narratives from the ancient Near East assumed the universe itself had always existed.

Contemporary creation myths abound as well. For example, many scientists consider the Big Bang to be the explanation of the origin of the universe. In this view, creation originates at a specific moment and establishes space and time as the creation expands from its starting point. Many combine this account with Darwinian evolution to explain the origins of biological life through random chance and the survival of the fittest. Such ideas are not just scientific theories; they are the foundations of an entire way of thinking about the world. These origin stories not only give an opinion about where the universe came from. They also shape people's beliefs about the way humans should live.

Genesis 1 is given for our instruction. As we understand God's creation, we come to better understand his character and his redemption. The chapter shows us the way he works in the world. It calls us to live in accordance with the way he designed it to operate. It shapes how we live out the call to leadership that he gave humanity.

God Forms the Created Kingdom
GENESIS 1:1-2

Genesis 1 fundamentally shapes the rest of Scripture. It is not a saga, legend, or creation myth like those linked to other ancient Near Eastern religions. Instead, it is history. It is written to reveal how the universe came into existence and how God will unfold his purposes for his people. Genesis 1:1-2 reveals that God forms the created kingdom with his purpose and his presence.

Where Genesis 1:1 says, "In the beginning," many readers wonder how long ago that beginning actually was. Genesis does not clearly say. Rather, the words are intended to call attention to the fact that God was the one present and active from "the beginning." Still, the age of the earth is an important question that merits consideration.

Some modern Christians tend to assume that because ancient people were less educated than people living today, we should be suspicious of the beliefs they held. Modern scientists, after all, claim that the natural order is much older than the genealogies of Genesis appear to indicate. This apparent certainty has caused many people either to abandon or to reinterpret the teaching of Genesis at this point.

In light of this, how should Christians think about the Genesis account and the age of the earth? Believers must recognize that people do not evaluate the natural order as neutral observers. We should not be surprised by efforts to reinterpret Genesis in ways that seem more rational or realistic to twenty-first-century minds, nor should we be discouraged by those who reject the Bible's creation account altogether. As the apostle Paul points out in Romans 1, God has plainly revealed himself to all humans in creation, but fallen humanity by nature "suppress[es] the truth" in "unrighteousness" (Rom 1:18-20). Thus, whatever questions we might have on this or other topics, we are wise to hold fast to the clear teaching of Scripture.

Several points should be emphasized concerning the age of the earth. First, God is the Creator, and the creation exists solely because of the creative work God began "in the beginning." Second, the Bible offers no precise timelines concerning the age of the earth. Whether the earth and the physical universe are to be considered relatively "young"—mere thousands of years old as the genealogies of Genesis seem to indicate—while appearing to be much older, or whether the created order is millions of years old, Genesis clearly affirms that everything that exists only does so because of God's creative act. Third, any interpretation of Genesis that rejects God's role as the Creator, or Adam and Eve as literal, historical human beings, is in conflict with the Bible's teaching. Finally, it should be stated again that Christians may reach different conclusions about the earth's age while still enjoying fellowship.

Genesis 1:2 speaks of the "Spirit of God" hovering over the waters in a way that signals a pattern appearing throughout the Bible. The Spirit brings order out of chaos. Where do we see this language about the Spirit hovering as an act of new creation again? When Gabriel tells Mary that the Spirit of the Lord will overshadow her. This is the same kind of language used in Genesis 1 (Luke 1:35). And when the Spirit "hovers" over Mary, she will conceive a male whose coming will ultimately launch a new creation, a new humanity. Moreover, when her son Jesus is baptized, the Spirit descends on him after hovering over the waters of the Jordan River. And similarly, Jesus is raised from the dead by the Spirit of God coming upon him and bringing him back to life (Rom 1:4).

Genesis 1:2 also reveals the Trinitarian nature of God's creation. Throughout the Scriptures, all three members of the Trinity are associated with creation. In addition to the role of the Spirit highlighted in Genesis 1:2, both Genesis 1 and Psalm 8 emphasize the role of Yahweh in creation. And in Colossians 1:16, the apostle Paul tells us of Christ's role in creation. He writes, "[A]ll things have been created through him and for him." The beginning of the Bible thus shows the centrality of Christ to its story. Christ-centered redemption comes for a universe established by Christ-shaped creation.

God Frames the Created Kingdom
GENESIS 1:3-13

After God forms the created kingdom, he frames it with *light*, with *limits*, and with *land*.

The First Day of Creation (1:3-5)

Beginning on day one of creation, God frames the kingdom with light. His speech calls the universe into existence, bringing order out of chaos through the power of his word. This, in fact, is why the New Testament authors credit creation to Christ. He is "the Word" that is creating all things (John 1:1-3). God saying, "'[L]et there be light,' and there was light," signals that Jesus, the Word who becomes flesh, is present at creation.

God's work in creation week also reveals God's wisdom. Proverbs 3:19-20 tells us, "The LORD founded the earth by wisdom and established the heavens by understanding. By his knowledge the watery depths broke open, and the clouds dripped with dew." Genesis 1 shows us that God established the heavens and the earth through wisdom.

The New Testament tells us the wisdom of God and the power of God are personal. Paul the apostle says "the Greeks" search after "wisdom," wanting to know the way the world works, and "the Jews" seek "signs" of power, wanting to know how to control the world. But we know that Christ Jesus is "the wisdom" *of God* and "the power" *of God* (1 Cor 1:22-25). When we see God speaking the galaxies into existence, when we see God speaking light and life, then we need to envision Jesus of Nazareth. And when we see God declaring his creation is good or declaring its wisdom, we need to envision the same. This is the wisdom and power of God at work, so much so that Paul, when talking about the wisdom of Christ, is talking about it in terms of an ancient "mystery" (1 Cor 2:7).

God's speech brings about God's results. That is true in the creation account. It is true of the calling of Abraham in Genesis 12. It remains so throughout the Bible. Scripture repeatedly shows God's power through the productivity of his word. When Jesus walks by the fishermen and tells them, "Follow me," they drop their nets and do so (Matt 4:18-20). When Jesus speaks to people possessed by demons and commands the evil spirits to come out of them, the demons obey (Mark 1:25). As Jesus, on a boat in the midst of wind and waves, commands, "Be still," nature calms (Mark 4:39). So the power of God's word first demonstrated in Genesis 1 is underscored throughout the Bible.

On the first day of creation, God creates light, separates it from the darkness, and gives them names. The light he calls "day" and the darkness "night." But some are troubled that God does not create the sun, stars, and moon until the fourth day. That seems absurd. How could day and night exist without the sun and moon? Why would God do things in such a way? Many of the religions surrounding Israel worshiped the sun, moon, and stars. In contrast, Moses shows Israel that there is no autonomous sun or moon worthy of worship. Instead, God shows his sovereignty over creation in a way that drives his people to worship him and not the creation.

God's authority over light and darkness in creation helps shape our understanding of the conflict between the kingdom of light and kingdom of darkness that rages throughout Scripture. Because we live in an electrified world today, we tend to miss the significance of light as a theme. The people originally hearing these words, however, do not. In Scripture, "darkness" provokes images of danger, opposition, and hostility. Yet God shows that from the beginning he created darkness and has ruling authority over it. We have a King who sovereignly stands against the darkness of Satan's work in the world.

The Second Day of Creation (1:6-8)

On day two of creation, God frames the kingdom with limits. God declares his sovereignty over the waters, over the skies, and over the atmosphere. This second day introduces the important theme of water in the Bible. Its importance is difficult to grasp in a culture like ours where seemingly endless supplies of drinkable water are available at every faucet. But this situation is far removed from what the Israelites experienced.

For Israel and others in the ancient Near East, waters are chaotic and dangerous. They are both the source of life and the threat of danger. There is, after all, a risk both in an abundance of water and its absence. It brings flood and famine. Water is viewed as a threat to the people of God, as seen in their recounting of the risks of the sea and respect for its monsters like "Leviathan" (Job 41:25; Ps 104:26). Water is also a threat to the people of God in the thirst they experience (Exod 17:2-3). The desperation for water God's people have, in fact, is precisely why these words by Jesus carry such force: "If anyone is thirsty, let him come to me and drink. The one who believes in me, as the Scripture has said, will have streams of living water flow from deep within him" (John 7:37-38).

In Genesis 1 God shows that he creates the waters and separates them from the expanse. This is preparation for life. It is preparation for the flourishing of his image bearers. Indeed, God's handiwork is for those made in his "image" (Gen 1:27). When God creates the waters, he is looking ahead to a coming day when Jesus will sanctify his church with "the washing of water by the word" (Eph 5:26). He also anticipates a coming new creation in which a river of endless, life-giving water is present for his people (Rev 22:1). Water and God's sovereignty over the waters are central themes that recur throughout the Bible.

The Third Day of Creation (1:9-13)

On the third day, God frames the kingdom with land. God divides the land from the waters while creating the earth, seas, and vegetation. His creation of the seas establishes an important motif connected to the water imagery in Scripture. At times the Bible portrays the seas as a hostile enemy that invokes fear. For instance, when Israel flees from Egypt, they panic as they are trapped by the sea, before God delivers them from their pursuing enemies (Exod 14). Throughout Scripture, warfare imagery often includes references to battling against the sea and its monsters (Ps 74:13). That, in fact, is why it is so significant that God promises to bring his people safely through the waters (Isa 43:2). In Genesis 1 God artfully assures his people they should not fear the sea because it would not exist apart from him. As its Creator, he is the sea's master.

Two sources of fear in ancient culture were the sea and the land— two of the things already covered in Genesis 1. Anxiety about the sea was related to protection: Will I be safe even in the dangers of the water? Anxiety about the land was related to provision: Will I have enough from the land to provide? Those same fears about protection and provision still show up today, even if in different ways. Day three should transform our perspective of our fears. If God created the seas, he can protect us from the dangers of the sea. If God created the land, then he can provide for us. The same is true today. We can trust God to protect and provide for us. Genesis 1 reminds us of Romans 8:31: "If God is for us, who is against us?"

When we understand God's role in creating the seas, it reshapes our understanding of baptism, too. Jesus foretells his death by declaring that he has a "baptism" experience to undergo; that is, he will experience the wrath of God (Mark 10:38). As new believers are baptized, they are plunged into waters representing judgment and brought through them as a symbol of God's conquest over Satan, sin, and death (Col 2:12).

When God produces vegetation during the third day, it sets the stage for the many ways plant life will shape the unfolding story of Scripture. Vegetation proves important from what happens in the garden of Eden, to building the ark of Noah, to providing the staff of Moses, to creating the ark of the covenant. All of this sets the stage for a coming Messiah, whom the prophets describe as a root, a branch, a stump, a shoot (Isa 11:1). How does Jesus describe himself? As a vine (John 15:5). This particular vegetation theme started on the third day culminates when Christ the Savior of the world is hung upon a tree (Acts 5:30; Gal 3:13). Vegetation plays a major role throughout the biblical narrative, and Moses shows us how it all starts on the third day of creation.

God Fills the Created Kingdom
GENESIS 1:14-31

After God frames the created kingdom, he fills it with creatures made through his provision and with humans made in his image.

The Fourth Day of Creation (1:14-19)

On day one, God says, "Let there be light" (v. 3). On day two, God says let there be limits. On day three, God says let there be land. Now, on days four through six, God says let there be *life*. Why is it that God creates vegetation on the third day but does not create the sun, essential to its flourishing, until the fourth? God brings forth fertility before he creates the sun to show that he alone is the giver of life. He, not the sun, is the sustainer of life. Ultimately, the vegetation is not dependent on the sun or the phases of the moon but on God.

This stands in stark contrast to the beliefs of the fertility cults that surrounded Israel. In writing Genesis, then, Moses shows Israel that fertility cults are not viable because life comes only through God. The manner in which the creation narrative is recounted shows the futility of seeking solace in anyone but him. The fourth day of creation enables us to resist other gods confidently and honor the second of the Ten Commandments.

The creation story was intended to shatter the allure of the false gods of Israel, and it should do the same for us today. In our culture, people still worship contemporary versions of these ancient fertility gods that promise things like the American dream. The creation story reorients us to resist this siren song by instead worshiping the God who spoke the sun, moon, and stars into existence. Genesis 1 shows that God is the Creator of all, from the smallest plant on earth to the largest star in the galaxy. God shows his sovereignty over all living things by sustaining them through the provision of water and light.

The Fifth Day of Creation (1:20-23)

God creates the creatures of the sea and the birds of the air, calling them to be fruitful and multiply. As God begins to create the diverse animals, it shows the glory of his creativity. God does not actually need six days to create the universe. He could have created everything instantly. But he does things over six days according to a process. He speaks, and the sea creatures and birds come into existence; he evaluates them and declares them good. Why does he do things this way? God is showing his glory through his creativity. Just think about it. The size of the blue whale. The brilliant colors of reef fish and parrots. The grace of the eagle. The playfulness of dolphins. Every creature in creation helps display the glory of God.

The fifth day shows that creation is not just intended for the presence of humanity. The creation, in all its vast array, is intended to be home to the animals and also a temple worthy of the presence of God. Genesis 1, in fact, describes the universe as the temple of God and Eden like the holy of holies. The creativity of his handiwork sets the stage for the worship of his glory. God creates the universe and fills it with his presence. God creates the world with such majesty because he is going to take up residence in it. This picture of the temple points ahead to the way Jesus speaks about himself as the temple of God (John 2:18-22). It also foreshadows wonders to come (Rev 21:1-4,22-23).

The Sixth Day of Creation (1:24-31)

When reading Genesis 1, we may be tempted to gravitate to the sixth day of creation because that is when God creates humanity. But we cannot understand what God does on the sixth day unless we see how it serves as the capstone of what God has done on the first five. From the tiniest plankton to the largest creatures ever to have lived, God creates all the wildlife on the earth. Mentioned here are the same kinds of animals that Adam names in the garden (2:19-20) and that Noah rescues on the ark (chs. 6–8). Then God declares that all his creation is good (1:25). But note he says this before he creates man and woman. By doing so, God sets the stage for the coming of the capstone of his creation.

God makes humanity in his image and likeness. What does that mean? My wife and I are raising four boys. Several years ago, we stumbled upon the ultrasound image of our oldest. Even when people look at grainy pictures like that one, they often try to discern any ways a child looks like his or her parents. What we inherently know is that every child, in a sense, is an image of his or her father or mother. That's what Genesis 1 is saying about all of humanity. Each of us is, in a sense, a picture of our heavenly Father. We're designed to reflect who God is and what he's like.

In contrast to the rest of God's creatures, humanity is designed to reflect him in our character, our convictions, our calling, and our community. Our lives are intended to image who he is, what he does, why he created us, and how he connects us. The Trinitarian overtones in this declaration ("Let us make") are significant because part of what it means to be made in the image of God is to reflect him in community, in relationship (v. 26). As the text shows us, both "male and female" reflect this image (v. 27). Since every person is made in God's image, then this truth should fundamentally shape how we engage with one another. As image bearers, all people have the same inherent dignity—regardless of their age, sex, ethnicity, or socioeconomic status.

The image of God is best reflected in the life of Jesus. As Genesis 3 will soon show us, the presence of sin now distorts the image of God in humanity. Just as the broken screen of a dropped phone makes it difficult to see things on that phone clearly, so the fall into sin shatters the image we are designed to display. But in Jesus, the God-man perfectly reflects his Father in his character, convictions, calling, and in the way he pursues community. This is precisely why Paul declares that Jesus is "the image of the invisible God" (Col 1:15). Genesis 1:26 thus anticipates the coming Messiah who would fully reflect the image that all of God's people are called to embody. Jesus is both the architect and the blueprint for what it means to be made in the image of God.

The sixth day of creation calls humanity not only to reflect God's image but also to rule his creation. This passage speaks of humanity's obligation to rule, to subdue, to be fruitful and multiply, and to lead. God calls people to take dominion over his creation for his glory and our good. Instead, Adam and Eve reject this instruction by eating of the one forbidden fruit in a way that seeks their own glory, forsakes God's mandate, and trusts the false promises of Satan. In the coming of Christ, however, the Bible records the restoration of this kingdom leadership. Jesus rules over his enemies, subdues death, and fulfills God's command to be fruitful and multiply by rescuing a people for himself who can thus fulfill the creation mandate by the power of his Spirit.

God declares the sixth day of creation not just good but "very good." We are tempted to assume the broken world around us is what is normal, what God always intended. But Genesis 1 shows us that is not the case. As God finishes his work of creating the universe, he declares the goodness of the glory it displays. And in it there is no sin, no death, no sorrow, no sickness, no failure. God has established his kingdom, raised up its rulers, and called them to reflect his image as they take dominion over it.

God Finishes the Created Kingdom
GENESIS 2:1-3

After God fills the created kingdom, he finishes it with his own rest. The climax of the Genesis creation story, then, is not the making of mankind but the Sabbath rest of God. Why? Because the primary purpose of the creation account is not *what* is created but *who* created it. The text declares, "[T]he heavens and the earth and everything in them were completed" (v. 1); therefore, the work lacks nothing, and there are no loose ends to tie up. Only one chapter into the Bible, we see proof that God accomplishes what he sets out to do.

What does it mean that God "rested" on the seventh day (v. 2)? Is God weary from his hard work? No. Instead, the passage picks up on a theme common to the ancient Near Eastern literature of Moses's day, in which divine rest is connected to the construction of a temple. In such narratives, when a temple for a god is finished, its deity is said to rest in it in order to recognize its goodness. Likewise, Genesis 1 tells the story of how God builds a temple for himself. The creation is not just designed to house creatures and humanity; it is also the place where God intends to dwell alongside his people. God celebrates the completion of this temple by resting in it, blessing it, and declaring it holy. In the New

Testament, Jesus rebuilds the temple through his death and resurrection (John 2:19) and ultimately restores God's original design to dwell with his people in the new heavens and the new earth (Rev 22).

Genesis 2 begins by declaring the creation "completed." In other words, God looks at the universe and says, "It is finished." Does that phrase sound familiar? We do not just see it here at the start of the original creation. We also hear Jesus echo the words "It is finished" on the cross as he ushers in the new creation (John 19:30). This inauguration of the new creation on the cross is not celebrated from the comfort of heaven but from the agony of earth.

Genesis 2 never uses the word *Sabbath*; nevertheless, it establishes a trajectory that shapes the biblical narrative. The Sabbath is *created* as God rests on the seventh day, Saturday. Soon we will see how the Sabbath is *corrupted* by sin as our rebellion ruins our rest. Later, the Sabbath is *commanded* for Israel to observe weekly. The Sabbath is *confirmed* in Jesus's life as he honors it as Lord of the Sabbath. The Sabbath is *completed* in Jesus's resurrection as he, according to Hebrews 4, becomes our Sabbath rest. The Sabbath is *converted* in the early church as Christians begin to worship weekly on the Lord's Day, Sunday. The Sabbath will be *culminated* in the new creation as we experience an everlasting Sabbath rest in Christ.

We often think of limits, rest, and Sabbath as unproductive inconveniences to be endured rather than beneficial gifts to be enjoyed. But in Mark 2:27 Jesus says, "The Sabbath was made for man." God finishing his work on the created kingdom sets the stage for our work in the created kingdom—work that is ongoing but also benefits from periods of rest.

Reflect and Discuss

1. God repeatedly declares creation "good" in the opening chapter of Genesis. Why is it important to grasp that he says this of matter and the human body in particular?

2. Christians of goodwill can disagree about the age of the earth. However, they must affirm the necessity of a Creator and his divine work in the creation of the cosmos. Why is it necessary to affirm the personal and intricate nature of this Creator God?

3. Paul says Christ is the means through whom God creates (Col 1:16). How does the presence of Christ at the beginning of Genesis set a pattern for the rest of Scripture?

4. God speaks the universe into existence in the opening chapter of Genesis. The Son of God will later be identified as the *logos* or "Word" of God (John 1). What benefits come of embracing this biblical parallel? How is Genesis anticipating the coming Word of God? How is John pointing back to the creation narrative in the opening of his Gospel?

5. Throughout the opening chapter, God displays his authority by bringing order out of chaos, such as with his taming of the water on the second day of creation. In what New Testament instances does Christ exercise his authority over nature? What does this reveal about his character and power?

6. As God continues to create, each day sees the planet moving toward a definite goal: chaotic seas give rise to dry land, giving rise to vegetation capable of sustaining life, leading to the establishment of animal and human life. What does this contribute to a discussion of God's providence and sovereignty?

7. As God creates birds of the air and fish of the seas, the limitless creativity and artistry of his character are on display. Provide examples of how we as image bearers continue to share in his creative work.

8. Before creating humanity, God makes all the animal kinds and declares creation "good" (1:25). In what way is it good?

9. As the capstone of his creation, humans share in the image of God. They are bestowed with honor and dignity as representatives of God on earth. How, in spite of the curse, do they still display this honor? How do they anticipate the future incarnation of God as the true representative of God on earth?

10. God chooses to rest or enjoy his creation on the seventh day. In what ways is rest a part of the holy order he has created? How is rest an act of worship?

Rulers of the Kingdom

GENESIS 2:4-25

Main Idea: After Genesis 1 provides a wide-angle view of God's creation, Genesis 2 focuses on how he creates, commissions, and connects the rulers of his kingdom.

I. **God Creates the Rulers of the Kingdom (2:4-9).**
   A. The creation of Adam (2:4-7)
   B. The creation of Eden (2:8-9)
II. **God Commissions the Rulers of the Kingdom (2:10-17).**
   A. Life in the garden (2:10-15)
   B. Forbidden fruit (2:16-17)
III. **God Connects the Rulers of the Kingdom (2:18-25).**
   A. The naming of the animals (2:18-19)
   B. The creation of Eve (2:20-22)
   C. The unity of marriage (2:23-25)

When we think of monarchies today, we usually envision either a ceremonial monarch like those in England, who carry little authority to lead, or we envision a power-hungry despot who rules with an iron fist. Neither helps explain the function of the rulers God raises up in Genesis 2. God creates human beings to lead his kingdom, literally and benevolently.

Though God remains ultimate Ruler, he nevertheless establishes Adam and Eve as king and queen of the universe. They are called to reflect God in their rulership over all things. Starting in the throne room of Eden, they are instructed to expand the dominion of his kingdom over all things. To accomplish this good work, they are expected by God to obey his commandment and fulfill his commission.

Genesis 2 is among the most consequential chapters in the Bible because it documents the origin and purpose of humanity and the origin and nature of marriage. It thus establishes themes that reverberate throughout the entirety of Scripture. In raising up rulers of the kingdom, God reveals how humanity is called to join his mission of leading his glorious creation.

God Creates the Rulers of the Kingdom
GENESIS 2:4-9

As God creates Adam and establishes the garden of Eden, this section's focus narrows to set a trajectory for how humanity is to rule.

The Creation of Adam (2:4-7)

In this passage Moses connects the creation of Adam with the creation of the universe itself by recounting in 2:4 how these are the "records of the heavens and the earth." He documents more specifically how the Lord made humanity and then ties the creation of Adam into the larger creation story. There is a sense in which Genesis 2 is a retelling of the Genesis 1 creation story that focuses on the way God raises up rulers made in his image to lead the new universe. If Genesis 1 provides a wide-angle view of creation, Genesis 2 offers a zoomed-in shot on the sixth day.

This is the first of several times Moses uses the phrase *these are the records* to note a key movement in the plot of redemptive history. In 2:4 we also see the first time he uses the personal name Yahweh (translated as "the LORD") to refer to God. It is not a coincidence that Moses uses God's more personal, relational name when highlighting the creation of those made in his image.

There are several significant aspects of Adam's creation. Whereas Genesis 1:26-28 anticipates humanity cultivating the ground, 2:5 tells us that, before Adam, "there was no man to work [it]." When the text speaks in 2:7 of how God "formed" Adam, it documents the meticulous, handcrafted nature of this moment, as if God is a potter fashioning his handiwork from the earth's clay (Ps 139:13-14).

Until this point, God has created all things out of nothing (*ex nihilo*). But with the creation of Adam, God does something different. He forms him "out of the dust from the ground" (v. 7). Why? God is showing that humanity is part of the created order yet also is called to rule over it. Humankind is distinct. In recording that God "breathed the breath of life" into Adam, Moses is connecting the way God speaks life into the universe with the way he speaks life into humanity. Jesus confirms the creation of Adam as the first human in Matthew 19:4-5. The literal, historical existence of Adam, then, is an essential part of our faith.

In the creation of this shared forefather, Scripture anticipates the coming of a second Adam who will restore the kingdom the first Adam would fail to rule well. Because of the fall, Adam eventually dies and returns to dust. Jesus walks earth's dusty roads and takes God's judgment against our sin at the cross so that he might save those who are formed from dust. Jesus forfeits the breath of life in his death so that, by his resurrection, he might be the forerunner of those who will experience newness of life. Genesis allows us to witness God imparting physical life to the first Adam, just as he will one day impart spiritual life through the second. As Adam becomes a "living being," Jesus becomes a "life-giving" one in order to rescue those who are spiritually dead (1 Cor 15:45).

The Creation of Eden (2:8-9)

Genesis 2 also speaks of how God creates the garden of Eden as a physical paradise for his people. Thus the chapter tells both of creating the ruler and the throne room from which he (and she) would rule. Whereas Genesis 1 quickly recounts the creation of the entire earth and cosmos, here Moses lingers over the establishment of one place on the global map. Yahweh himself "planted a garden in Eden," revealing the special interest he has in this place. In one sense, Eden serves as the throne room of his own kingdom; the garden is the most holy place in the Edenic temple God establishes.

God fills the garden of Eden with evidence of his goodness. He places the man in the garden in order to rule over it, to establish his dominion over creation as God's vice-regent (vv. 7-8). But God also causes "every tree pleasing in appearance and good for food" to grow there (v. 9). Discerning readers cannot help but notice a foreshadowing of Genesis 3:6 in 2:9. Is it not significant that part of what lures Eve to eat the fruit of the tree of the knowledge of good and evil is that it is a delight to the eyes and good for food (3:6), when every tree God created there had those same attractive characteristics?

Moses mentions two trees among the lush abundance that are particularly significant. God places the tree of life in the "middle of the garden" to denote its centrality. He also establishes "the tree of the knowledge of good and evil," which anticipates the coming kingdom conflict that unfolds in Genesis 3:1-6. It is no accident that at the heart of God's kingdom his throne room centers on two trees representing eternal life and divine wisdom.

Eden becomes a powerful theme throughout Scripture. For instance, the prophets of God look back to Eden as they document what the people of God have lost (Joel 2:3). They look back to Eden as they celebrate the way God will comfort his people (Isa 51:3). The prophets also look back to Eden as they anticipate future redemption (Ezek 36:35). John, in fact, looks ahead to the restoration of Eden in the new heavens and the new earth. There, he says, the "tree of life" bears fruit every month (Rev 22:1-3). The second coming of the new and better Adam will one day restore the glory of Eden lost in the fall of man.

God Commissions the Rulers of the Kingdom
GENESIS 2:10-17

In Genesis 2 God does not just create Adam; he commissions him to rule over his kingdom.

Life in the Garden (2:10-15)

After further describing the setting of Eden, Moses highlights what God intended life in the garden to be like. Though the location of Eden described in Genesis 2 is not easy to pinpoint on today's post-flood map, its precise coordinates are not the focus of Moses's attention. Instead, he highlights the abundant resources that exist in this Edenic outpost of God's kingdom. In addition to the rivers that run through Eden, Moses speaks of the plethora of precious metals in this holy sanctuary. This description anticipates the imagery of the coming new creation, which will overflow with water and precious resources, too (Rev 21:15–22:2)

In the midst of the Edenic setting, God calls Adam to a life of faithfulness in productivity. In fact, God "placed" Adam in the garden for a specific purpose. What is it? "To work it and watch over it" (v. 15). Thus, in the beginning God places his people in the throne room of his kingdom to take dominion over his creation in a practical sense. The Hebrew words for "work" and "watch over" are used later in the Old Testament to speak of how the priests are to minister in and guard the tabernacle (Num 3:7-8). This connection implies that Adam is carrying out a priestly work in Eden as he tends to the holiest place in God's divine temple.

That God gives humanity the call to work *before* the fall leads to sin and brokenness is significant. It means labor is a part of God's good design for humankind. It is not simply a necessary evil we must endure because of the fall. Work is a key component in God's design for humanity; it is part of bearing his image in our daily lives. Indeed, even Jesus fulfills this particular creation expectation through working with Joseph as a carpenter and later in his ministry labors (Mark 6:3; John 5:17). Whereas Adam worked to protect the kingdom, we who trust in Christ now work to reflect the kingdom. This reflection happens best at the intersection of one's purpose, passions, and within his or her place. In other words, we believers reflect the kingdom most clearly when we serve at the nexus of why God created us, how God has equipped us, and where God has rooted us.

Forbidden Fruit (2:16-17)

God calls Adam to faithfulness not just in his work but also in his obedience. God commands Adam not to eat from one particular tree. Yet before God speaks of what Adam can't do, he highlights what he can. God "commanded" Adam to freely enjoy "any tree of the garden" (v. 16). God designed Eden in such a way that Adam can enjoy its fruits. There is freedom in obeying the commandments of God.

But there are also restrictions in God's commands. God tells Adam not to eat from the "tree of the knowledge of good and evil" (v. 17). Why? God warns, "[O]n the day you eat from it, you will certainly die." Disobedience will lead to death. This is the first time the idea of death is introduced in the Bible. The idea that disobedience will lead to death recurs throughout Scripture.

Most people assume the commands of God are either necessary evils to curtail the effects of sin or unnecessary inconveniences that rob us of the good life. But Genesis 2 shows us that faithfulness to God's commands is the key to the good life. Even before the fall, God's commands include both freedom and fences, liberty and limits, rights and restrictions, guidelines and guardrails—all for our good and his glory. God creates humans in his image with responsibility for their choices. Then God gives this restriction about the tree of the knowledge of good and evil to allow only one test of their obedience. At the heart of this test is a question: Who will define good and evil—God or us? Throughout the Scriptures, there is an anticipation of a coming Messiah who would faithfully keep the commandments of God.

God Connects the Rulers of the Kingdom

GENESIS 2:18-25

The last part of Genesis 2 documents the creation of Eve and the unity of marriage as the man and woman made in God's image reflect his Trinitarian community by becoming one flesh.

The Naming of the Animals (2:18-19)

Before God provides a helpmate for Adam, he shows him there is not a helper suitable for him among the animals. Moses records the words of Yahweh: "It is not good for the man to be alone" (v. 18). This statement stands out in the text because it disrupts the pattern of God declaring his creation "good." When God declares he will provide a "helper" as Adam's complement, he is revealing humanity's need for community. Even though God's created order is "good," Adam's experience is "not good" yet. He is designed to take dominion over creation within community.

This episode also demonstrates humankind's authority over God's creation. God brings every animal to Adam to "see what he would call it." Indeed, "whatever the man called a living creature, that was its name" (v. 19). Imagine you meet someone new and he tells you his name is Matthew. If you respond and say, "No, your name may have been Matthew. But now I have decided your name will be Jedidiah," he will think you have lost your mind. Why? Because you do not have the authority to give another adult a new name—though you can name your own child or a pet. Similarly, Adam has the right and responsibility with regard to all the animals, and he carries out this authority as part of his duty to take dominion over creation.

Adam's naming the animals anticipates the coming of a second Adam (Jesus Christ) who would carry out a similar mission. Whereas the first Adam provides names for the creatures, this new Adam gives a new name to his people by faith; it is the family name of our heavenly Father. And while the first Adam demonstrates his authority over creation, the Bible anticipates a second Adam who will exert his own authority by ushering in a new creation.

The Creation of Eve (2:20-22)

God provides a helpmate for Adam to join him in the call to dominion that he has given to humanity. Though God knew the man would not find a suitable helper among the animals, he allowed Adam to name them, in part, to confirm that need in Adam's mind as well. The text tells us "no helper" was found for Adam. So God crafts one for him (1 Cor 11:9).

In a final act of creation, God fashions the woman. How? While Adam stands among the trees, he is overcome with a deep sleep as he is pierced and a rib is removed. In other words, a bride comes from his side. Does this sound familiar? Later, when Jesus the second Adam is on the cross, he is not standing among the trees but hanging on a tree. He is not in a deep sleep but in deep agony when his side is pierced for our transgressions (Isa 53:5). By God's design, another bride—the church—comes from his side.

What is the relationship between the man and the woman? Technically, she is intended to be a "helper . . . corresponding" to the man, a complement (v. 20). This does not imply that Eve is inferior to Adam either in her inherent dignity or in her standing before God. Instead, it reveals that her role is to assist and serve alongside her husband as she partners with him to carry out God's call to dominion. The man and woman are equal in value yet distinct in roles. Genesis 2 shows us that even before the curse of sin corrupted the relationship between man and woman, God's good design for marriage included male leadership and female support. The complementary roles of husband and wife are not a product of the fall. They are not something we have to apologize for or minimize. Instead, male leadership and female submission are part of God's good design for the home.

The Unity of Marriage (2:23-25)

The marital union between Adam and Eve is so familiar to Christians that we can easily overlook its significance. Hearing this passage frequently referenced in wedding ceremonies and sermons can lead us to quickly gloss over its importance to the flow of Genesis and even to the entire Bible. So, what is God doing here? He does not just offer Adam a helper; God gives him a bride. God is not giving Adam a business partner; he gives him a life partner. Yahweh seals the sacred bond between this man and woman through the covenant of marriage.

Adam recognizes the significance of this marital union in verse 23. Since the woman is created from Adam's rib, she is, quite literally, "bone of [his] bone." And as Adam demonstrated his authority in naming the animals, he again displays authority and leadership by declaring, "This one will be called 'woman.'" Adam's relationship to Eve reveals God's pattern for relationships in the context of the marital union.

Moses's additional comments here also shed light on the covenant of marriage beyond that of Adam and Eve. When a man and woman marry, for instance, they are to leave "father and mother" (v. 24). The first marriage thus establishes a pattern in which a newly married couple transcends their former responsibilities and relationships in order to adopt and concentrate on new ones. The husband leaves the headship of his father, becoming the head of his own new home. This text implies that should husbands fail to take on that new leadership by continuing to cling to their parents, danger is ahead. Though the husband and wife are called to continue to honor their parents, they are expected to leave their authority and establish a home of their own.

As the husband and wife set out to form a new family, they find help in the distinct roles God designs for each person within the marriage relationship. The husband is called to headship, in which he leads his household by providing and protecting. Headship should be a loving leadership that glorifies God by seeking the good of the family. The wife is called to submit to her husband's leadership as she serves as his helpmate. Part of this involves nurturing and caring for her spouse and any children they might have. The primary disposition of the husband is never to be selfishness but sacrifice. The primary disposition of the wife is not to be skepticism but support. Both husband and wife glorify God by delighting in the roles he has designed for them.

In marriage, a husband "bonds with his wife" (v. 24). As a result, the two "become one flesh." That is, the man and woman unite in community through a holistic relationship consummated through their sexual intimacy. By God's good design, two distinct people are joined together in a one-flesh union through the marriage bed. Husband and wife are called to lives of sexual purity, which resist the pull to satisfy their sexual appetites outside the bounds of marriage (1 Cor 6:16-17). They honor God's design by pursuing faithfulness with each other through intentionality.

Moses confirms the goodness of this one-flesh union by choosing this point in the text to declare that the "man and his wife were naked, yet felt no shame" (v. 25). He also tells us this precisely because we will soon learn that nakedness, from the point of the fall onward, is associated with shame (3:7). Sin brings a disruption of intimacy; it brings a shame to nakedness. But Adam and Eve initially experience the goodness of their covenant without either.

The one-flesh relationship between husband and wife also provides for us a window into the relationship of the Trinity (Father, Son, and Spirit). In both marriage and the Trinity, there is unity and community. Yet there is also distinctiveness. The husband is still man; the wife is still woman. But they are one flesh. Likewise, each member of the Godhead remains distinct, even as they are one in essence. And though the husband and wife are equal in essence and dignity, they are distinct in roles. The same is also true of the Trinity.

Jesus shines greater light on the pattern of marriage established in Genesis 2 when he responds to questions from the Pharisees about divorce in Matthew 19:5-6. Jesus quotes this text to point out that, from the beginning, God has established marriage to be a lifelong heterosexual monogamous covenant between one man and one woman. Jesus recognizes a pattern in the first marriage that should shape every other. Over against today's cultural uncertainty about marriage, Jesus could not be more clear about what God designed marriage to be.

In an era filled with cohabitation, no-fault divorce, and same-sex unions, the picture of marriage described in Genesis 2 is under assault. In Scripture, such deviations from the biblical design for marriage are portrayed as disruptions of God's intentions. In cohabitation, a couple simulates the one-flesh union in a way that converts it into a relationship of convenience that awards all the benefits of marriage without the commitment and responsibility. In no-fault divorce, two people rip apart the one-flesh union in an act resulting in further chaos. In same-sex unions, the relationship between two men or two women ruptures the creational pattern of marriage between one man and one woman.

When Paul reflects on marriage in Ephesians 5:22-33, he reveals that the Lord created biblical marriage not just for the reasons above but to reflect the relationship between Christ and the church. Jesus is the bridegroom who lovingly leads his church by sacrificing for her, even to the point of dying on the cross, so that he might sanctify her. The church is the bride who willingly submits to her groom by following him in obedience and joining him in his mission. The relationship between husband and wife, then, is intended to reflect the cosmic mystery of the gospel. Genesis 2 anticipates the coming Messiah who would rescue his bride and establish an everlasting union with his church.

Reflect and Discuss

1. God gets into the dirt and forms Adam. Unlike the rest of creation, God molds, rather than speaks, humanity into existence. How does this contribute to humanity's uniqueness?

2. This first Adam will ultimately fall. However, the second Adam who will come will redeem fallen humanity. In what ways does the second Adam better fulfill the commands given to the first Adam to take dominion over creation?

3. After creating Adam, God places him in Eden. Its garden, the most holy place in the temple of creation, is filled with goodness. What does this show about how God desires to relate to humanity?

4. Adam is placed in the garden to work and care for it. Work is therefore not an effect of sin; it is part of humanity's creation mandate. What is helpful about this revelation?

5. God gives Adam the freedom to enjoy the garden and all its fruitful trees with one exception. What does this situation reveal about the commands and law of God?

6. The command not to eat the fruit of one tree is not meant to curtail Adam's joy. What is it intended to accomplish? And why does obedience to the commands of God lead to greater joy in the life of the believer?

7. As Adam names the animals, he exercises dominion over them. Even though some are stronger, faster, and larger than he. What evidence of humanity's special role over creation do you see today? Focus on positive examples.

8. How does Eve's creation signify her special role as a complement to Adam? In what ways is she to partner with him in the call to take dominion?

9. The relationship of Adam and Eve sets a pattern for marriage. In what ways do modern husbands and wives continue to follow the biblical pattern?

10. Explain how the marriage of Adam and Eve foreshadows the relationship between Christ and the church.

The Clash of the Kingdoms

GENESIS 3

Main Idea: The serpent's tempting of Eve and Adam to embrace sin launches an ongoing clash between two kingdoms that will culminate in the messianic arrival of the woman's ultimate offspring, who will one day crush the head of the serpent in victory.

I. **The Cycle of Sin and the Judgment of God (3:1-13)**
   A. Doubt (3:1-5)
   B. Deception (3:6a)
   C. Disobedience (3:6b)
   D. Disgust (3:7-8)
   E. Destruction (3:9-13)
II. **The Curse of Sin and the Promise of God (3:14-24)**
   A. The curse of sin (3:14,16-19)
   B. The cure for sin defeats our enemy (3:15).
   C. The cure for sin disarms our shame (3:20-21).
   D. The cure for sin delivers us from our exile (3:22-24).

The word *fall* has a widely understood meaning in our culture. We talk about someone's fall from grace or fall from stardom, and we all instinctively know we are talking about something that started off good turning bad. The word *fall* carries with it the idea of humiliation or demotion. A fall often leads to brokenness.

In Genesis 3, the fall of Adam and Eve into sin results in the brokenness of creation; it shatters their ability to reflect the image of God clearly as they were designed to do. The serpent's temptation and its sad results set the stage for the ongoing clash between the kingdom of darkness and the kingdom of light that unfolds throughout Scripture. In Genesis 3 the biblical narrative shifts from creation to corruption, from integrity to insurrection, from rule to rebellion. Genesis 3 describes "the curse" that has come not just upon human beings but also upon the entire creation.

God created the universe "very good," putting Eden at the center of it. In this garden sanctuary he meets with his priest-king, Adam, and the queen, Eve. From the throne room of Eden, they are called to rule, under God's care, over all of creation. But what happens in Genesis 3 as Adam and Eve fall into sin proves a serious disruption to all the goodness, eventually affecting not just humans but the entire created order. The first promise of rescue in the Bible, however, fuels a messianic hope that shapes the entire storyline of Scripture.

The Cycle of Sin and the Judgment of God
GENESIS 3:1-13

Genesis 3:1-13 describes how the temptation from the serpent leads into a cycle of sin for God's vice-regents, ushering in the collapse of the kingdom under the judgment of God. The unfolding narrative illustrates that while the schemes of Satan are often effective, they are not particularly creative. Instead, from this first encounter forward, Satan uses the same tactics over and over to lead people away from God's design. The sin cycle that repeats itself throughout fallen human history, in fact, follows a common five-step pattern we first observe in Genesis 3.

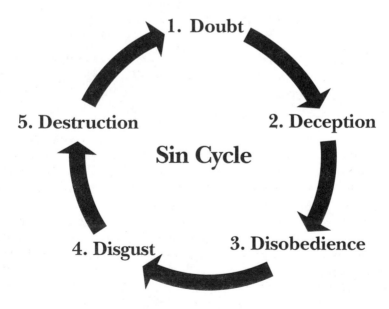

Figure 1: The Sin Cycle

Doubt (3:1-5)

The first step in the sin cycle is *doubt*. When examining Genesis 3, it is tempting to focus only on the fall itself. But the enemy knows forbidden fruit is tempting because of forgotten faith. He knows doubt drives deception. So he often slithers into our lives, sometimes unnoticed, and whispers in our ears. This is much like what he does to Eve in Eden.

The text describes the serpent as "the most cunning of all the wild animals that the LORD God had made" (v. 1). And this crafty creature invades Eden not by mustering troops but by slipping a sleeper cell of skepticism into Eve's psyche. Genesis 3 thus warns us he is calculating and crafty, detached and deceptive.

The first book of the Bible does not give us the true identity of this particular serpent. Not until the book of Revelation is it confirmed. John describes him as the "ancient serpent, who is called the devil and Satan, the one who deceives the whole world" (Rev 12:9). Therefore, just as demonic possession takes place elsewhere in Scripture, as when Jesus casts demons into pigs (Matt 8:28-34), Satan possesses this animal, and the evil one appears in the form of a cunning snake. Why a serpent? Scholar Leon Kass explains:

> [T]he serpent is a mobile digestive tract that swallows its prey whole; in this sense the serpent stands for pure appetite. At the same time, the serpent is cold [blooded], steely-eyed, and unblinking; in this respect he is the image of . . . icy calculation. (*Beginning of Wisdom*, 81)

The clash of the kingdoms is, at its root, a war of words. After all, how is everything made that is made? Through a Word, a Word that, as John will say, becomes "flesh" (John 1:14). That's how God brings the creation into order. The serpent imitates his approach but parodies it by using words to create destruction. He uses words to corrupt.

First, Satan tempts Eve to doubt the *word* of God. The serpent hisses, "Did God really say?" He is introducing doubt by questioning the revelation of God. Notice how cunning the serpent is. Rather than making a statement, he asks a question that leads to doubt. He then twists and perverts the actual instructions found in Genesis 2:16 so that God's command appears more restrictive than it is. He still employs this approach today.

Satan also tempts Eve to doubt the *wisdom* of God. When Eve replies to the serpent, she inadvertently allows his question to become a whole conversation. As a result, Eve begins to question what God really meant. This tells us the serpent successfully shifted the command of God to seem like something less potent. Now, Eve gets more focused on what God commanded than why he commanded it. Losing sight of the purpose of God can cause us to question the wisdom of God, too.

Satan even tempts Eve to doubt the *way* of God. He stokes suspicion about God's design for Eve's life. When he asserts in 3:4, "You will certainly not die," he suggests that God will not follow through on his promises. He also tests Eve's devotion by making it appear as if the way of God is not a pathway to her good but a barrier when he suggests, "[Y]our eyes will be opened and you will be like God." Satan thus turns the way of God upside down, making it seem a problem rather than a blessing. Today, he continues to insist that God is not holding humanity up but is holding us back, that rejecting God's way won't bring judgment from God but equality with him, and that rebelling against God's way won't blind our eyes but will open them to truly see.

This garden scene marks the first time people in the Bible doubt God, but it is not the last. For instance, after the storm rages on the sea, the disciples on the boat doubt Jesus enough to despair. After the arrest of Jesus, Peter doubts Jesus enough to deny him. Even after the resurrection of Jesus, Thomas doubts Jesus enough to dismiss him. So we Christ followers must not expect to be immune to doubt. Rather, we must remember that the serpent always initiates the sin cycle with suspicion.

One glaring problem in the Genesis 3 scene is that Eve is talking to Satan about her problems with God instead of talking to God about her problems with Satan. Every person in human history, though, tends to follow this same tragic pattern. At least until the arrival of Jesus. In the wilderness temptations, Satan sows suspicion with the repeated phrase, "If you are the Son of God." The enemy tempts Jesus to doubt the *word* of God through self-provision, the *wisdom* of God through self-protection, and the *way* of God through self-promotion. But Jesus knows distrust leads to disobedience. So he resists doubt through devotion and later empowers us, his followers, to do the same through the Holy Spirit. Nevertheless, every one of us—in countless situations—must decide if we will listen to the whisper of Satan or heed the words of our Savior.

Deception (3:6a)

The second step in the sin cycle is *deception*. Satan doesn't just test our devotion through planting doubt. He also tempts our desires through active deception. Satan seduces Eve by tempting her to satisfy good desires through consuming forbidden fruit. In every era of spiritual warfare, doubting the wisdom of God makes one ripe to fall for the deception of Satan. The technique of temptation employed in Genesis 3 reverberates throughout human history because the serpent still seeks to seduce us toward sin.

Satan often deceives with relation to our appetites. Eve, for instance, sees that the fruit is "good for food." Generally, the desire for food is good. As Adam and Eve live in Eden, they experience rhythms of being hungry then full, hungry then full. The appetite for satisfaction, then, is not part of the curse but part of how we are created. Yet the serpent deceives the couple into satisfying their appetites through eating forbidden fruit. The New Testament says all who are apart from Christ have a god, ultimately their own bellies (Phil 3:19). Indeed, people tend to serve their appetites. While in the garden, the appetites are subject to the word of God, but since the fall it's now typically the other way around. Whether it is the temptation toward consuming illicit fruit from a tree or the temptation toward viewing illicit images, a deceptive appeal to the appetites is at work. The serpent tempts us to find satisfaction through substitutes.

Satan deceives our desire for significance through our approval. Eve saw that the fruit was "delightful to look at." Isn't beauty a good thing? Yes. At the heart of our recognition of beauty is the desire for approval—to value or be valued, to affirm or be affirmed, to see beauty or be beautiful. Satan deceives her into seeking significance through forbidden sources. The problem is that the serpent's seduction causes her to desire approval from the creation instead of the Creator. Proverbs 29:25 warns, "The fear of mankind is a snare, but the one who trusts in the LORD is protected." This longing for significance through the approval of others starts in Eden, but it echoes through human history.

Satan deceives our desire for success through our ambition. Eve saw that the fruit was "desirable for obtaining wisdom." Wanting wisdom is good; after all, God is pleased by King Solomon's asking for it (2 Chron 1:7-12), and Colossians 2:3 says that in Christ are "hidden all the treasures of wisdom." The problem here isn't the ambition to pursue wisdom and power, then. The problem is the ambition to pursue wisdom and power through the path of the serpent rather than the path of God. Satan tempts us to seek wisdom through forbidden means, to seek power via forbidden paths, to seek ambition by traveling forbidden avenues. Eve is deceived into believing that caving in to seduction will supply the understanding she wants. But what happens as a result brings humanity face-to-face with a question Jesus will later ask in Mark 8:36 (ESV): "[W]hat does it profit a man to gain the whole world and forfeit his soul?"

Paul further warns us about the danger of the sin cycle as he explains Satan's pattern of deception in the New Testament era. In 2 Corinthians 2:11 Paul tells the Corinthian church that he has given them particular instructions "so that [they] may not be taken advantage of by Satan. For we are not ignorant of his schemes." He later adds, "But I fear that, as the serpent deceived Eve by his cunning, your minds may be seduced from a complete and pure devotion to Christ" (2 Cor 11:3). Paul thus warns that what happened to Eve can happen to any of us, too: we can embrace the message of a false gospel based in ungodly wisdom and reap devastating results.

God had given a good news message to Adam and Eve. In essence he said, "Trust me. Obey me. Eat of all of this fruit. Eat of the tree of life, but don't go near that tree of the knowledge of good and evil at this time, and I will bless you." Similarly, the church at Corinth had been told to believe the gospel of a crucified and resurrected Christ and be blessed by him. But as he did in Eden, the serpent came in and planted a seed of doubt. He uses this same tactic to tempt each of us away from pure devotion to Jesus and the true gospel. As Christians, we must be alert to the devil's cunning schemes and resist them.

Disobedience (3:6b)

The third step in the sin cycle is *disobedience.* Disobedience happens when deception drives us forward from desire to decision. It shifts us from seduction to sin. And with this shift, everything changes. Don't miss the way Eve slowly moves toward sin. Before she eats the fruit, she holds it. Cupping that fruit in her hand is the setup before the submission to sin. It's as if in taking the fruit, the fruit takes hold of Eve.

Can you imagine the impact felt as she bites down for that first sinful taste? No sooner does she shatter the skin of the fruit than does sin start to shatter the world around her. As juice trickles down her chin, certain death trickles into her heart. When Adam and Eve eat of the fruit and fall into sin in Genesis 3, we see a complete reversal of Genesis 1 and 2. Everything moves toward corruption and guilt, away from peace to strife and eventual war, and away from life to death. God's good design was for humanity to submit to him, for the wife to submit to the husband, for the beasts to submit to the humans. But in this one swift incident things change. The woman submits to a beast. The man submits to the woman. And no one submits to God. Eve, in fact, doesn't just engage in sin against God herself; she encourages it in Adam. Thus, this couple that starts out united in marriage is divided by sin. One of my friends offers an apt comment on this point: "Sinning together is the fastest way to tear two people apart."

What happens when the man, who does not appear to have engaged in conversation with the serpent, eats of the fruit? For him, at least for a moment, it seems as if the serpent is right. God had told Adam and Eve they would die if they ate the fruit, yet they don't. The consequences of their sin are not immediately evident. Nevertheless, from the moment Adam and Eve eat of the forbidden tree, they introduce death into the world. They—and any offspring to be born to them—are under a curse of death. "[I]n Adam," Paul says, "all die" (1 Cor 15:22). Death comes for all through one man (Rom 5:12). Adam is the head of the human race, so when he intentionally violates this headship by doing the one thing God said not to do, the consequences are catastrophic. The fallout will affect the entire created order and the rest of human history (Rom 8:20-22). Adam's doubt about God's word too, it seems, leads to his embracing deception, which ultimately gives birth to dis-obedience. With that disobedience comes death. Thus, though we as the descendants of Adam and Eve should reflect God just as humanity is still intended to do, we now default to rejecting God and failing in our chief purpose.

Disobedience does not just affect the human family. It brings a curse into the world. Under it, Satan now exercises dominion over the man and the woman, which means he also has dominion over the entire created order. One taste of forbidden fruit fractures the universe and brings about brokenness. What man and woman were given to rule, they no longer rule. Now, the entire universe is enemy-occupied territory. And this is the terrible reality behind suffering.

The coming of Jesus, however, changes everything again. The second Adam recapitulates the life of the first Adam. The temptation of Jesus doesn't start in a garden like Eden surrounded by abundance but in a desert surrounded by nothing. The wilderness temptations of Jesus in Matthew 4 mirror the temptations of Eden. In the first temptation, Satan tempts Christ's *appetites* by luring him to turn stones into bread. But Jesus resists the temptation to seek satisfaction through a forbidden substitute. In the second temptation, Satan tempts his *approval* by luring him to cast himself down from the temple and yet miraculously survive it. But Jesus resists this temptation to seek significance through forbidden sources. In the third temptation, Satan urges Jesus to receive the kingdoms of the world by bowing down to worship him, the devil. But Jesus resists this temptation to find success through Satan's forbidden solutions. This man alone stays faithful to God. Thus, the second Adam succeeds where the first Adam fails. And renewed hope for the human family—indeed for creation itself—is born.

Disgust (3:7-8)

The fourth step in the sin cycle is *disgust*. Disobedience isn't the end of the sin cycle. Instead, sin, after all, smuggles in shame. Disobedience dredges up disgust. After Adam and Eve grab and eat the forbidden fruit, guilt grabs them. Genesis 3:7 says, "[T]he eyes of both of them were opened, and they knew they were naked." In other words, their sin brings a sense of exposure and shame. What is shame? Disgust over having disobeyed. Shame tells us we are nothing better than our worst moments. In this fourth step of the sin cycle, Satan shifts from using his powers of deception to instead accuse (Rev 12:9-10). This tactic, too, can prove devastating. The serpent easily moves from seducing to shaming, from deceiving to devouring, from alluring to accusing.

Have you noticed that every children's book of Bible stories uses strategic placement of vegetation to cover the nakedness of the first couple? Without the fall, no one would think twice about a lack of clothing. Deep within ourselves, we have a sense of shame about nakedness that begins with Adam and Eve. They came to think of themselves in a new way as a result of their sin. Thus, when they look at each other, they don't primarily see the image of God anymore. They see reminders of sin.

What do they do in response to their shame? They respond in the two common ways we often react when we desire to disguise our self-disgust. First, we respond to our shame through control. They "sewed fig leaves together" to cover their bodies (v. 7). They try to manage their sin and mask their shame by controlling their circumstances. Typically, we too would rather cover our shame than crucify the underlying problem. We would rather manage the results of our sin than destroy it. But the only path past our shame is to quit running from it and start wrestling with it. That's what Paul declares in Romans 8:1: "Therefore, there is now no condemnation for those in Christ Jesus."

Second, we respond to our shame through escape—or at least a poor attempt at it. The brokenness that occurs after the fall results not just in an alienation from each other. It causes alienation from God. When the pair hears God walking in the garden, they spring into action (v. 8).

The Lord's entry into the garden foreshadows the special presence of God that would later come to rest in the temple of Israel. The Lord enters his most holy place to be present with his people. But Adam and Eve now have a problem. Their disgust fuels alienation, and they no longer want to be in God's presence, precisely because he is holy and they no longer are.

Where do Adam and Eve hide? "[A]mong the trees" (v. 8). Don't miss how important this detail is in the text of Genesis. God has just told them they may eat from all of the trees of the garden—except for the one of which they have now rebelliously partaken. And in their efforts to avoid confrontation on the matter, they flee into the abundance God has provided for them. There they cower, trembling in the presence of God, not wanting to come out and see him because of their shame. How often do we hide behind abundance for similar reasons?

Genesis 3 puts in front of us two ways we can respond to our disobedience: with disgust or with dependence. Every one of us, since we are all descended from this first couple, is a sinner (Rom 3:23). And by default each guilty party is either hiding from God with Adam or chooses to hide "with Christ," who can cover our shame with his own righteousness (Col 3:3).

But what if we trust in Christ yet still feel our shame? How can we embrace freedom? Hebrews 12:2 tells us that it comes by *keeping our eyes on Jesus, the pioneer and perfecter of our faith. For the joy that lay before him, he endured the cross, despising the shame, and sat down at the right hand of the throne of God.*

Hebrews 12 thus challenges us not to look inward at our sin but to look upward at our Savior. Shame focuses on our sin. Freedom focuses on his salvation. Shame focuses on our past. Freedom focuses on our future. Shame is defined by our failures. Freedom is defined by our faith.

Destruction (3:9-13)

The fifth step in the sin cycle is *destruction*. The sin cycle doesn't stop with disgust. Disobedience also brings destruction. In other words, sin leads to shame that culminates in sabotage. The effects of sin don't stay compartmentalized to one area of life; rather, sin affects everything. Genesis 3 describes how disobedience destroys our relationship with God, our relationships with one another, and our relationship with the creation we are called to rule.

Understanding the destructive nature of sin is fundamental. God calls to the first couple and asks, "Where are you?" (v. 9). Can you imagine the trembling in Adam's voice as he responds? Don't miss how abnormal this is: the human king who rules under God and enjoys audience with him is now afraid of him! Genesis 3 reveals a tragic shift in Adam's role: from ruling with God to running from God, from fearing (i.e., respecting) God to being afraid of God. In verse 11 God responds to Adam's fearful answer this way: "Who told you that you were naked?" Right away, then, he confronts the couple in their shame.

The alienation between God and man shows itself again in how Adam and Eve react. Keep in mind, Adam is still the king over the earth, appointed by God to be accountable and responsible for everything. Yet how does he respond to God's first and, more alarming, second question in verse 12: "Did you eat from the tree that I commanded you not to eat from?" Adam blames the woman ("[S]he gave me some fruit"), and then he essentially blames God ("[T]he woman you gave to be with me")! The woman, apparently following his lead, then blames the serpent (v. 13). Ever since, the tendency to shift blame to cover sin's shame has echoed throughout history. If the first sin is devouring the forbidden fruit, the second sin is devouring one another.

If you look back at figure 1, you will notice that the fifth step of destruction is not the final step in the sin cycle. Rather, the arrow goes from destruction right back to step 1. Why? Because destruction drives us back to doubt, and that supercharges the next round of the sin cycle. And with each loop around the cycle that we make, Satan pulls us further down the path of rebellion that first appears in Genesis 3.

So, how can we escape the cycle? Romans 5:15-18 shows us that it is not through our own strength but through accepting by faith the free gift of the gospel that was secured by the second Adam, Jesus Christ. Jesus endured the shame of the cross so we can be set free from the shame of our sin. Jesus endured the judgment we deserved so we can receive the righteousness we don't. Jesus endured the sabotage of Satan so we who take refuge in Jesus by faith can experience the freedom of salvation.

The Curse of Sin and the Promise of God
GENESIS 3:14-24

In the aftermath of sin, God's promises of judgment and salvation reshape his relationship with his people and his creation.

The Curse of Sin (3:14,16-19)

After Adam and Eve's sin, God puts a curse on the serpent that foretells certain judgment for Satan and coming salvation for God's people. He tells the snake, "Because you have done this, you are cursed more than . . . any wild animal" (v. 14). Why is it that many people feel great revulsion for snakes? In part because the serpent is cursed by God. There is, perhaps, even an underlying sense of rage that humanity feels toward them thanks to what happened in the garden. Regardless, as Satan spoke a word of deception and led mankind into sin, God speaks a word of judgment and places serpent-kind under a curse. Though Romans 8:19-23 speaks of a day when such curses will be lifted, there is no promise of redemption for this particular serpent. As the writer of Hebrews says, God does not provide redemption for the fallen angels (that is, the devil and his cohorts) but only for Abraham's offspring (Heb 2:16).

The first aspect of the curse is that the serpent will crawl on its belly, indicating that it did not do so prior. It should come as no surprise that, in Leviticus 11, God declares that animals that crawl on the ground are "unclean" and "abhorrent" (Lev 11:41-47). Snakes who "eat dust" are unfit food for the people of God in their pursuit of holiness because these animals would defile them. This is a continuation of the curse pronounced in Genesis 3:14.

Moreover, God's saying the serpent will eat dust emphasizes that it is now in a position of subservience because of the curse. What is the significance of dust? When the psalmist speaks about how the son of David will redeem God's people through victory, he declares in Psalm 72:8-9, "May he rule from sea to sea and . . . to the ends of the earth. May desert tribes kneel before him and his enemies lick the dust." Licking dust, then, is a sign of defeat. Likely remembering the curse of Genesis 3 as he composes, the psalmist declares that the defeat of God's enemies will include eating dust. They, like snake-kind, will be made lowly in the presence of the conquering King. In that day, God will defeat the ultimate serpent who initiated all the trouble, and he will do it through a coming son of David who will—to use more modern vernacular—make him bite the dust. Interestingly, Isaiah speaks of the restoration of dominion that occurs in the coming messianic kingdom. He notes the "serpent's food will be dust" then too (Isa 65:25). That particular judgment on the serpent always remains in effect.

In Genesis 3:16-19, the curse of God swiftly stretches beyond the serpent to affect the woman, the man, and the entire creation. What is the curse that comes on the woman? She will experience both pain in childbearing and a "desire" for her husband, who "will rule over" her (v. 16). This means the curse will affect Eve right down to her calling. What, after all, remains her great privilege long after being expelled from the garden? She is "the mother of all the living" (v. 20). She is the one who brings forth more human life. But thanks to the curse of sin that her disobedience welcomed into the world, she will experience pain and sometimes even sorrow in this childbearing act.

But notice that God does not curse Eve by making her barren. If God had done that, what would he be doing? He would be sentencing Adam and Eve to death because the only hope God gives them is the promise of an offspring who can redeem them by defeating the serpent. If God made her barren, the curse would bring a judgment that would nullify the promise of salvation he is making.

What does God mean when he says, "Your desire will be for your husband, yet he will rule over you" (v. 16)? Does this suggest Adam and Eve experienced an equal relationship before the fall but now the man will have headship over the woman? No, Genesis 2 presents the leadership of the husband over the wife as a glorious part of God's good creation. He is created first; she is taken from him; he names her and has headship over her. But theirs is a loving relationship prefiguring Christ's relationship with his own bride, the church.

So, what does God mean when he says, "Your desire will be for your husband"? Rather than referring to sexual desire, the language here is similar to what Genesis says later with relation to sin and Eve's son, Cain (4:7). This is important because it suggests Eve will desire to dominate and destroy Adam in much the same way sin would desire to do that to their son Cain. Before the fall, Adam and Eve lived in a sense of marital harmony as two become one. They built each other up. But ever since then, husbands and wives tend to use their desires and powers to break each other down. Instead of naturally supporting each other, they often subvert each other. Thus, the curse fractures that one-flesh union functionally as it creates discord through the struggle for power. Both the agony of giving birth naturally and the animosity that tends to arise in marriage point to humanity's need for the curse to be reversed.

To the man, God issues a curse in 3:17-19 that exposes his sin and also focuses on his vocation. When God confronts Adam's sin, he shows how the man has rejected his responsibility to rule over creation and protect his wife. The man surrenders his authority, falls into sin, and then blames her when God confronts them. God tells him that, because he abandoned his leadership and ate of the tree, a curse is coming upon the ground.

Why does God curse the ground? The curse falls on the soil to reflect the fact that God created Adam from the ground and called him to take dominion over it. This particular aspect of the curse means creation will now resist Adam's rule. As Paul points out in Romans 8, the entire created order now fights back against humanity's rulership as it groans under the curse of sin (Rom 8:23). Thorns, thistles, tempests, and tsunamis all reflect the curse of the ground Adam earns. This, in fact, is part of why the disciples find Jesus so remarkable when he can stand before the waves and command them to "be still" (Mark 4:39). As so many of the second Adam's miracles do, this one shows that he has the power to reverse the curse on the creation that came about as a result of the sin of the first Adam.

By this point in history, humankind has lived under the curse of the ground for so long that we assume it is normal for the creation to fight back against its rightful ruler. But when God tells Adam there will be "thorns and thistles" and that he will bring forth food by "the sweat of [his] brow," it shows us that many frustrations we commonly fight are not part of God's original good design for the world. They are reminders of the broken state of things. Reminders of the heavy—and often unforeseen—costs of sin as humanity seeks to carry out its calling.

The curse the man receives also carries with it a restatement of the promise of death warned about in Genesis 2:16-17. As if to make sure the couple grasps just what a sobering penalty this is, God tells Adam, "For you are dust, and you will return to [it]" (3:19). The thorns and thistles are symptoms of the decay that is pointing to death.

Today the curse of sin touches every part of our lives, from our closest relationships to our greatest responsibilities to our deepest fears. Signs of it both point back to how humanity abandoned its dominion at the fall and point ahead to how humanity will experience the judgment of sin in death.

The Cure for Sin Defeats Our Enemy (3:15)

In verse 15 God meets the couple's pain with a promise. With news of a coming cure for the curse of sin. This promise of judgment for the serpent, though, is behind the clash of the kingdoms appearing throughout the storyline of Scripture. God declares that he will defeat the serpent. But he will not do it unilaterally. Rather, he graciously promises victory over his enemy through the offspring of the woman. Satan deceived her, leading humanity into sin and fracturing creation. But her seed, her descendant, will be the one to restore all things and crush his villainous head.

In verse 15 God really makes the first promise of salvation. In Genesis 3:15 God makes the first promise of salvation. It is the seedbed for the gospel proclaimed throughout the storyline of Scripture. Every passage of Scripture is transformed by this verse. This promise of vicarious victory radiates throughout the entire Bible. When John the apostle looks at the history of redemption in Revelation 12, for instance, he depicts the kingdom conflict between the ultimate seed of the woman and the serpent. Starting with a reference to the woman experiencing the curse via the pain of childbearing, Revelation 12 displays the clash of Genesis 3. In light of Genesis 3:15, it is no surprise that the serpent seeks to "devour" the offspring of the woman (Rev 12:4).

In a sense, the entire Bible displays the ongoing kingdom warfare between the seed of the woman and the seed of the serpent. The exodus is about that; the Canaanites battling against the Israelites is about that; Herod's seeking to destroy the little ones of Bethlehem is about that. Over and again and through varied means, the dragon of old seeks to devour the offspring of the woman, specifically the one who is to rule all nations with a scepter of iron (Ps 2:9). (But he's pleased to destroy her other children too.) The whole Old Testament, beginning with Genesis 3:15, anticipates the coming, ultimate offspring of the woman who will destroy Satan. The head-crushing imagery shows up in the Old Testament's messianic prophecies (Num 24:17) and its messianic patterns (1 Sam 17:49).

Genesis 3 describes the first salvo in an ongoing war between the kingdom of light and the kingdom of darkness. Though Adam and Eve were called to dominion, they surrender their rulership when they fall into sin through embracing the deception of the serpent. The rulers thus become his slaves. The Bible repeatedly warns us, in fact, that we are slaves to sin and slaves to the one who is a liar from the beginning. How does the serpent exert such rule over humanity? Through his hold on our desires. The one who is made low to eat the dust of the ground now rules over God's creation in such a way that he is exalted as "the prince of the power of the air" (Eph 2:2 ESV). The only thing that can deliver creation from him is the fulfillment of the promise of Genesis 3:15.

Satan wars against humanity because he recognizes the threat of Genesis 3:15. He therefore seeks to subvert, deceive, and destroy humanity because he recognizes the head-crushing promise of the seed of the woman. He wants humanity destroyed because he does not want his head crushed. But Genesis 3:15 declares that one day God will raise up a deliverer who will restore God's people by defeating God's enemies. That's exactly what we see in the cross of Christ as he destroys the work of the devil (1 John 3:8). The nails on the cross that bruised Christ's heels remind us of the victory that crushes Satan's head. Jesus destroys his power to deceive and devour. The whole Bible is designed to tell the story of how Genesis 3:15 becomes a redemptive reality.

The Cure for Sin Disarms Our Shame (3:20-21)

That Adam is said to give his wife a name meaning "mother of all the living" right after the curses are spoken is a note of hope. It suggests to the reader that her identity is not to be defined by her shameful past but her hopeful future, which is secured in light of verse 15.

Despite God's words of judgment, he displays several other acts of kindness that foreshadow the mercy he will show his people as he restores his broken kingdom. For instance, when Adam and Eve sew "fig leaves together" to try to cover their shame, they fail (v. 7). But God does for them what they can't do yet on their own: he makes "clothing from skins" so they can cover their nakedness adequately. This starts a pattern of sacrificial substitution in the Bible in which sins are covered through the shedding of blood (Heb 9:22).

This pattern of sacrificial substitution culminates in the cross of Christ. Whereas in the garden God provides clothes to cover the shame of sin, Jesus is stripped of his clothes before the cross and takes on the shame of sin there. Not only is he naked, but as one who is publicly crucified, he is in the greatest position of shame a human can be in—so much so that the rest of the New Testament speaks about how Christians should not be ashamed of the scandalous idea of the cross with relation to the gospel (Rom 1:16). He is taking that aspect of the curse upon himself.

Other links to the tragic events of Genesis 3 are seen throughout the Passion Narrative. For example, it is no accident that the promised restoration of the kingdom begins in *the garden* of Gethsemane (John 18:1). And innocent Jesus literally takes the curse upon himself as he is crucified on *a tree.* "Cursed is everyone who is hung on a tree" (Gal 3:13). That a crown of *thorns* is placed on his head brings to mind God's curse involving the ground (Gen 3:18). In death, he is laid to rest with the expectation his body will return to *dust* like any other man's. Yet while Jesus chose to live under the curse and even die, he nevertheless triumphs. He is the rescue plan.

The Cure for Sin Delivers Us from Our Exile (3:22-24)

Though God graciously covers the shame of their sin, he exiles Adam and Eve—and all of humanity with them—out of his kingdom. This is the first exile mentioned in the Bible. God is not just saying that since Adam and Eve won't live by his rules under his roof, they must get out. Instead, God is protecting them and thus all humanity. He prevents them from eating the fruit from the tree of life so that they are not able to perpetuate their own lives in their fallen, broken state (v. 22).

Banning humanity from the tree of life is actually an act of grace. Should the man and the woman maintain access to the tree now that they have enslaved themselves to the serpent, to the evil one, only further wickedness, evil, and sorrow can result. As God has made clear, they must die. But dying is not the worst thing that can happen to them. Living perpetually under the serpent's dominion, separated from and at enmity with God is.

Nevertheless, God wars against his unfaithful people in exiling them from the throne room of Eden and setting up warrior angels to block them from the tree of life. These cherubim are warriors of light who block the entry to Eden with whirling swords of fire, keeping sinful humanity away from God's presence. Later, when Solomon builds the temple, images of these warrior angels are embroidered on the veil (the heavy curtain) that separates the holy of holies from the rest of the temple (2 Chr 3:14). But at the death of Christ, the temple's embroidered veil is torn in two. Why? Because God has made a way for humanity to get back into paradise and back to the tree of life (Matt 27:51; Rev 21:3-4; 22:1-4).

The second Adam experiences the same type of exile on the cross that the first Adam experiences in the garden. As he, the second Adam, is nailed to the tree, Jesus sorrows over the sense that God has abandoned him (Matt 27:46). Because at the time he wears the sins of the world, he too is driven from the presence of the Father, just like Adam and Eve. He is cursed, just like Adam and Eve.

Today, we are all in exile because of our sin. But the beauty of the gospel is that Jesus restores those who trust in him to the kingdom by taking on the shame and penalty of their sin. Ultimately, faith in what he accomplished on our behalf defeats our enemy, disarms our shame, and delivers us from exile. The clash of the kingdoms that begins in Genesis 3 finds its climax in the triumphant, curse-reversing victory accomplished by Christ.

Reflect and Discuss

1. God uses words to create; the serpent uses them to destroy. What might this suggest about how Christians should use the power of words?

2. The serpent's deception is to question the goodness of God. Why would the serpent begin here? In what ways do we question God's goodness in our actions?

3. From Eden onward, Satan uses the same sin cycle to lead us into disobedience. Which of the five steps in the sin cycle stood out to you the most? How does each step pave the way for the next one?

4. Give an example of how the serpent twists the good desires of Eve to bring about destruction. What does this reveal about the nature of sin?

5. The effects of the first couple's sin include the cursing of creation itself. How do our sins have consequences for not just us but others as well?

6. With the recognition of their nakedness comes shame. Why are they ashamed? How does sin corrupt the unity and innocence of Adam and Eve's existence prior to the fall?

7. Fallen Adam and Eve flee from the presence of God where they previously walked daily with him. How does sin distort the relationship between God and humanity? Why are they afraid?

8. Adam and Eve both attempt to shift their blame. What does this show about the nature of their own relationship with each other and also with creation? How has sin broken even the most intimate bonds?

9. The curse on creation also carries a promise of future victory. Explain what is promised in Genesis 3:15. When is this promise fulfilled?

10. God provides a sacrifice for Adam and Eve and uses the animal's skin to make clothes for them. How is this initial substitute pointing toward the perfect substitute of Christ?

Family Matters

Main Idea: The battle between the offspring of the woman and the off-spring of the serpent explodes as Cain murders his brother Abel. This scene displays the depth of the curse and the hope of God's promise as it reveals two ways humanity can leave a legacy.

I. **The Way of Cain and the Way of Christ (4:1-16)**
   A. The way of Cain leads to sin (4:1-7).
   B. The way of Cain leads to death (4:8-12).
   C. The way of Christ leads to new life (4:13-16).
II. **The Legacy of Cain and the Legacy of Christ (4:17–5:32)**
   A. The legacy of the way of Cain (4:17-24)
   B. The way of Christ shapes our family legacy (4:25–5:11).
   C. The way of Christ shapes our future legacy (5:12-24).
   D. The way of Christ shapes our faith legacy (5:25-32).

My family is filled with sons. As my wife and I raise four boys in our house, we are finding it nearly impossible to keep the pantry stocked. Our home is full of noise but, more importantly, also lots of fun. Nevertheless, there is potential for ongoing strife among the brothers. The curse of sin often shows itself through sibling conflicts.

When reading Genesis 4, we may think it is simply a passage about a sibling rivalry that gets out of hand. But something deeper is going on in the text. Behind the first rivalry between brothers recorded in Scripture, a spiritual war is raging. A war between the kingdom of darkness and the kingdom of light. The worship of God, after all, is often met by the warfare of Satan. Any time sin crouches nearby, the hidden dragon does too (v. 7; Rev 12:9). Adam and Eve may have left the scene of the first crime, but they couldn't get away from the presence and influence of the serpent.

In this brief passage Moses highlights the new normal of life as the first family begins to grow east of Eden. Now corrupted by the curse, humanity swiftly turns from living in community to contempt, from enjoying dominion to being dominated. Abel's blood cries out for justice, and the judgment of God thunders down upon Cain for the first murder.

In the midst of the carnage of Genesis 4, however, a gospel promise remains. Moses recounts Adam's genealogy in part to demonstrate how God will faithfully preserve the Genesis 3:15 promise to raise up an offspring from the woman, who will crush the head of the serpent. The text shows us how to embrace the image of God, walk in the presence of God, and cling to the rescue of God in spite of the curse. And while this section of Genesis shows that we are all capable of doing greater sin than we could ever imagine, it also proves God is capable of extending greater grace than we could ever deserve. What makes the difference is whether we follow the way of Cain, which leads to sin and death, or the way of Christ, which leads to new life.

The Way of Cain and the Way of Christ
GENESIS 4:1-16

After Adam and Eve are exiled from Eden, two of their children, Cain and Abel, choose two different ways to live (cf. Gen 5:20). The result is a narrative showing that God's plan to use Eve's offspring to crush Satan's head is at work despite the accumulating effects of the curse.

The Way of Cain Leads to Sin (4:1-7)

Though many rightly focus on the tragedy of Genesis 4, the first thing to notice is that the passage starts with the good news of the gospel. Why? Adam "was intimate with his wife" (v. 1). That is gospel. How? When Adam and Eve relate to each other sexually, they are rolling back the judgment of the curse. The coming of the curse of sin injects shame, disunity, unhealthy desires, and pain, which no doubt disrupted their relationship. Nevertheless, Genesis 4:1 proves theirs is still a one-flesh union. And through this intimacy, Adam and Eve begin to fulfill God's original call: that they be "fruitful and multiply" (1:22 ESV).

Genesis 4:1 is also a gospel message because it initiates an important step toward the fulfillment of the Genesis 3:15 promise: an offspring of the woman will defeat the devil. When Eve bears Cain, she recognizes the potential that his birth might have. In declaring, "I have had a male child with the LORD's help," she may be hoping this is *the* promised male offspring.

There is significance to the occupations of Cain and Abel, as each seeks to carry out the Genesis 1:26 call to dominion through his labors. Abel pursues the dominion goal in his role as a shepherd. He seeks to subdue, tame, and care for animals, despite the opposition the curse creates. Also imaging their father Adam, Cain works the ground (cf. 2:15). The cultural mandate to take dominion over creation does not stop with Adam but continues with his offspring. In both of Adam's children, the call to dominion is at work. As the text unfolds, we see these two men making two different offerings that show they choose two different ways to live. Ultimately, each person faces a choice of which of these ways to take.

It is notable that before Genesis 4 speaks of sin, it speaks of sacrifice. Many people tend to focus on the bad news of this passage. Before that, however, Cain and Abel still have a relationship with God that is expressed through their worship. This should capture our attention because after Adam and Eve are driven out of the garden, there is scant indication of what humanity's relationship with God is like. Nevertheless, their sons still call on the Lord, and he responds to their sacrifices.

Cain is a farmer, and his offering likely includes things like broccoli and brussels sprouts, "some of the land's produce." Abel is a shepherd, and his offering includes things like chops and shanks from "the first-born of his flock and their fat portions" (vv. 3-4). To these two offerings God responds differently. Though "the LORD had regard for Abel and his offering," he did "not have regard for Cain and his" (vv. 4-5). The text does not definitively declare why or how God showed his regard for one and not the other, but Cain's reaction reveals the problem is not just Cain's offering but Cain himself.

The way Cain responds contemptuously to God's lack of regard for his offering sets a trajectory for the entire storyline of Scripture. It introduces a way of life that reacts to circumstances with sin. Jude 11, in fact, speaks of "the way of Cain," recognizing that his behavior in Genesis 4 stands as an example of those who choose to live by a pattern of sin. I say "pattern" because a sequence emerges in the lives of those who respond to God's displeasure over their actions with further rebellion rather than repentance. Cain is "furious" and "despondent" that God finds in him (or at least his offering) room for improvement. And to the gentle wisdom God offers him, he responds not with any sign of turnaround but with the intent to murder (Gen 4:5-8). This extreme reaction may suggest Cain had tried to put God in his debt by offering him a sacrifice. And when God does not bless him as a result, he lashes out with jealous rage.

Abel and his offering represent another way of life that appears throughout the Bible, one of faith that looks toward the climax of what God will do to restore his kingdom. Abel, in a move reminiscent of how it took a blood sacrifice to clothe his parents just after their initial sin, brings the firstborn of his flock (the best of what he has) and offers fat portions along with the meat. (In ancient times, fat was considered the best portion.) Moreover, he gives it with what seems like a sense of humility, and God regards his offering. This first recorded animal sacrifice for the worship of God sets a precedent that permeates the sacrificial system of the Old Testament and finds its fulfillment in the sacrifice of "the Lamb of God" (John 1:29).

The way of Cain and the way of Abel are opposites. Cain's way of pride dishonors God and leads to further sin and death. Abel's way of faith taking action honors God and leads to blessing in spite of death. Whereas Cain may give an offering to put God in his debt, Abel provides a sacrifice in the belief that God one day will reverse the curse. Thus, Abel "offered to God a better sacrifice than Cain did" (Heb 11:4). In fact, in contrast to Cain, Abel gets "approved as a righteous man," according to the same passage. Therefore, "even though [Abel] is dead, he still speaks through his faith" (Heb 11:4). Millennia after his death, Abel is thus a force for good. People choosing to follow the way of Cain is a problem that continues throughout biblical history and even into our own day. But the way of Abel does too. A day came when the ultimate example of those who walk by faith, the Lamb of God, came and offered himself as a sacrifice. This offering God regarded so highly that he raised Jesus from the dead and extends the gift of life to all who trust in him (John 3:16; Rom 1:3-4).

The text also suggests that the problem with Cain's sacrifice is not just Cain's motive but also his mindset. What does Cain offer? Vegetation. In the law provided to Moses and Israel, God often requires the fruit of the ground as part of the sacrifices given to him (Lev 2:1; 19:24; Neh 10:37). Yet in this case, notice that right before Cain makes this offering, God has clothed Adam and Eve by replacing their garments of vegetation with animal skins acquired through the shedding of blood (Gen 3:21). This bloodshed is central to the Old Testament sacrificial system. Without its shedding, Hebrews 9:22 says, "[T]here is no forgiveness" of sins (cf. Lev 17:11). It is possible, then, that the main problem with Cain's offering is not so much what he offers as it is that he generally acts as if the fall has not occurred, as if the curse does not exist, as if there is no need for blood to be shed.

Interestingly, the New Testament shows the convergence of these rival offerings of vegetation and bloodshed in the Lord's Supper. In the symbolic meal that Jesus gives the church to eat in order to proclaim his death and remind them of the coming of his kingdom, it is bread (made from the produce of the land) and wine (from the fruit of the vine, but representing his blood) (Luke 22:14-20). It is vegetation. It is a restoration of the failed sacrifice of Cain. Yet that is not all it is. Jesus teaches that when believers come to the Lord's Table, they are eating his flesh and drinking his blood (John 6:53). In taking the Supper the church is proclaiming the same thing Abel did, though from a more informed perspective. Though we are under the curse of sin, the Creator keeps his word to send an offspring of Eve to crush the serpent's head. And through blood sacrifice—Jesus's own—humanity's standing in the kingdom of God can be restored.

A motif that emerges in Genesis 4 and runs throughout the rest of the book is the idea of the firstborn versus his brother. It shows up in the account of Ishmael and Isaac, of Jacob and Esau, and is central to the narratives of Jacob's sons. In the ancient Near East, the firstborn son normally receives the primary blessing from the father. He becomes the leader of the next generation of the family. Yet repeatedly in Genesis, this cultural pattern gets reversed: a firstborn fails and one born later is exalted. The early readers of Genesis would've found this shocking. To them, the unexpected reversals would sound like warnings.

Also important in this passage is that when God confronts Cain in his contempt, he warns him of the threat of sin. He asks Cain, "Why are you furious?" (v. 6). God implies that Cain has no right to be angry with Yahweh. The real issue is with Cain and his heart. God knows that in Cain's heart, "sin is crouching at the door" (v. 7). Behind fury, sin is lurking, as if hiding behind a door, waiting to pounce and cause new damage. We have already seen this crouching sin and the hidden dragon behind it in Genesis 3:1-6, as the serpent lured Adam and Eve into sin. God's warning to Cain parallels Jesus's warning to Peter when he was tempted to think more highly of himself than he ought: "Satan has asked to sift you like wheat" (Luke 22:31). Just as Eve will have a malicious desire for her husband that will lead to sinful conflict (Gen 3:16), so too will Cain—and all of humanity—because sin has a malicious desire to destroy us. In the call for Cain to "rule over" sin (4:7), God foreshadows the spiritual warfare all the people of God will face, seeking to follow the way of God and resist the deception of Satan (see Eph 6:11-18).

The Way of Cain Leads to Death (4:8-12)

The way of Cain is marked not only by sin upon sin. It always results in death. Since we live in a world in which news of death and murder fill the headlines, it can be easy to miss the shock of this first murder occurring only a few verses after the record of the fall. But Genesis 4 should appall us. A child of Adam and Eve, not the parents themselves, was the first person to die as a result of their choice to sin. And he was killed by his own brother.

Here we see the clash of the kingdoms of light and darkness at work outside of Eden. As a male offspring of the woman, Cain is supposed to crush the head of the serpent in bloody victory, but instead he crushes the head of his brother in bloodlust. Why? As the author of Hebrews tells us, Cain is jealous because "Abel offered to God a better sacrifice than [he] did" (Heb 11:4). The underlying problem, then, is not mere sibling rivalry. The problem is not that Adam and Eve did a poor job raising their sons. Instead, as the apostle John explains, Cain "was of the evil one," and his brother, as proven by his actions, was "righteous" (1 John 3:12). That is, Abel was a man of faith.

This murder is the opening salvo in the ongoing kingdom conflict between the offspring of the woman and the offspring of the serpent. Cain is of his spiritual father, "the devil" (John 8:44). So the issue is not just that he hates Abel but that he hates God. Behind anyone's hatred of others is really a loathing of God. Cain is so furious when God rejects his offering that he works against God's stated plan by killing another male offspring through whom God might have fulfilled the Genesis 3:15 promise. He thus does the bidding of the serpent. When anyone hates another person, he is following in the way of Cain. Such is a manifestation of the warfare between the serpent and the offspring of the woman. When Cain comes against Abel, he does the bidding of the serpent. It is a partial fulfillment of the Genesis 3 statement to the serpent that "you will strike his heel" (3:15). Cain is not just murdering his brother; he is murdering the offspring of the woman.

Cain escalates the sinful pattern of his father by shedding blood. He murders Abel, and Abel goes back to dust. Even before Adam draws his last breath, his son dies. This is a fulfillment of the Genesis 3 curse. Can you imagine Adam and Eve's horror when they learned the news that Cain has escalated the sinfulness of his father by shedding the blood of Abel? At the sight of their son's blood running into the dust, they come face-to-face with the reality that their sin not only ensured their own future deaths; it has now led to the death of one who was not party to their fateful choice.

Cain continues to follow in the sinful footsteps of Adam in what he says to God with regard to the murder. With echoes of God's question of Adam in Genesis 3:9, the Lord asks Cain, "Where is your brother Abel?" (4:9). In simply asking, God is exposing Cain's sin. Like Adam did in chapter 3, Cain deflects blame, asking, "Am I my brother's guardian?" (4:9). In the original Hebrew, Cain's question is a play on words: "Am I supposed to watch over the shepherd?"

God confronts Cain in his sin and curses him for his rebellion. How does God know Cain has sinned? "Your brother's blood cries out to me from the ground" (v. 10). Just as the consequences of Adam's sin spread to the entire universe, evidence of Cain's sin against Abel is spreading across the ground. Thus, humanity's sin once again causes the creation to groan in bondage, to accept things that never should have been (Rom 8:22). In Genesis 4 the ground groans because of the blood of an innocent man murdered.

Though the Bible does not have much to say about Abel's life, it repeatedly refers to his death. Jesus, for instance, acknowledges Abel as the first murder victim (Matt 23:35). Yet Jesus recognizes that Abel is actually the first martyr, too. Jesus says that when you look at all the prophets of God who have been killed, righteous Abel is the first (Luke 11:51). Thus, Jesus sees this first murder for what it is: the beginning of a pattern of spiritual warfare waged against his people.

The New Testament also presents the death of Abel as a type of the death of Christ. In Hebrews 12:24 the text speaks of how Christians have come "to Jesus, the mediator of a new covenant, and to the sprinkled blood, which says better things than the blood of Abel." There is a connection between the shed blood of Abel and the shed blood of Jesus, then. Abel's blood cries out from the ground because of the curse of sin. Jesus is the new and better Abel whose blood cries out from the ground as he becomes the curse of sin so that he might reverse the curse of sin (Gal 3:13). Abel is an early offspring of the woman who is struck by the offspring of the serpent. Jesus is the new and better offspring of the woman, and he crushes the head of the serpent. Abel the shepherd lays down the life of a sheep to offer a blood sacrifice that God regards. Jesus is the good shepherd who lays down his own life for the sheep, offering a blood sacrifice God regards once and for all (John 10:14-15).

God specifically condemns Cain for murdering his brother, his kin (Gen 4:10-12). As Scripture progresses, it speaks of kinship that is not just biological but ethnic and then spiritual. The church, for instance, is a spiritual family (1 John 3:1-2). Just as there is a heightened condemnation for Cain because he does violence to his kin, Scripture speaks against doing harm to our spiritual brothers and sisters in Christ. Therefore, conflicts in the church are not just a matter of clashing personal preferences. Instead, they are acts of spiritual warfare that undermine the gospel unity God has designed for his people to experience with one another. This is precisely why Paul repeatedly addresses ongoing conflicts in the early church. According to the New Testament, the problem in those situations is not human nature but satanic nature guiding people's actions. This is not just conflict. Instead, as Jesus says in the Sermon on the Mount, it is murder (Matt 5:22). In the church we are guilty of following the way of Cain when we slander, gossip, lie, divide, or quarrel. When Christians hate their brothers and sisters, they are actually hating the one who loved them to the point of death—Jesus himself. Such embodies the murderous spirit of Cain, not the merciful spirit of Christ. But the way of Christ is to wage warfare as a church community in order to put to death the destructive way of Cain and walk in the united way of Jesus.

It is easy to look on Genesis 4 and condemn the obvious sin of Cain. Yet Scripture teaches that every one of us has followed this path, though often in ways we may never even recognize (Rom 3:23). Those who face judgment apart from the mediation of Christ will be confronted with this question: How can you come into the presence of a new creation when you are still bearing a curse? Blood cries out against you because you, like Cain, have responded to God in rebellion.

How can someone know whether he or she is following in the way of Cain? Jesus, when speaking of "sheep" and "goats" in Matthew 25, shows us that the way of Cain appears when people see the needs of others and turn away from them (Matt 25:31-46). The apostle John frames it this way in 1 John 3:17: "If anyone has this world's goods and sees a fellow believer in need but witholds compassion from him—how does God's love reside in him?" When people are suffering or in need, then, do you open your heart to them or close it? The answer to that will help reveal whether you are walking in the way of Cain or of Abel.

The way of Cain leads to exile and death; the way of Abel can lead to Christ. True, on the one hand, Cain and Abel are already experiencing exile from God because their parents were cast out east of Eden for their sin. But notice that part of God's curse on Cain is that he is now "alienated from the ground" and destined to be a "restless wanderer" (vv. 11-12). A restless wanderer banished from the "presence" of God (v. 16). In this judgment, then, we see that the way of Cain leads to sin, leads to death, and ultimately leads to hell.

The Way of Christ Leads to New Life (4:13-16)

This passage displays several dimensions of the way of Cain that contrast with the way of Christ modeled throughout the storyline of Scripture. Cain's response to God's judgment turns inward in self-preservation rather than upward in self-surrender. Cain responds to God's judgment in fear. By this time, the population of the earth has grown to the point where he now is afraid that, in his exile, "whoever finds [him] will kill [him]" (v. 14). Cain panics because he believes someone who was close to Abel will seek to avenge his death. It is entirely reasonable for Cain to have this fear because we see kinship-related vengeance happen repeatedly in Scripture, beginning later in Genesis.

While the way of Cain is remorse, the way of Christ is repentance. Cain responds to God's judgment by saying, "My punishment is too great to bear" (v. 13). There is sorrow in his voice. But it is the anguish of remorse, not repentance. Ultimately, Cain is more concerned about how much his sin affects him than he cares about how much it affects God. Remorse groans at the consequences of sin, but repentance grieves at the commission of sin. When Cain resists repentance, he is missing the way of Christ captured by Paul when he says, "God's kindness is intended to lead you to repentance" (Rom 2:4).

While the way of Cain is violence, the way of Christ is mercy. This text reveals the depth of God's mercy. How does God respond to Cain's fear? Not with justice but with mercy. It would be reasonable to expect God to tell Cain that, if someone else kills him in an act of revenge, he is getting what he deserves. After all, as God says later, the penalty for shedding blood is having your blood shed (9:6). But that is not what

God does. Instead, God "placed a mark on Cain so that whoever found him would not kill him" (4:15). God shows mercy in protecting him.

While the way of Cain is sin, the way of Christ is surrender. This text reveals the depth of humanity's sin. Cain reflects the same corrupted, sinful nature that mars Adam and Eve after the fall. That sinful nature is embedded in each one of us (Rom 3:10,23). Cain follows in the sinful way of Adam by seeking to become his own God by rebelling against his word. Cain carries on the curse introduced by Adam's sin. That same curse affects every one of us. It is easy to ignore our particular sins because we live in a culture that wraps them up in a therapeutic package and justifies them with all kinds of explanations. But the Bible does not do that with Cain's sin or with ours. Apart from Christ, we are prone to the same violent vengeance. Every sinner is confronted with a choice: crucify the flesh or the flesh will crucify you.

The Legacy of Cain and the Legacy of Christ
GENESIS 4:17–5:32

In Genesis 4:17–5:32 Moses documents the emerging rivalry between the offspring of the woman and the spiritual offspring of the serpent as he records new developments in the legacy of the descendants of Cain and revisits Adam's line with relation to his son Seth.

The Legacy of the Way of Cain (4:17-24)

So far, Genesis has told the story of two ways to live. Now it tells the story of two legacies—the legacy of Cain and the legacy of Christ. What do we mean by legacy? Our legacy is our long-term impact from our short time in this world. Every one of us is leaving a legacy with our life. The question is, What type of legacy will it be? This passage shows us that one's legacy will prove either negative or positive. Genesis reveals that the type of legacy is often made apparent in a person's descendants (biological or otherwise). That is, legacy shapes lineage.

Moses portrays Cain as the first in a line descended from Adam and Eve that nevertheless shows itself to be spiritual offspring of the serpent. As previously noted, Cain does the work of the serpent by murdering his brother, proving himself to be a spiritual descendant of his "father the devil" (John 8:44). Genesis 4:17-24 documents the development of Cain's family line to show how the serpent's lineage perpetuates itself through him, effectively continuing the ongoing conflict with the offspring of the woman. What emerges in Genesis 4 and continues throughout Scripture is seed warfare—the seed of the woman battles against the seed of the serpent in an ongoing clash of the kingdoms.

There are several important things to notice about Cain as the text describes his legacy. Paralleling 4:1, verse 17 speaks of how "Cain was intimate with his wife." But, if verse 1 signals a message of hope through the birth of Adam's child, verse 17 warns of conflict through the birth of an offspring to one who remains unrepentant. Notice also the shift in Cain's occupation. He begins the chapter as a farmer working the ground (v. 2) but becomes "the builder of a city" (v. 17). The abrupt change makes it seem as if the trend toward sin not only affected his decision in the moment to murder his brother and reject God but also shaped the entire trajectory of his future. What is the name of this city? Enoch. So, rather than honor God in an act of humility, Cain honors his son through naming the city pridefully. Cain is trying to forge his legacy through his family. One who pursues legacy as Cain did seeks success through work and significance through the future of his or her family instead of finding those things from God.

Cain's attempts to build a legacy in part through outward successes leads to brokenness in a number of ways. Broken relationships are among them. Cain's descendant Lamech, for instance, becomes the first polygamist: "Lamech took two wives for himself" (v. 19). Thus, the seed of the serpent not only endangers the gospel hope through committing the first murder, but this rebellious approach to life contributes to fracturing the gospel picture of marriage through the first act of polygamy.

The legacy of Cain also leads to broken purpose. Technological advances that occur through Cain's descendants include the design of musical instruments and the use of bronze and iron tools (vv. 21-22). Even broken sinners in a line of rebellion against God, then, are able to reflect his image through the creation of new inventions and tools. But the problem is that those made in the image of God sometimes use such things in opposition to the purpose of God.

The legacy of Cain that Moses records is intended to reveal a pattern of generational sin that escalates the rebellion that has already emerged in the first few chapters of the Bible. Lamech, for example, reports the second murder recorded (v. 23), and he boasts of his actions to his wives! He also escalates the pattern of vengeance that Cain inaugurated, claiming that he will "be avenged" not just seven times like

Cain but "seventy-seven times" (v. 24). This attitude of escalated violence and vengeance sets the stage for the kingdom conflict that further
unfolds throughout redemptive history as the seed of the serpent wars
against the seed of the woman.

The Way of Christ Shapes Our Family Legacy (4:25–5:11)

In contrast to one following the way of Cain, one who follows the way
of Christ charts a different course for his or her family. The family line
of Adam experiences fresh hope with the birth of Seth, as Genesis sets
the stage for the good things yet ahead for humanity. Imagine, though,
the heartache of Adam and Eve. God has exiled them from Eden for
rebelling against him. God had promised them he would defeat their
enemies through the offspring of Eve. They likely hoped deliverance
would come through Cain or Abel. Instead, their firstborn murders
his brother. With one son disobedient and off to wander and the other
dead, it seems that all hope is lost.

Yet a new birth leads to new hope. When the text says, "Adam was
intimate with his wife again" (4:25), it is hinting that God is nevertheless faithful to his promise made in Genesis 3:15. Notice what Eve says
of Seth's birth: "God has given me another offspring in place of Abel"
(v. 25). Adam and Eve thus recognize the significance of this latest birth.
It signals another chance for the promise to come to fulfillment. By the
time this male grows up and fathers a son of his own, in fact, "people
[begin] to call on the name of the LORD" (Yahweh; v. 26).

Genesis 4:25-26 has the restoration of Eden in view as it not only
records God's faithfulness to his promise in Genesis 3:15 but also documents an emerging pattern of worship that will one day culminate in
the restoration of God's presence with God's people in God's kingdom.
Through a new birth, a substitute, an offspring of the woman. That is
exactly how he establishes our family legacy today—by the new birth of
salvation that only comes through Jesus, our substitute, who is the offspring of the woman who will crush the head of the serpent.

With the words "the family records of Adam," in fact, 5:1 signals the
next major section of Genesis. It documents the faithfulness of God as
he preserves the bloodline through which redemptive bloodshed would
come. While for many the genealogies are their least favorite parts of the
Bible, given their boring repetition, intimidating names, and seemingly
uncertain purpose, this passage is significant. Why? Because it presents

an early genealogy for the people of God. Some genealogies, like this one, exist for the sake of the gospel. They help explain the legacy of the people of God by offering a wide-angle view of redemptive history. They provide a picture of our past and a window into our future. The reason Genesis 5 is in the Bible is to demonstrate how God fulfills his word so that eventually Christ "would be the firstborn among many brothers" (Rom 8:29). Every name in it is pointing ahead to Jesus, the name above all names (Phil 2:9).

For those in Christ, Genesis 5 is an early family tree. It connects God's faithfulness from Adam through Noah and ultimately to all who belong to him through their faith in Jesus. This passage records ten generations of Adam's descendants in a manner that helps drive the biblical plot forward. Genesis 5 opens by echoing chapter 1, noting that (1) God "created man" by (2) making him "in the likeness of God," (3) establishing them "male and female" as (4) "he blessed them" (5:1-2; cf. 1:26-28). It records that Adam fathered offspring and sets an important trajectory for the way the Bible portrays families in the future.

One thing important to notice while reading genealogies is what features are distinct from the typical pattern that the passage and similar chapters follow. In the case of Adam's descendants in 5:3-5, one unique inclusion is that Adam "fathered a son in his likeness, according to his image." Just as God fathers Adam and makes humanity in his likeness, so Adam reflects the image of God by fathering a son who embodies his own likeness and image. The most shocking aspect of Genesis 5, however, is that it bluntly documents a series of deaths, reminding us that things are not the way they were originally designed to be prior to the fall. When this passage speaks about Adam, it notes that after 930 years, "he died" (5:5). God, after all, had warned Adam and Eve that they would die if they ate from the tree of the knowledge of good and evil (2:17). But the serpent deceived them into believing they could sin without consequences—which is still how Satan often works—and they ate forbidden fruit (3:4-6). From that point forward, humanity is "held in slavery all their lives by fear of death" (Heb 2:15). Genesis 5:5 shows Adam receiving the wages of sin (Rom 3:23). Yet while the first Adam tastes death as judgment for sin, Jesus comes as a second Adam who not only tastes death but overcomes it and will reverse the curse (Rom 5:12-21).

The Way of Christ Shapes Our Future Legacy (5:12-24)

If we want to understand the genealogies of the Bible, we don't just need to know their purpose but also their patterns. There are around twenty-five genealogies in the Bible, and this first one shows some common dimensions of their pattern. When they recount deaths, it is a reminder that things are not the way they are supposed to be. But when they recount births, it is a reminder that God has not given up on us. What should most stand out among the genealogies are the uncommon elements—those included people or asides that break from the typical script. This should catch our attention because it often happens for a reason. Each person's family tree has certain people who stand out more prominently, after all. Maybe one's ancestor was a French conqueror. Perhaps a grandmother's relative was Bonnie, from the outlaw duo Bonnie and Clyde. Such people stand out in a genealogy because there is something distinct about them. Adam's descendant Enoch, born of the line of Seth, is one of these uncommon people (v. 21). So far, the recorded trajectory for each generation has been that a man lives, fathers at least the son mentioned, lives longer, then dies. Yet a disruption appears with Enoch's name. What is it?

Enoch shows us that the way of Christ shapes our future legacy when we walk with God. Enoch had a close relationship with God. How do we know? Because the text interjects an unexpected comment, declaring, "Enoch walked with God" (v. 24). This revelation suggests a sense of intimacy unseen since before the fall (cf. 3:8). Notice the contrast: in Genesis 3, post-fall Adam hides from God in his sin; in Genesis 5, Enoch walks with God. This suggests the righteousness that comes by faith and anticipates a "walking" motif that permeates the New Testament to describe the intimate relationship Christians should have with God (Rom 6:4; 8:4; 2 Cor 5:7; Gal 5:16; Eph 2:10; 4:1; 5:2; Col 1:10; 2:6; 1 Thess 2:12; 4:1; 1 John 1:7; 2 John 1:4; 3 John 1:3-4; Rev 3:4). Christians, in fact, can walk with God the Father because Jesus walked the earth as God in the flesh. He was cast out from the presence of God in his crucifixion, so that we who place faith in him might experience intimacy with God through sanctification.

Enoch also shows us that the way of Christ shapes our future legacy when we are welcomed by God Instead of facing death, in fact, Enoch gets raised to newness of life. The passage tells us that rather than dying like Adam's other descendants, Enoch gets taken by God (v. 24).

Imagine how shocking this turn of events would have been for Enoch's family and friends. Hebrews 11:5 sheds further light on what happened in Genesis 5 by noting,

> By faith Enoch was taken up so that he should not see death, and he was not found, because God had taken him. Now before he was taken he was commended as having pleased God. (ESV)

The faith of Enoch, then, led to the favor of God. Enoch was pleased to walk with God, so God was pleased to welcome him.

What the Bible says about Enoch stands in stark contrast to the way of Cain. The legacy Cain sought to establish for himself and his progeny was all about outward success, advancements, and accomplishments. But Enoch's life shows that one seeking to establish a legacy in Christ goes about things differently. The believer's future is not based on his or her work but on his or her walk. It is not based on credentials but on character. It is defined not by pleasing others but by pleasing God. The way of Christ, foreshadowed in the life of his ancestor Enoch, tells us that one's walk with God is essential to shaping that person's legacy.

The ascension of Enoch anticipates the later ascension of Jesus. Christ is the new and better Enoch who doesn't just walk with God but walks as God. Just as Enoch pleased God and ascended to his presence, Jesus pleases God and ascends to his side (Acts 1:9-11). In focusing on the centrality of Christ's death and resurrection, it is easy to miss the significance of the ascension. But it shows that Jesus, as the fulfillment of the Genesis 3:15 promise and descendant of Enoch, conquered Satan, sin, and death and is now restoring the kingdom. Thanks to the ascension, the Messiah is currently "seated at the right hand of God" where he rules over the kingdom (Col 3:1). The ascension positions Jesus to pour out on his people the Holy Spirit as the spoils of his redemptive victory so that they too might experience the newness of life that comes with walking with God (Acts 1:8; 2:33). The way of Enoch anticipates the way of Christ.

The Way of Christ Shapes Our Faith Legacy (5:25-32)

If we want to understand the genealogies of the Bible, we don't just need to know how they relate to the purpose of God but also how they relate to the promises of God. In the genealogies, God shows himself faithful to the promise he has made in Genesis 3:15 to raise up a deliverer for his people. Had he failed to do so, you and I would be headed to hell. Death would have the last say in the human story. But the genealogies prove that God is not a liar. He keeps his promises in Christ. Many of the Bible's genealogies serve as the blockchain of redemptive history, recording the lineage of the people of God to verify God's faithfulness. Knowledge of the fulfillment of his promises strengthens our faith.

One specific way the genealogy of Genesis 5 shapes our faith is through hinting at a new hope grounded in a new rest. This passage concludes with the birth of Noah to set the stage for the flood narrative to come in Genesis 6–9. In this way, Genesis 5 provides a wide-angle link between the creation of all things in Adam's day and the judgment of all things in Noah's day. But in the original language, Noah's name means "rest." As Lamech names Noah, he hopes that somehow Noah will restore the Sabbath rest the people of God experienced before the rebellion of the fall. The whole Bible repeatedly tells the story of those made in God's image seeking God's rest, either failing to find it through idolatrous pursuit or actually experiencing it through faith (Heb 4:1-11).

Genesis 5 displays humanity's longing for God to reverse the curse of sin. The passage declares that at Noah's birth, his father Lamech says, "This one will bring us relief from the agonizing labor of our hands, caused by the ground the LORD has cursed" (v. 29). He hopes, then, that the curse of the ground inaugurated by Adam's sin (3:17-19) and amplified by Cain's rebellion (4:11-12) will perhaps be reversed by Noah's life. While things do not play out as he hopes, something fascinating nevertheless does. As Genesis 6–9 will document, Noah—descendant of Adam through Seth and Enoch and also ancestor to Christ—passes through the waters of judgment on an instrument of wood so that through him God might start to address the curse of sin. In this way, he anticipates the coming of the Messiah who, in the crucifixion, passes through the waters of judgment by being nailed to an instrument of wood so that ultimately he might reverse the curse (Luke 12:50).

Throughout the major developments of the family line recorded in Genesis 5, Seth's genealogy anticipates the coming of a Messiah who would finally fulfill God's victory promise of Genesis 3:15.

Reflect and Discuss

1. Genesis 4 begins with news of renewed intimacy between the husband and wife. Why is this hopeful news? How does it contrast with their actions in the previous chapter?

2. How does the call to taking dominion through work evidence itself in the lives of Cain and Abel? What does it suggest about the mandate to flourish and take dominion over creation?

3. God accepts both grain and animal sacrifices throughout Scripture (Lev 2:1; 19:24). So, why does God accept Abel's sacrifice but reject Cain's offering?

4. The response of Cain to God's preference for the sacrifice of Abel is not repentance but rebellion. Why do you think that we are so prone to continue in our rebellion rather than repent when faced with consequences for our sinful actions?

5. The pattern of the younger brother being blessed over the older begins in the Bible's first sibling narrative. But why does God choose to bless this particular younger brother? What might this suggest about God's plan and grace?

6. Ultimately, the murder of Abel by Cain is an attack by the serpent on the seed of the woman, though both men are her full biological offspring. What does this reveal about the continual struggle between these two lineages?

7. How is God's judgment on Cain also merciful? What does this reveal about the character of God?

8. The line that descends from Cain, who follows the way of the serpent, is a line of broken and sinful people but also creative people. What does this suggest about God and how he deals with those who bear his image?

9. The birth of Seth leads to the birth of Enoch, during whose lifetime people first call on the name of the Lord, "Yahweh" (4:26). What is worship? Why is worship the proper response to God's faithfulness?

10. The genealogies of Scripture serve to advance the story while also drawing attention to important figures. These are our spiritual ancestors. What is significant about the names included in this genealogy? How do you see the promise being fulfilled?

The Judgment of God and the Rescue of Noah

GENESIS 6–9

Main Idea: The story of Noah pictures in miniature the entire biblical narrative of the judgment of God against sin and the redemption of God's people through judgment. The Noahic narrative points toward the future salvation-through-judgment concept found in the Old Testament that culminates in the person and work of Christ.

I. **Noah and God's Judgment (6:1-22)**
   A. The purpose of God's judgment (6:1-7)
   B. The patience of God's judgment (6:8-16)
   C. The promise of God's judgment (6:17-22)
II. **Noah and God's Rescue (7:1–8:19)**
   A. God rescues us from the penalty of his judgment (7:1-16).
   B. God rescues us from the power of his judgment (7:17-24).
   C. God rescues us from the presence of his judgment (8:1-19).
III. **Noah and God's Covenant (8:20–9:29)**
   A. The Lord and the covenant with creation (8:20-22)
   B. The Lord and the covenant with Noah (9:1-11)
   C. The Lord and the sign of the covenant (9:12-17)
   D. The Lord and the lineage of the covenant (9:18-29)

In some ways, the Noah narrative is a return to the opening chapters of Genesis, when God calls the earth out from water and populates the planet with creatures. Repeatedly, Moses uses language that links Noah to Adam as a kind of second chance. Post-flood, Noah is told to "be fruitful and multiply" and receives a call to subdue the earth (9:1). Also, in his story it is reaffirmed that humanity bears God's "image" (9:6).

Noah represents a chance to succeed where Adam failed. Yet, in spite of getting many things right, even Noah will fail. And if Genesis 1–2 is the story of God's creation, then Genesis 6–9 is the story of the world's de-creation and fresh, though nevertheless broken, restart. In the end, the account of Noah further points toward the need for a future Adam who will undo the curse and fulfill the 3:15 promise of God. The narrative specifically foreshadows what is to come in the giving of the Noahic covenant.

Noah is portrayed as a person of righteousness who, like his ancestor Enoch, walks "with God" (6:9). His obedience to build the ark, seemingly in the face of scorn and ridicule, is evidence of his faith in God. Ultimately, Noah receives a covenant of blessing that will find its fulfillment in the person of Christ, who will be the means for the salvation of all peoples from God's coming judgment.

The Noahic narrative not only points ahead to the first coming of the Messiah but also to his second coming. Evidence of this is seen as Jesus refers back to Noah's story as an example of the judgment of God coming at the end of time (Matt 24:37-38; cf. Luke 17:26-27). The "coming of the Son of Man" will be much like "the days of Noah" in that people were "eating and drinking" and living their lives unaware of what was about to take place. In this way, the Noah narrative is not just a nod to what happened in the beginning but an anticipation of the end and what follows.

What is the story of Noah really about? Judgment for God's enemies. Rescue for God's people. A covenant based on God's promises. It is the story of God's redemption of humanity told in miniature. And for the reader, it offers both warning and hope.

Noah and God's Judgment
GENESIS 6:1-22

The opening of the Noah narrative unveils a pattern that will be found throughout the Bible. God is patient toward the sinfulness of humanity, but their growing rebellion will eventually result in his just judgment. Nevertheless, there remains the promise of a preservation of the righteous in the midst of that judgment and the hope for a future restoration after it.

In chapter 6, Moses repeatedly points back to the sinfulness of humanity, the corruption of the created order, and God's much-deserved judgment against all wickedness and evil. Genesis 6, noting that by Noah's day "every inclination of the human mind [had become] nothing but evil all the time," reveals the dark prevalence of sin (v. 5). From Eden onward, in fact, the darkness of sin expanded. The shadow of sin spreads. It seems as if there is no hope to stop it, until God steps into the picture. Noah first appeared in the text in 5:29, where we learn his name is related to rest and relief. But the relief his father Lamech hoped for when he named him does not show up as planned in Genesis 6. Instead, God's judgment falls and kicks off a new era.

The Purpose of God's Judgment (6:1-7)

Following the genealogy introducing Noah, Moses offers a broad perspective on the state of mankind in Noah's day. He speaks of the protagonist against the backdrop of increasing wickedness on the earth. God originally commanded humanity to increase and multiply to promote their flourishing and stewardship of creation. Yet here we learn that after the fall, such expansion of the human race led to an increase of wickedness, violence, and disorder across the planet.

Moses offers a striking example to illustrate the state of things. He writes of "the sons of God" taking in marriage "the daughters of mankind" (vv. 1-2). Great speculation has long surrounded the precise identity of these "sons of God" in particular. Every time the phrase "sons of God" is used in the Old Testament, it is in reference to angelic beings, and the New Testament authors seem to confirm that is the case in this situation (2 Pet 2:4-5; Jude 6). While their identity may be unclear, what is clear is that this development parallels the narrative of the fall. Just as Eve *saw* the fruit was *good* and *took* it, the sons of God *saw* the daughters were *attractive* [good] and *took* them "as wives" (Gen 6:2). Creatures, it seems, are continually being led astray by desires and appearances. At the opening of this chapter, only Noah stands apart.

What about "the Nephilim" (v. 4)? There is not sufficient space here for a full analysis of the Nephilim and their nature. This term itself is unclear too, and it is used in the Old Testament only one other time (Num 13:33). There the spies of Israel may have been connecting the native people of Canaan to these great "men of renown" known in previous days. Regardless, these people are said to be the products of the sinful union of the sons of God and daughters of men, and their appearance here accentuates the increased wickedness of Noah's time. What Moses focuses on is not the stature of their size but the stature of their sin.

This passage reveals that the purpose of God's judgment is not just to confront the breadth of humanity's sinful actions. He also means to deal with the depravity of our sinful thoughts. This section points to the fact that God cares not only about the outward actions of people but also the internal reality of their sin. Further, the sinfulness is not fleeting but the single motive for every thought: "[E]very inclination of the human mind was nothing but evil all the time" (v. 5). God declares that sin has infected every person, every moment, every intention, every thought, and every heart. Wickedness has become a way of life.

Moses characterizes God's response to this as one of sorrow and regret (v. 6). Thus, God is not pictured in the flood account as a disinterested Judge but as a grieving Father. This image of a God who is grieved by sin will continue throughout the Bible. Jesus, for instance, grieves over unrepentant Israel (Matt 23:37). Paul warns Christians not to "grieve" the Holy Spirit (Eph 4:30). God's grieving will result in judgment against sin and the near destruction of humanity from the face of the earth. The judgment seen here is not rash or arbitrary, however. In play are the thoughtful actions of a patient God who is also completely just.

The Patience of God's Judgment (6:8-16)

Humanity had deserved the type of sweeping judgment seen in the Noah account ever since that first sin in the garden. Yet God, Scripture reveals, often delays destruction not because he is weak but because he is merciful. The apostle Peter writes that God does not want "any to perish but all to come to repentance" (2 Pet 3:9). The entrance of Noah in verse 8 demonstrates this in that while *all* of creation is under judgment because of the wickedness of sin, the imperfect man Noah is said to find favor with God. The next three verses continue this contrast, describing Noah in ways that shed light on the special relationship he has with God.

God's patience protects a righteous remnant. The description of Noah continues by calling him "a righteous man" (v. 9). Importantly, this righteousness is not based on his works or lack of sinfulness but on his faith (Heb 11:7). Moreover, Noah is "blameless," a person of integrity in contrast to his peers. Noah is also one who experiences communion with God. Like Enoch, who walked with God (Gen 5:21-23), Noah experiences God's favor and enjoys fellowship with him. God's favor is the foundation of Noah's faith. God's righteousness is the root of Noah's righteousness. God's character is the catalyst of Noah's seeking communion.

This man's walk with God is uncommon, and it leads to a result that introduces another biblical concept. As 1 Peter 3:20 says, "God patiently waited in the days of Noah while the ark was being prepared."

Why is God said to be patient with regard to this time? For the same reason he is patient now—because he desires to protect a righteous remnant for rescue.

God's patience preserves a corrupted creation. The next section of verses returns to the wickedness of the created order by describing not only the corruption of humanity but of all creation (Gen 6:11). As the wickedness of humanity increases, so too does the corruption of the earth as a result of events in Genesis 3. Christians should not be surprised by this given the apostle Paul's insight that the entire creation is "groaning" for redemption (Rom 8:19-22).

In the flood narrative, everything comes under God's judgment. This foreshadows the total nature of God's wrath that is poured out on Christ at the cross. But God does not give up on creation. In his patience, he preserves it. Just as the flood of waters cleanses the earth and launches a new creation in Noah's day, the judgment events described in Revelation will cleanse the corruption of sin from it again and usher in a new creation at Christ's return.

God's patience provides an unexpected deliverance. What follows is a description of the command from God to Noah to build the ark (Gen 6:14). His building the massive vessel likely appeared ridiculous to Noah's neighbors, and he may have faced ridicule, particularly if his land was near no large body of water. Regardless, to onlookers there would have seemed no need for this ark, which was longer than an American football field. What matters most in this passage, however, is not the size and shape of the boat but the size and shape of God's patience and plan that leads to rescue. The vessel is large enough to house Noah, his family, two of every land animal kind, and birds too. There is also plenty of room for food stores to see them through the coming storm (vv. 19-21).

God promises a deliverance Noah did not deserve through a rescue he did not expect. This deliverance from the waters of judgment foreshadows the unexpected deliverance God would one day offer through his Son. Just as God rescues Noah from his wrath via an instrument of wood, God rescues the believing masses from the waters of judgment through events involving another instrument of wood—the cross of Christ.

The Promise of God's Judgment (6:17-22)

Despite the difficulties and demands the building of this ark poses, Noah perseveres because of the reason for the command: God is sending a flood to wipe out humanity and animal life (v. 17). *Certain judgment* is coming. Keeping in mind the context of the larger picture (the coming flood) helps Noah persevere in the smaller pictures of his everyday life (accumulating materials and workers to build the boat, collecting food, etc.). Believing what God says about the flood and embracing what he is to do in the meantime causes him to press on in the mission. This reflects the way God wants to work in our lives today. As we believers come to understand the larger narrative of what God is doing through Christ for the world and actively set about the mission of sharing the gospel so that others might be spared God's wrath, we find it easier to remain faithful to that calling no matter the difficulties.

This chapter culminates with the promise of *covenantal judgment*. In verses 18-21, we see the initial promise of the covenant, which is later given to Noah in full (8:15-22). It is the promise of a future for humanity through Noah and his family. Restoration will follow the judgment. The covenant is not only for humanity, however, but for all of creation. This theme carries on throughout the Bible: God preserves a righteous remnant for the restoration of creation in the wake of his judgment. In this instance, not only is the family of Noah saved, but also at least two of every animal is spared.

The response of Noah to this command and covenant promise is obedience. Twice in verse 22 Moses highlights the obedience of Noah. This points to the truth that it is not enough to have knowledge of the calling of God for our lives. We must also act in obedience to that calling.

This chapter concludes with the promise of *coming judgment*. The sweeping wrath mentioned in it points to the truth of humanity's universal need for salvation. Just as sin is widespread and universal in the time of Noah, it is much the same today. In fact, Paul the apostle notes that "there is no one righteous" (Rom 3:10). The hardness of heart at work in the time of Noah is not unique to his time in history. But the declaration of the gospel is that hardened hearts that lie under judgment are offered salvation through the person and work of Christ. Jesus makes clear in Matthew 24:36-44 that the story of Noah doesn't just point ahead to his own first coming but also to his second. God's judgment in Genesis 6 is a preview of the judgment that awaits the whole world at the return of Christ. The waters of judgment are gathering above. So the question each person must wrestle with is this: Am I in the boat? That is, am I trusting in Jesus, the only way of rescue from the judgment?

Noah and God's Rescue

GENESIS 7:1–8:19

If Genesis 6 shows us the need for salvation, this section shows us the way of salvation. In the narrative, the complete salvation God gives to Noah and his family is paralleled with the complete judgment against the wickedness of the rest of humanity. As judgment arrives in the form of a total flood, God chooses to extend grace to faith-filled Noah and his family. This starts a pattern involving the redemption of a righteous remnant that will continue throughout Scripture.

God Rescues Us from the Penalty of His Judgment (7:1-16)

Humanity's salvation depends on God's rescue from the penalty of his own coming judgment. Noah has lived by faith and in obedience to God's direction for many years. Now God commands Noah to enter the ark because it is time for the promised rescue, time for him to be spared the penalty of his judgment that the whole world outside the ark faces. This passage answers several questions about the nature of God's rescue of people from the penalty of judgment.

First, why does God rescue anyone? The end of verse 1 explains why God rescues Noah. The Lord says, "I have seen that you alone are righteous before me in this generation." And what is the basis of Noah's righteousness? It is tempting to assume it is based on Noah's obedience, since he did all the Lord commanded him (6:22; 7:5). As we live in a dark culture just like Noah, there is, after all, an ongoing danger in believing that one can be saved if his or her actions are better than those of others. Yet that was not the case with Noah, and it is not the case with us. Hebrews 11:7 shows us why God saves anyone from the penalty of his judgment. It says,

> By faith Noah, after he was warned about what was not yet seen and motivated by godly fear, built an ark to deliver his family. By faith he condemned the world and became an heir of the righteousness that comes by faith.

Noah, then, had unwavering faith in an unseen future. What is true of Noah's day is true in our own. We cannot be saved by our behavior but only by our belief, specifically our belief in Jesus and what he did for us. Active obedience to God is not the root but the fruit of our rescue from the penalty of judgment.

A second question this passage answers is this: Whom does God rescue from the penalty of judgment? Genesis 7:7 helps address it: "Noah, his sons, his wife, and his sons' wives entered the ark because of the floodwaters." The seven people spared besides Noah, then, must share his faith in God's plan and role as their rescuer. How tragic that all the other people are left behind, a stark sign of not just their wickedness but unbelief.

The eight humans, of course, were not the only ones on the boat. Verses 8-9 tell us that land animals and birds of every type enter the ark. How did they all fit? How did they get along? How did the turtles and slugs get there on time? The text does not tell us. But what we do know is that God preserves the life of every kind of animal so that he can launch a new creation after the judgment.

A third question this passage addresses is, How does God rescue people from the penalty of his judgment? The answer is in this section's ending statement that God "shut" them in the ark (v. 16). As the drops start to fall, Noah can't shut the door to his own boat. But God steps in to do what man can't do on his own. This verse is significant because it points to the truth of salvation—that it is all of God. Those God calls, he keeps. God offers both provision and protection as he rescues Noah from his own wrath. That's exactly what he does for those who, by faith, are in Christ. After the filling of the ark finishes, the flood flourishes.

Although outside the ark the initial downpour may have been welcomed as a source of relief and blessing, the continual and excessive deluge would have eventually become a source of fear and anxiety over the coming weeks. The rain, after all, continues to fall for "forty days" and nights (v. 17). Though no doubt literal, this number is also significant because it is used throughout Scripture to signify times when God is testing or refining his people. The Israelites are in the wilderness forty years after their flight from Egypt (Num 14:33). The beginning of Jesus's ministry is marked by his spending forty days in the wilderness where he is tested and tempted by Satan (Matt 4:1–11).

God Rescues Us from the Power of His Judgment (7:17-24)

Noah's story shows that salvation depends on God's rescue from the power of his own wrath. The surging waters lift the ark and eventually cover the highest mountains by over "twenty feet" (v. 20). Without this boat and God's protection of it, humanity is lost. Noah overcomes the power of the judgment in surviving the flood not because of the strength of his boat or even the strength of his faith but because of the strength of his God.

From this point forward in the Bible, the image of water will carry with it the connotations of judgment and wildness. Asaph the psalmist, for instance, will describe the waters as the place of "monsters" (Ps 74:13-14). David, too, picks up on this theme of wild water that can be traced back to Noah's flood. He writes, "Save me, God, for the water has risen to my neck" (Ps 69:1). If today you feel the waters of turbulent circumstances are up to your neck, take heart in knowing that just because a person like Noah or David is in the boat of ultimate safety by faith does not mean he or she won't still feel the effect of choppy waves. The believer must endure the storms of life because God uses them to deepen our faith and make us more like Jesus. This refining is part of the rescue. Christ is our sure and steady anchor amidst the power of the storm.

Eventually, the destruction of everything on what was dry land comes about by the waters of Noah's flood. And before it is complete, life outside the ark is no doubt terrifying and chaotic as people and animals seek higher ground to save themselves. All such efforts, however, prove fruitless. In the end, there is nothing anyone can do to save himself. Outside the ark, with the exception of the fish and sea creatures God protects throughout the storm, no person or animal "with the breath of . . . life" is left alive (v. 22). God's judgment as decreed in 6:13 is total and devastating (7:23).

This pattern of divinely decreed destruction in the wake of great wickedness continues throughout the storyline of Scripture, particularly in the holy wars of the Old Testament. It reminds us that although God is patient, when his judgment arrives, it is complete. As sure as God fights for his people in their faithful obedience, he also fights against those who prefer to live in sinful rebellion.

This pattern culminates on the cross. That God pours out the full force of the flood of his wrath upon Jesus for others' sins is the greatest evidence of how he protects those who turn to him in faith. The breath of life in Jesus was wiped out so that we who trust in him can live. He took the punishment we earned so that we can find deliverance like Noah did. After the flood, "only Noah was left" (v. 23), along with the others who were united to him. Similarly, only those in faith union with Jesus will be saved from the power of God's judgment against their sin.

God Rescues Us from the Presence of His Judgment (8:1-19)

After the waters have surged for "150 days," God remembers Noah and those inside the ark, rescuing them from the presence of the flood, from the presence of active judgment (vv. 1,3). It is not as if God has forgotten them, however. "Remembering" in this sense is not about God's memory but his mission. In his perfect timing, he brings to bear the covenant promise he has made to Noah.

Beginning with this passage, a biblical pattern emerges in which remembering leads to rescue. In Genesis 19 God remembers Abraham in connection with bringing judgment to Sodom and Gomorrah and thus rescues his nephew Lot. In Genesis 30 God remembers Rachel (and Jacob) and opens her womb. In Exodus 2 God remembers his covenant with Abraham, Isaac, and Jacob and rescues Israel from Egypt. Later, the thief on the cross pleads with the Messiah, saying, "Jesus, remember me when you come into your kingdom" (Luke 23:42). Each instance speaks to the way God remembers his covenant or promise and rescues his people from the presence of his judgment.

In the flood narrative, God removes "the breath" (*ruach* in the original language) of life through his judgment (Gen 7:22). Now, he relents from his judgment as the "wind" (*ruach*) begins to blow (8:1). In other words, God breathes new life into a new creation.

As Noah and his family prepare to leave the ark, Noah sends out both "a raven" and "a dove" (vv. 6-12). The two types of bird would respond differently to the outside world. The first, the raven, is omnivorous and a scavenger. Because of the corpses he no doubt finds, the raven is able to sustain himself until the waters recede. The dove, a herbivore, goes out and returns bearing vegetation, signifying that the waters have receded to a limited degree. When it does not return later, Noah knows that God has removed the presence of his judgment and revealed the gift of a new creation. If the raven's absence confirms the presence of death, then the dove confirms that life arises after it. Where else do we see the imagery of a dove hovering over the waters of judgment in a way that signals new life? In the baptism of Jesus (Matt 3:16-17), the one who rescues us from the presence of judgment and raises us to new life.

As the people disembark, there is a mirroring of the creation story. Genesis 1 begins with a description of the waters on the face of the earth and the Spirit of God hovering over them (1:2). Now, somewhere above this scene a literal dove hovers over the waters of the earth, scouting out the best places to rest (8:12-19). Also, just as Adam was the head of humanity, so Noah is now head of the human race. One difference between the two men is striking, however. Whereas Adam began his work innocent and untried, Noah starts out this new season of life having endured much. Regardless, in verse 17 Noah receives the same creation mandate stated in Genesis 1. God has not given up on humanity. Instead, Noah, like Adam, is called to take dominion over the new creation (9:1). In this way, Noah gives us a glimpse of what God does for us in the gospel of Christ. Jesus is a new Adam, a righteous man who experiences favor with the Lord as he walks with God. He obeys all that God commands, and, ultimately, Jesus saves us from the waters of judgment by an instrument of wood. Noah's rescue from judgment anticipates all believers' rescue from judgment, as well as the purposeful activity that lies beyond it.

Noah and God's Covenant
GENESIS 8:20–9:29

The covenant God makes with Noah and the world after the exit from the ark teaches us about the way God deals with his creation. There will be kindness and favor on the people of God because of the covenant. It will not only apply to them, however, but to the whole created order. This promise of protection, even in the face of deserved future judgment, foreshadows events linked to the coming of Jesus the Messiah. In him will be the culmination of this promise of blessing and favor.

The Lord and the Covenant with Creation (8:20-22)

What is the first thing you do after finishing a long road trip? Do you stretch? Eat? Unpack? Upon exiting the ark, the first thing Noah does is construct "an altar" and offer sacrifices to God (v. 20). The blood offering serves as a propitiation, ensuring that God is not angered with Noah and his family, who survived the flood not by merit but by grace. This instance of humans sacrificing animals in worship to God anticipates the coming Old Testament sacrificial system that ultimately culminates in the self-sacrifice of Christ.

These particular sacrifices are made during a time of limited availability since so few animals survived the flood. Noah, then, is not offering burnt offerings from abundance but rather from scarcity. Just like the widow who gives out of her poverty as recorded in Mark 12:41-44, Noah chooses to make an offering that is "pleasing" to God, regardless of his lack. By sacrificing from one of every clean animal, Noah is also showing the totality of the sacrifice. This is a sacrifice encompassing all creation.

The sacrifice itself is said to rise as a "pleasing aroma" (Gen 8:21). Repeatedly throughout Scripture, the idea of a pleasing scent is used to characterize an acceptable sacrifice made to God. Both in the Old Testament (Lev 1:9) and in the New (Eph 5:2; 2 Cor 2:15), the satisfying fragrance is connected to God's blessing. The New Testament passages especially connect the image to Christ as the "fragrant offering" made on behalf of those who trust in him.

Noah's sacrifice results in the promise that God will never again curse the ground because of humanity (Gen 8:21). This removes any threat of God's repeating the planet-wide destruction announced in 6:7, but it does not reverse the curse pronounced on Adam in 3:17. Thus, Noah does not fulfill the hope expressed by his father Lamech that he would "bring . . . relief from the agonizing labor . . . caused by the ground the LORD has cursed" (5:29). Rather, the whole creation continues to suffer under that curse to this day (Rom 8:22). The yearning for that relief looked forward to the Messiah. Yet now God in Christ has brought about assurance of the reversal of the curse of sin and death. The return of Christ will bring about the reversal of the curse on the ground. It will end "agonizing labor" forever (5:29).

The Lord and the Covenant with Noah (9:1-11)

The covenant with Noah doesn't just reverse the curse of God's judgment by flood. It also restores the calling of God's people. The command to "multiply and fill the earth," for instance, is again repeated as God blesses Noah and his sons in the opening of the chapter (v. 1). God also gives the animals back into the care of Noah and his descendants. But this time humanity is told that they may eat the animals (cf. 1:28-30). Along with this change comes the animals' fear and dread toward humanity (9:2). Even today, despite advances in science and technology, humanity does not have complete control over animals as Adam first did.

Next, God's instructions for Noah shift from the significance of the sacrifice to the significance of the blood (vv. 4-6). One dietary restriction laid on humanity by God is that they are prohibited from eating the blood of the animal. With this prohibition, God is limiting the wildness of humanity. But more importantly, the command helps establish the importance of blood, which will form the center of the later sacrificial system (Deut 12:23). God is thus paving the way for a system in which blood is to be held in awe. The blood, after all, stands as a sign of the life of a creature. And this ultimately points to the high value of the blood of Jesus, which cleanses from sin. Jesus makes the connection explicit in the new covenant when he says of the wine of the Supper, "This is my blood of the covenant" (Matt 26:28). Thus the importance of abstaining from blood—it is where life is found.

In Genesis 9 God also calls for respecting the blood of people made in his image. Those who take the life of another human are to know their lives will be demanded in return (v. 6). The act of murder is an attack on the very image of God.

God's words in this passage point to two things. First, they show that God expects the violence that occurred with Cain, and that was prevalent before the flood, to continue. The injunction against violence is made because violence will continue even in this new created order. Post-flood humanity still has a sin nature that must be restrained (8:21). The second thing to note is that because of the presence of sin, a system of law will prove necessary to govern the behavior of humanity. In the case of Cain, God dealt with him directly and offered protection from vengeance. But God here gives a law that is universal in its scope. Everyone is accountable to it. And it is given as both a warning and a restraint. That the image of God remains in every person despite the fall means every person should be treated with dignity and respect.

God's covenant with Noah represents an important development in God's ongoing relationship with mankind. After God's judgment comes God's covenant. Genesis 9:11 sees the convergence of the two promises

God made in this section of the Genesis narrative. The promises made in Genesis 8:22-23 and 9:11 are affirmations that God will not destroy the earth again with a flood, and there has never again been such a catastrophe on the earth. The promise of peace in Genesis 9:11 serves as the foundation for God's ongoing promise of peace to his people in the future. He says,

> *"For this is like the days of Noah to me:*
> *when I swore that the water of Noah*
> *would never flood the earth again,*
> *so I have sworn that I will not be angry with you*
> *or rebuke you.*
> *Though the mountains move*
> *and the hills shake,*
> *my love will not be removed from you*
> *and my covenant of peace will not be shaken,"*
> *says your compassionate LORD.* (Isa 54:9-10)

As sure as the entire planet will never again experience flood, God's steadfast love will never leave. His covenant of peace will never expire. How is this possible? As Isaiah points out elsewhere, it is because of the steadfast love of the Messiah, who is the Prince of peace (Isa 9:6). The Noahic covenant prepares the way for the new covenant.

The Lord and the Sign of the Covenant (9:12-17)

Genesis 9 reveals the "sign of the covenant" God makes not just with Noah but with "every living creature" (v. 12). The symbol is a rainbow. And the "bow . . . in the clouds" serves as a reminder, not to Noah and his descendants primarily, but to God (vv. 14-16). This is the purpose of all the signs that God gives in covenants. They exist primarily for God, not the other parties of the covenant. The point that the people of God are to remember is that God remembers. Noah and his descendants are to notice rainbows appearing naturally in the sky and know that God chooses to keep his covenant not to destroy the whole earth by water again.

When the church participates in the Lord's Supper, we are not just reminding ourselves of the suffering of Christ on our behalf and that God chooses to credit his righteousness to us who place faith in him (Luke 22:19-20). Rather, just as God looks on the rainbow and remembers the covenant he made to spare the whole earth from flooding, God sees us participate in this sign of the new covenant and remembers. He recalls that we sinners are righteous by our faith in Jesus. That is, he stands by his decision to honor the substitutionary sacrifice of the mediator of his people.

The mediator stands before him continually because this is an everlasting covenant. Likewise, Genesis 9:16-17 speaks of the everlasting nature of the covenant between God and Noah and all of creation. It is a covenant that cannot be revoked or changed. We will soon see another example of "a permanent covenant" as God establishes one with Abraham in 17:13.

God's "bow" in the sky is both a sign and a confirmation of this covenant. While the natural rainbow is indeed a beautiful wonder, it bears striking resemblance to a sobering image. The bow shape resembles a weapon of war turned away from the earth. In fact, it points upward toward God, who would himself bear the judgment for his people at the cross instead of pointing down toward those who deserve his wrath on account of their sin.

The Lord and the Lineage of the Covenant (9:18-29)

When the flood subsides, the ark is not the only thing that had a crash landing. Noah's life comes crashing down in sin as well. Though Noah escapes the presence of God's judgment, he doesn't escape the presence of sin. This is the first time we see sin up close outside the garden. After Noah and his sons leave the ark, Noah plants a vineyard. Noah steps into a new role, but he is still the same sinner. As he is partaking in the fruits of the vineyard, he becomes drunk. Noah follows the same sin cycle as Adam and Eve. Just like Adam, Noah takes the fruit, and then the fruit takes him. Just like Adam, Noah is deceived by the enemy to follow his own desires rather than God's design. And just like Adam, Noah's sin leaves him naked and ashamed.

Why does Moses record this incident? It would have been easy for Moses to whitewash the life of Noah and leave this out. Why is it there? It reminds us that there are no perfect people in the family of God. Adam followed the serpent. Noah was a drunk. And Moses himself, as we will see later, was a murderer. Even King David, a man after God's own heart, was an adulterer. Here is the key: the people Jesus *came from* reveal the people he *came for*. All the people listed in Luke's genealogy of Jesus, from Joseph back to Adam, needed a Redeemer (Luke 3:23-38).

News of Noah's actions grows more troubling in light of the way Noah's son Ham reacts to the episode. Ham, the father of a man named Canaan (who will prove important to the story later), spots his father naked and goes to tell his own brothers. This may suggest voyeurism, but it definitely indicates dishonor of an elder and gossip. It is, in fact, the first direct example in the Bible of someone not honoring his or her parent (Exod 20:12).

Instead of exposing what was uncovered like Ham did, Shem and Japheth cover what was exposed. Theirs is the first biblical example of bearing with others in their sin (Eph 4:2). It is also reminiscent of the way God compassionately covered Adam and Eve in their shame.

These two reactions lead to two responses from Noah once he is sober (Gen 9:24-27). As Noah offers blessings to two of the sons (and, by extension, their progeny) and a curse on the line of third son, we see that the rivalry between the spiritual seed of the serpent and the fallen but faithful seed of the woman, dating back to the 3:15 promise given in Eden, did not end at the flood. The New Testament, in fact, makes clear that this rivalry of the seeds continues even today (2 Cor 11:3).

This section that finishes the narratives from Noah's lifetime includes what has become known—erroneously—as the curse of Ham. But while what is said in verse 25 points to the birth of the institution of slavery in general, it is Ham's line—continuing through his son Canaan, that is in view. Moreover, while the so-called curse of Ham has been sinfully construed as a justification for slavery and racism in the past, such uses involve a complete misreading of the text. The curse that comes on Ham's son Canaan is not based on the color of Ham's skin but the consequence of Ham's sin. It is all about the fact that Ham's sin has far-reaching, generational consequences.

It is helpful to keep in mind Moses's original audience. His Israelite readers received this book while preparing to enter the land of Canaan. Its native Canaanites, descended from the man by that same name, stand boldly against God in their idolatry. The point is their wickedness continues a tradition that goes all the way back to Ham, and it is about time for that pattern to be addressed.

Not long after experiencing God's protection and grace in the matter of the deluge, Noah and his family evidence sin, leading to a further curse and condemnation. In including these insights, Moses is making clear that the post-flood world is not the final new creation where the serpent's head is crushed and sin and wickedness no longer exist. For that state to arrive, humanity will need the first and second comings of Jesus. For this reason, the author of Hebrews tells his readers to fix their eyes on Jesus, just as Noah was looking forward to a coming city and a new creation (Heb 11:7-10).

Reflect and Discuss

1. After the fall, humanity is described as sinful in both their actions and their thoughts (6:5). Why is attention given to both thoughts and actions? What does the New Testament have to say about the relationship between sinful thoughts and behaviors (Matt 15:19)?
2. Moses describes God as being grieved over the sin of humanity (6:6). Why does sin grieve God? What might this reveal about how God responds to human action? Is he distant or personable?
3. Noah is described as righteous, not because of word or deed but rather because of his faith (Heb 11:7). What does this suggest about the underlying problem leading to the destruction of his contemporaries? Does his faith come from a pure heart or from God's graciousness?
4. Noah's obedience to build the ark likely made him appear ridiculous to his neighbors. Which faith-based habits that Christians practice today are strange to the surrounding culture?
5. God's judgment is total in the flood. Why do you think the flood was so severe, its effects so total?
6. God seals Noah and his family and the animals into the ark. What does this suggest about the role of God in salvation? What does the flood account reveal about his ability to ensure salvation?
7. Noah represents a new Adam and a new beginning for humanity. However, he will also prove to be sinful. What does this reveal about fallen human nature?
8. Noah's worshipful sacrifice is made in a time of scarcity. Why do you think he felt the need to give in spite of his limited resources? How should his example inform the modern Christian practices of giving and worship?
9. The Noahic covenant places importance on the blood of both animals and humanity. How does this point to the coming salvation offered through Christ?

10. God is shown throughout these chapters as a just God. The Noahic covenant serves as a law after the flood. What does this show about the character of God and the source of law and justice?

Many Nations and the Father of Many Nations

GENESIS 10–11

Main Idea: The genealogies of Noah and Shem, as well as the episode at the Tower of Babylon, point to the continuing faithfulness of God to bring about his promise of an offspring of the woman who will crush the serpent's head. The genealogies demonstrate God's faithfulness to protect the line that will give rise to this Messiah. What happens at Babylon is another picture of judgment tempered by the grace of God.

I. **The Table of Nations and the Future of the Covenant (10)**
   A. The Table of Nations anticipates the Bible's unified message (10:1-10).
   B. The Table of Nations anticipates the Old Testament's unparalleled Messiah (10:11-20).
   C. The Table of Nations anticipates the church's unstoppable mission (10:21-32).
II. **The Tower of Babylon and the Judgment of God (11:1-9)**
   A. The power of pride to undermine God's design (11:1-4)
   B. The power of the gospel to overcome our pride (11:5-9)
III. **The Descendants of Shem and the Coming of Abram (11:10-32)**
   A. The shape of our story (11:10)
   B. The shape of our identity (11:10-26)
   C. The shape of our future (11:27-32)

Moses interrupts the Genesis narrative to show how humanity proliferates, operates, and rebuilds after the flood. This section tucked between the accounts of Noah and Abram (who becomes Abraham) is bookended by two strategic genealogies. The first is somewhat expected. It is a record of the early people groups who descend from Noah's boys. This genealogy provides insight into the background of many of the nations and place-names that will figure prominently in the later chapters of Genesis, as well as in the rest of the Old Testament: Babylon, the Philistines (10:14), and Sodom and Gomorrah's origins (10:19) are all addressed here.

Moses then resumes the narrative of mankind's earliest post-flood years by focusing on one particular instance of rebellion: the building of the Tower of Babylon. (The name of the tower and the name of the city in which it stands are identical in Hebrew: *babel.*) This episode chronicles the sinful and clumsy efforts of Noah's descendants to protect and exalt themselves in the aftermath of the cataclysmic flood. That sin violates God's command to "fill the earth" (1:28; 9:1). Instead, they settle as a group in a valley and intend to make a name for themselves, refusing to "be scattered throughout the earth" (11:2–4).

God extends a lavish measure of grace to humanity even as he addresses their sinfulness. Rather than destroying any of the people involved in making these decisions, God works through creative means to make sure everyone will disperse across the face of the earth as he intends. This points back to the promise God made to Noah that he would not destroy the earth by flood, even though the people were deserving of such punishment.

The narrative culminates in a more focused genealogy of the descendants of Shem. The focal point of this genealogy is the person of Abram and his wife Sarai. This particular genealogy is prominent because of the way the story of God's redemptive work is advanced in the life of Abram. From Abram's line come the remaining patriarchs— Isaac and his son Jacob (later renamed Israel)—the kingly line of David, and eventually Jesus.

The repeated back-and-forth between global perspective and micro attention in the lives of individuals and episodes reveals the way God is working at both the cosmic and the personal levels to accomplish his plan for redemption. God is at work overseeing the course of human history while simultaneously attending to the lineage and future of the promised Messiah. Both the genealogies and the short episodes presented in this portion of Genesis between Noah and Abram illustrate the faithfulness of God in bringing about his promises.

The Table of the Nations and the Future of the Covenant
GENESIS 10

This genealogy known as "The Table of Nations" lists seventy names that help explain the origins of the earliest post-flood nations on earth. While we might feel tempted to skip over it because its names are often difficult to pronounce, this passage is important and worth the read. First, it sets the scene for the story that unfolds throughout the whole Bible, one in which the Creator seeks not only to redeem a certain family line but faithful persons from "every" tribe and nation (see Rev 7:9). Second, it reminds us that all people on earth are extended family, having both Adam and Eve and Noah and his wife as shared ancestors. And third, it introduces us to many names and places that show up later in Scripture. For instance, verse 13 speaks of a man named Mizraim. Given that early cities often shared the names of their founders, this sheds light on the origins of Mizraim the place. It's the Hebrew word for "Egypt."

The Table of Nations Anticipates the Bible's Unified Message (10:1-10)

Many scholars theorize this Genesis 10 genealogy comes chronologically after the Tower of Babylon story in chapter 11. So, why does it appear first? In part because the sequence helps us understand what happens in Genesis 11. But the order here also contributes to the unified message of Genesis and the entire Bible—sinful humanity remains under a curse and maintains its desperate need for a Savior who can set things right. To begin with, Genesis 10 serves as a subtle reminder that all are descendants of Adam. But it also anticipates readers' encountering the particularly troublemaking people groups found throughout the Bible. For instance, as noted, it gives insight into the origin of places that show up in important ways throughout it, from familiar locations like Egypt ("Mizraim" in v. 6) to less familiar ones like "Heth" (v. 15). Later, we will meet "the Hethites" (23:3). These are the descendants of Heth, just as the later Israelites will be so named because they are the descendants of Israel.

Genesis 10 also helps get to the bottom of more specific problems that will serve to underscore the Bible's unified message. The first of these problems emerges from the line of Ham (vv. 6-20). The trouble starts with a man named "Nimrod," who is known as "a powerful hunter" (vv. 8-9). But since humanity has received clearance to eat meat by this point, the problem is not that Nimrod hunts. It is what he builds, specifically because of the impact it later will have on the people of God. Like his forefather Cain, Nimrod is a builder of cities (vv. 10-11). Yet he is not just a city builder. He desires a kingdom. One that starts "with Babylon" (v. 10) and extends "to Assyria" (v. 11). These two places would later house two of Israel's greatest foes in the Old Testament. The two nations would not only brutally abuse but also force the people of God into exile. Nimrod thus establishes outposts for the kingdom of darkness that work against the faithful people of God.

This leads into the next specific problem the passage helps introduce to the biblical narrative: those who align with the kingdom of darkness will face dire consequences. When God establishes the Abrahamic covenant in 15:18-21, it is a promise of deliverance, a promise of military victory. Over whom? Over the outposts of darkness and rebellion I've mentioned and others, too. Half the nations mentioned in Genesis 15's covenantal promise of conquest, in fact, appear in the Table of Nations. So, just as the genealogy shows a continuity between the covenants of Noah and Abraham, it also speaks to the continuity of the struggle introduced in chapter 3. Babylon, Assyria, the Philistines, and the Canaanites will all prove to be enemies of God's people, Israel. Yet throughout the Old Testament, God preserves his people from these enemies so that one day he can bring forth his Messiah (Josh 3:10).

The Table of Nations Anticipates the Old Testament's Unparalleled Messiah (10:11-20)

Redemptive history does not go around the genealogies. It goes through them. The genealogy in Genesis 10 anticipates an unparalleled Messiah expected throughout the Old Testament in several ways. To begin with, the Table of Nations anticipates the preservation of God's Messiah in the Old Testament. Genesis 10:15 brings us face-to-face with Israel's biggest rival in the Old Testament, Canaan. Genesis 10 is like a preview of the enemies the people of God will face: Babylon, Assyria, the Philistines, and the Canaanites. Yet throughout the Old Testament, God preserves his people from these enemies so that one day he can bring forth his Messiah (Josh 3:10).

Genesis 10 anticipates the prophecy of God's Messiah in the Old Testament. Prophecy after prophecy about the Messiah in the Old Testament references the people and nations first mentioned in Genesis 10. As already noted, when Genesis 15 unfolds the covenant with Abraham, it mentions five of these nations. When Micah 5 prophesies that the Messiah will come from Bethlehem, it mentions Assyria and the land of Nimrod. When Psalm 72 anticipates the coming of the Messiah as a righteous king, it speaks of his victory over Tarshish, Seeba, and Sheba. But perhaps the most important connection between the Table of Nations and future prophecy about the Messiah is found in Isaiah 11:10-12, where God promises rescue for his people from multiple nations first mentioned in Genesis 10. After Genesis 10:18 tells us the enemies of God are scattered, the Old Testament recounts how the people of God are dispersed in judgment for their sin. Now, in Isaiah 11:12, it uses the same root word for scattered as it unfolds God's promise of a Messiah who will rescue his people and gather the dispersed. Who will the root of Jesse rescue them from? Isaiah 11:11 lists eight places and seven of them show up in Genesis 10. We can't fully make sense of this promise of deliverance apart from Genesis 10. The Table of Nations helps to lay the foundation for the messianic expectation of the Old Testament.

The Table of Nations Anticipates the Church's Unstoppable Mission (10:21-32)

Why is Shem's family listed last in this genealogy? After all, he is the firstborn of Noah, so it would be normal to list him first. But Genesis 10 saves the best for last because it is preparing for the promise of the Messiah and the purpose of our mission to run through Shem and his offspring. Genesis 10 anticipates our unstoppable mission in several ways. To start, Genesis 10 anticipates the unstoppable mission of Jesus. Beginning in 10:21, two descendants of Shem receive focus. They break the script, disrupting the normal flow of the genealogy. When that happens, the text is usually shining a spotlight on that person. First is Eber, whose name is likely where the term *Hebrew* originates. Even though Eber is four generations away from Shem, he is listed immediately. Then, in verse 25, Eber's son Peleg is mentioned, along with the added commentary "for during his days the earth was divided," which is a play on words with the meaning of his name in a way that foreshadows the Tower of Babylon story in Genesis 11.

When these two descendants are spotlighted in the genealogy, how does that anticipate the unstoppable mission of Jesus? The genealogy of Jesus in Luke 3 gives us the answer. In the long list of names, both Peleg and Eber are mentioned in Luke 3:35. From Eber, the man whose name became synonymous with the Hebrews, the hope of the Hebrews will come. From Peleg, the man whose name means "divided," a Messiah would come who would break down the dividing wall of hostility and reconcile us to God and one another in fulfillment of Abraham's promise. The sequence of Luke is different from the other Gospels at this point. Luke 3 starts with the baptism of Jesus. But before it gets to the start of his mission in Luke 4 with the wilderness temptation, there is an interlude to give this genealogy that runs through Peleg and Eber. In other words, Luke builds off of Genesis 10 to confirm Jesus is the unparalleled Messiah in order to prepare the way for his unstoppable mission.

Genesis 10 also anticipates the unstoppable mission of the church. The chapter concludes in Genesis 10:32 with the statement, "The nations on earth spread out from these after the flood." The total number of all the nations represented in Genesis 10 is seventy, which is a number of completeness. But in the Septuagint, the total number of nations listed is seventy-two. When Jesus sends his people out on mission for the first time in Luke 10:1-2, how many does he send out? "After this, the Lord appointed seventy-two others, and he sent them ahead of him in pairs to every town and place where he himself was about to go" (Luke 10:1). This is not a coincidence. Instead, Jesus is reaching back to the Table of Nations the first time he sends the church out on its unstoppable mission to the nations.

The Tower of Babylon and the Judgment of God
GENESIS 11:1-9

The structure discussed in this story has traditionally been called the "Tower of Babel." That name is a transliteration of the Hebrew name for the tower: *babel*. That same Hebrew name *babel* is used in the rest of the Old Testament to refer to the city of Babylon, home to enemies of the people of God (2 Kgs 20:17; 24:1; Jer 21:7; Ezek 17:12). It is, in fact, the earliest people of Babylon who are building this tower. We will gain a deeper understanding of this event by connecting it to the rest of the history of the city of Babylon (Gen 10:10; Dan 4:30; also 1 Pet 5:13; Rev 14:8; 17:5; 18:10,21).

The building of the tower at Babylon is a picture of humanity's continuing rebellion against God. If the presentation in Genesis 10 helps establish the idea of unity in the human family, Genesis 11 is a story of division. In it we see humans seeking to elevate themselves and acting dismissively toward God. And as a result, this civilization that starts out aligned and united quickly becomes a place of confusion and division.

It is sobering to realize our contemporary American culture has much in common with Babylon. In a way, the confusion and division regarding everything from politics, to what constitutes a certain gender, to race relations, to whether abortion should be a right reflects their story. If we can understand how Babylon collapsed, then perhaps it can shape how we live in an American Babylon today.

The Power of Pride to Undermine God's Design (11:1-4)

Why did Babylon's project unravel? Because of the soaring heights of their pride. The Tower of Babylon narrative, in fact, is primarily a story about the power of pride. What is pride? It is one of those concepts that is easy to understand but harder to define. But for our purposes, pride is the decision to put self at the center of the story instead of God. It is being more concerned with fulfilling our own desires than with honoring God's design. At the heart of pride is a selfish answer to this question: Who will be the center of my life, God or me? Pride is thus the soil of our sin, the roots of our rebellion.

Pride turns inward instead of upward to find satisfaction, success, and significance. Before you think a Bible passage on pride does not apply to you, just remember that pride can show up in our lives in more than one way. Of course, pride can show up in arrogance, as we visibly think of ourselves more highly than we ought and seek to elevate our status in the eyes of others. But pride can also show up in self-pity, as we think of ourselves in a lesser way than we should. In those cases, we want others to find ways and words to help us elevate our status in our own eyes. Pride turns inward or outward instead of upward to find satisfaction, success, and significance. And such is the widespread state of affairs behind this story of early Babylon. They aim to put themselves on higher ground because they think of themselves more highly than they ought.

If you don't know the end of the narrative, what unfolds in Genesis 11 does not seem so bad at first. After all, people are being fruitful and multiplying and seem to be taking dominion over the earth by imaging God through their creative abilities. So, what is the problem? The problem in Babylon is not what they are doing but why they are doing it. A careful read of the passage makes clear that things are not as they should be. For instance, they are not building a tower because one is necessary. And they are certainly not erecting it to make a name for God but to make a name for themselves. Their motivation is not praise but pride, not humility but hubris, not virtue but vanity. It is a perfect picture of humanity's ongoing rebellion against God rooted in pride that continues even today.

How does their pride make itself apparent? First, pride seeks satisfaction through *self-provision*. And in verse 3 they leverage God-given resources and God-given creativity not to honor God but to benefit themselves, to satisfy their appetites, and to meet their craving for renown. Whereas in Genesis 3 humanity tries to become like God by seizing fruit, in Genesis 11 humanity tries to become like God by seizing the opportunity to make bricks that might withstand the test of time and catastrophe.

Second, pride seeks success through *self-promotion*. Verse 4 reveals that is just what the builders wanted, saying, "Let's make a name for ourselves." People today often desire to do the same. Only now, it isn't through the size of our towers but through the size of our social media following or our bank account or our job title.

Third, pride seeks significance through *self-protection*. In a time so close to the terrible events of Noah's day, it might make sense for people to build tall towers out of fear of another flood. But that's not the driving factor behind this particular construction project. The real motivation behind it surfaces in verse 4: "Come, let's build ourselves a city and a tower with its top in the sky. . . . [O]therwise we will be scattered throughout the earth." So they want self-protection against being dispersed. Separating, after all, might lead to feelings of insignificance and irrelevance. Pride's pull toward self-protection causes them to seek self-centered community. What brings the people of Babylon together, then, is not a common focus but a shared fear.

The result of doing this is having proximity but lacking intimacy. We face the same danger of establishing self-centered community today, and it leads to the same results. This may be why it sometimes seems that while our lives have never been closer in some ways, our hearts have never been at risk of being further apart.

The pride of Babylon stands in stark contrast to the way of Jesus. In the wilderness temptations (Matt 4:1-11), in fact, Jesus experiences the same pulls from pride mentioned but resists them. Just as the people of Babylon turn mud into bricks in an effort at *self-provision*, a hungry Jesus gets tempted to turn stones into bread. Yet he will not. Just as the people of Babylon hope to ascend to the pinnacle of the tower to deliver themselves from danger, even as they draw attention to their own greatness, Jesus is tempted to ascend to the pinnacle of the temple to deliver himself from danger through an act of *self-protection that would highlight his own greatness.* Yet he will not. And just as the people of Babylon seek *self-promotion through building,* Jesus gets tempted to build a kingdom for himself apart from the cross. Jesus succeeds where humanity fails by resisting the pull of pride.

Jesus doesn't just combat the pride common to Babylon in his daily life, however. He also crucifies it in his death. When Jesus is on the cross, for instance, he resists the prideful pull of *self-provision.* The religious leaders mock him, saying, "He saved others, but he cannot save himself" (Matt 27:42). Nevertheless, he refuses to pursue his own deliverance outside God's perfect plan. Also, when Jesus is on the cross, he resists the pull of *self-protection.* In Matthew 26:53 Jesus had informed his disciples that he could have requested twelve legions of angels to defend him. Yet he refuses to do so. When Jesus is on the cross, he resists the prideful pull of *self-promotion,* too. Paul describes how Jesus emptied himself, humbled himself, and sacrificed himself so that, ultimately, God could highly exalt him (Phil 2:1-11). Even in his dying, then, Jesus resists Babylon's deepest problem and also makes a way of salvation through *self-sacrifice.*

The Power of the Gospel to Overcome Our Pride (11:5-9)

Proverbs 16:18 says, "Pride comes before destruction, and an arrogant spirit before a fall." As the pride that built Babylon collapses under the judgment of God in Genesis 11, that maxim is proven true. The hopeful news is that the Tower of Babylon account is not just a warning story about the power of human pride. It is pointing to the power of the gospel.

The pattern of how God responds to the pride of the people is much the same way he still confronts pride today. First, God personally *recognizes* the pride and the harmful effect it can have. He doesn't just let it unfold outside his notice as if it didn't matter. In verse 5, "the LORD came down to look over the city and the tower that the humans were building." The phrase "came down" is both an echo of what God does after Adam and Eve sin in the garden and a preview of what he will do later in the case of Sodom and Gomorrah (18:21). He takes an up-close look at the builders' sinful solidarity and knows it signals only the start of even greater rebellion (v. 6). The planned height of the tower, after all, reveals the the depth of their pride.

Second, God *reckons* with their pride. In the days of Noah, God's judgment came in the form of sweeping destruction. But in the days of Babylon, God's judgment comes in the form of disruption. God's reckoning with their pride shatters one language into many, with the result of scattering family groups to their new locations on the world map. In verse 9 the name *Babylon* (Hb. *babel*) sounds like the Hebrew word for confusion (*balal*). Imagine the mass confusion arising right after God shatters the unified language!

When God scatters their location, he doesn't send a flood upon the people of the world to destroy them. Instead, God sends a flood of people into the world to disperse them. True, their fear of being scattered and vulnerable (v. 4) becomes a reality, but so does their obedience to God's plan for humanity to spread and fill the world.

Just as with Adam and Eve in the garden, God, in his mercy, prevents them from continuing in their sinful behavior by saving them from themselves. And he does the same thing for us. God casts us out of the towers of our own strongholds to sin so that we might be brought into his kingdom.

Third, God *reverses* their pride. Acts 2 reveals that Genesis 11 is not the end of the story for how God confronts our pride. Pentecost is a reversal of Babylon. In Acts 2:4-6 God reverses the shattering of the languages by restoring them from many unintelligible conversations back into one clear message. In Acts 2:5 God reverses the scattering of their location by gathering together the many nations that were dispersed. In Acts 2:6 God reverses the confusion of their lives by providing clarity. In verse 11 God reverses the pattern of humanity seeking to make a name for itself.

The gospel proclaimed at Pentecost doesn't just confront us in our sin. It challenges the pride underlying it. That pride may show itself following a presentation of the good news. It can appear as either a self-righteousness that says, "I don't need Jesus," or a self-pity that says, "I'm not good enough for Jesus."

What happened at Babylon addresses the former: we cannot find salvation by climbing to the heavens through our own efforts. It doesn't matter how many good works we do, how much money we give, or how many times we go to church. Even if we pile our good deeds as high as the sky, they will just collapse like a house of cards should we try to stand on them. But God doesn't require us to make a way to him, which is excellent news for those who fear they'll never be good enough. Instead, the truth of the gospel is that God has come down to us sinners. Jesus took on flesh and dwelled among us so that he could make a way through his death and resurrection to bring us to God (John 1:14). All he asks of us is that we repentantly believe.

Unlike the Babylonians who amassed bricks to build a tower of pride, God is gathering and assembling living stones as he builds his humble church (1 Pet 2:5).

The Descendants of Shem and the Coming of Abram
GENESIS 11:10-32

This last major genealogy in this section of Genesis is a bridge between the first part of the book that begins with the creation of the universe and the second part that begins with the calling of the man best known as Abraham. It also functions like a gateway from where we believers came from (being in Adam) and the pathway to where we are going (being fully in Christ). If the first section of Genesis 11 reveals that pride comes before the fall, this section reveals that promise comes before fulfillment.

The previous genealogy focused on all the nations descended from Noah and his sons. This one focuses the reader's attention on the lineage of Shem's descendants as it prepares the way for a focus on one in particular. The shape of this genealogy shows us several dimensions of the shape of our lives.

The Shape of Our Story (11:10)

The genealogy of Shem begins with the phrase, "These are the family records." This is a translation of the Hebrew word *toledot*. Why draw attention to this phrase that seems insignificant? Because it shows up approximately ten times in Genesis. And each time it serves as a marker signaling a shift in the shape of the story (DeRouchie, "Blessing-Commission"). It serves two functions, narrating and narrowing the story of Genesis.

The *toledot* helps us track the turning points that define the shape of the book. So far, that shape has unfolded in six phases:

- *Phase 1: The purpose of God in our origins (1:1–2:3).* In the section of Genesis occurring before the first *toledot*, God creates the universe and establishes his kingdom for his glory and our good.
- *Phase 2: The patience of God in our sin (2:4–4:26).* In this second section of Genesis, marked by the first *toledot in the book*, God creates humanity in his image, calls humanity to his mission, commissions humanity for his kingdom, confronts humanity in our sin, comforts humanity with his promise, and consoles humanity in our brokenness.
- *Phase 3: The providence of God in our pain (5:1–6:8).* In this third section of Genesis, which opens with a *toledot*, God demonstrates his faithful providence. This first genealogy reveals that God's promise to the woman that he will raise up a deliverer is on track. He meets human failure with his faithfulness. He meets our pain with his providence.
- *Phase 4: The promises of God in our brokenness (6:9–9:29).* In this fourth section of Genesis, also opening with a *toledot*, God pictures in miniature the entire biblical narrative of salvation through judgment. Despite our brokenness, God keeps his promise to rescue his people.
- *Phase 5: The pattern of God for our future (10:1–11:9).* In this fifth section, which opens with a *toledot*, God doesn't provide only a picture of our past but also a preview of our future. What happens at Babylon reveals a pattern of pride that shapes our sin. Nevertheless, the genealogy of Noah's family hints that God's promise to secure our salvation remains on track.
- *Phase 6: The plan of God for our lives (11:10–25:11).* In this sixth section (including a *toledot* at both 11:10 and 11:27), God shapes the story of Abraham and his family through the genealogy of Shem. It helps reveal the plan of God for the people of God.

The *toledot* structure of this book doesn't just shape the story of Genesis. It shapes our own stories as well. How so? Because the story of universal scope that we live within should shape the stories we choose to live out.

The Shape of Our Identity (11:10-26)

Shem's name actually means "name" in the original language. In fact, 11:4 tells us the people built the Tower of Babylon to "make a name (*shem*) for" themselves. But when humanity tries to make a name for itself, it fails. By contrast, when God makes a name for Shem, he and his line flourish.

There is a notable difference between this genealogy and the two prior genealogies in Genesis. The difference involves who is presented. The genealogies in Genesis 5 and 10 are like a "who's who" of the Bible. Genesis 5, for instance, records familiar names like Adam, Enoch, Methuselah, and Noah. Genesis 10 lists significant figures like Canaan, Babylon, Mizraim (Egypt), and the Philistines. But Genesis 11 is more of a "who's he?," being filled with what seem like unnecessary, and unfamiliar names.

So, why are these names given? Not because of the men's personal significance, not because of their successes. Rather, these largely unfamiliar names are listed because of the Messiah the men are connected to biologically. Their names are written down in Scripture not because of their extraordinary fame but—at least generally speaking—their ordinary faithfulness. The people of Babylon sought to make a name for themselves and failed. Now no one knows them. But the people of Shem's genealogy (again, for the most part) apparently sought to bring up each successive generation of their family tree in such a way as to ultimately help make a name for Jesus. Now the whole world can know of them.

We live in a culture in which people want to make names for themselves. Their pride is driven by a fear of insignificance, a fear of being forgotten. But this passage shows us that what matters is not one's credentials but his or her connection to Jesus. Since that's true, then it should free us Christians from the pressure of performance that might urge us to try to make a name for ourselves.

Genesis 11 subtly calls us to ordinary faithfulness combined with a next-generation focus, all for the sake of Christ. In him we believers have our identity. Thus, every diaper you change, every task you complete, every Bible study you teach, every friendship you build—when done as an act of faithfulness to God—is valuable, whether or not anyone else notices.

The Shape of Our Future (11:27-32)

A new genealogy begins with another *toledot* in verse 27. While the genealogy of Shem is filled with names we rarely encounter in the rest of the Bible, the genealogy of Terah is marked by three names significant to the storyline of Scripture.

First is Terah himself. What does Terah become known for? Joshua 24:2 notes he "worshiped other gods." This, then, is the first documented example of idolatry in the Bible that is associated with the people of God. Terah intends to live in the land of Canaan but eventually settles in the land of Haran (Gen 10:31). Though Terah does not make it into the land of Canaan, the idolatry typical of Canaan makes it into him. Terah thus serves as a warning that all of us, no matter our family connections, are susceptible to the seduction of idols. Despite Terah's failures, however, God still uses him to raise up his chosen one, Abram.

The next familiar name appearing in the genealogy of Terah is Sarai. Her introduction is distinct because she is female. Rarely in the genealogies of the Bible, particularly in Genesis 10–11, are women highlighted in the lineages. But Sarai's introduction is even more remarkable in that the woman is later associated with being unable to conceive. A genealogy, after all, is meant to show the continuation of a line. As Genesis 17:19 later reveals, her barrenness is not the end of her story, though. Her barren state gets undone by the promise of God, when Sarai the barren becomes Sarah the mother.

The final widely recognized individual who receives special attention in the genealogy of Shem is Abram. It is noteworthy that in the genealogies of Genesis, there are ten generations from Adam to Noah and now ten generations from Noah to Abram.

The story of Abram that begins here is marked by several gifts from God that don't just change this man's life but reveal the shape of our future as believers. The first is *a new place to live.* When his story begins, Abram, his father, and their family have traveled out of Ur to reside in Haran, but Abram is told he will eventually become "a great nation" in the land of Canaan (12:2). This, according to Nehemiah 9:7-8, is one of the ways God demonstrates his covenant faithfulness to Abram. The second gift is *a new name.* When first introduced to the reader, Abram is described in relation to his family as being the son of Terah, who has a wife named Sarai. Later, however, Abram will be renamed Abraham because of God's promise to make him the "father of many nations" (17:5). Finally, God gifts Abram with *a new promise.* Genesis 12:1-3 presents the call for Abram to leave Haran to pursue God's promise of a hopeful future: "[A]ll the peoples on earth will be blessed through [him]." In Acts 7 Stephen's speech informs the reader that Abraham's story is intended to teach that hope is found in God's faithfulness to his promises.

Abram grew up in a difficult situation: he was raised in a family running from God by worshiping idols. Then his Uncle Haran died. Then his wife turned out to be barren. The man faced several circumstances that could have kept him from wanting anything to do with God. Yet the Lord welcomed him into his own family by wooing him with a promise and providing him with a purpose greater than his struggles.

You may find yourself in the same situation as Abram: growing up in a family that is running from God and battling brokenness in your life that is the result of death, despair, disappointment, or disobedience. But in the same way God pursues Abram and changes everything for him, he is doing the same thing for you through the death and resurrection of Jesus Christ, the son of Abraham.

Reflect and Discuss

1. The genealogies of Scripture link the covenants of Scripture together. But how else do they prove helpful to Christians?
2. How do the genealogies in Genesis help reveal God's providential working in history to accomplish his purposes?
3. What do the genealogies discussed in this chapter contribute to your understanding of the promised seed?
4. The descendants of Noah gather together to build a tower reaching to the heavens, an action in opposition to God's stated will. What does their activity suggest about fallen human nature?
5. God intervenes and limits the way worship can occur for humanity. Must we conform our worship to God-directed methods? Are there limiting factors on what constitutes worship?
6. The judgment of God is merciful in its scope. In judging the Babel incident, God does something to prevent people from gathering together en masse. The aim is to slow humanity's self-destructive decision making. How have you seen God's judgment as a merciful means of preventing your own further self-harm?
7. The very thing the builders at Babylon sought to prevent by building the tower (being scattered) was in fact the result of their actions. What's another example of how sin can cause what we hoped to prevent?
8. Terah desired to live in Canaan but settled in the land of Haran. How does the fact that the father of Abraham was susceptible to the

impulse of worshiping other gods enrich your understanding of the
biblical narrative?

9. At first, Sarai is known for her barrenness. But that is not the end of
her story. In what ways have you seen God use an initial problem or
flaw to pave the way to blessing or new identity?

10. With the introduction of Abram, Moses moves us to the next period
of redemptive history. But Abram, for the reasons discussed, is an
unexpected person to be used for God's purposes. Why might God
choose unlikely people to accomplish his plans?

Walking by Faith

GENESIS 12–14

Main Idea: God calls Abram and promises to bless both him and the nations through him. This call and blessing establish the pattern of the favor of God toward his people that continues throughout the book.

I. **The Call of Abram and the Promise of God (12:1-9)**
   A. The promise of a new place
   B. The promise of a new people
   C. The promise of a new purpose
II. **The Testing of Abram and the Provision of God (12:10–14:16)**
   A. Abram's calling is tested by adversity (12:10-20).
   B. Abram's calling is tested by abundance (13).
   C. Abram's calling is tested by attack (14:1-16).
III. **The Blessing of Melchizedek and the Favor of God (14:17-24)**

The call of Abram recorded in chapter 12 centers the Bible's story of redemption on the life of a single person. It marks a shift in Genesis that turns away from the origins of shared human history to document the origins of God's chosen people. Previous chapters are concerned with representatives or heads of humanity among the nations of the world. Similarly, the story of Abram focuses on the head of a specific people group, the Hebrews (later known as the Israelites and then the Jews). Through them would come the key human offspring promised in Genesis 3. Without Abram, then, no lineage leads to Isaac, Jacob, Judah, David, and eventually Jesus the Messiah. Abram's calling is thus a major hinge on which the story of redemption turns.

Featured in these chapters are two important themes. The first is that the story of redemption is solely based in God's action on behalf of his people. The calling of Abram, after all, is based solely on the divine mercy and goodwill of God toward him. It is not based on Abram's worthiness. Notice that at this point in the Bible there is no description of Abram being a person of righteousness, despite Moses's inclusion of such a description for a previous key figure, Noah (6:9). True, Abram will later be described as righteous, but only after exhibiting belief

(15:6). Foremost in Abram's story is the reminder that God is working out his plan of redemption on behalf of an unworthy people and for his own glory.

The second theme is that God's blessing to Abram is more than just a promise of land, though that is important. Instead, it is the greater idea that through Abram being blessed, all the nations will be blessed. The ultimate offspring of Abram, who is the guarantee and fulfillment of this blessing, of course, is Jesus Christ (Gal 3:16).

Although Abram did not see the fulfillment of all the Genesis 12:1-3 promises in his lifetime, he was unwavering in his faith that things would be accomplished as God said. Abram thus stands as the paragon of faith in the Old Testament and remains an excellent example for Christians today. We too are called by God and must hold fast to God's promises because of unwavering trust that the promise giver will fulfill them. As sure as many of his early promises were fulfilled to Abraham and Israel, so too will his promises to us in Christ be fulfilled.

The Call of Abram and the Promise of God
GENESIS 12:1-9

Remember that the call of Abram is based solely on God's grace and not Abram's righteousness. God's purposes in his call to Abram are made clear in this passage: God will bless the whole world through Abram and his descendants. The latter includes not only the man's biological descendants but "all the peoples on earth" who will unite to him through placing faith in his ultimate descendant, Jesus of Nazareth.

The Promise of a New Place

The call of Abram marks one of the most important moments in God's plan for redemption. But interestingly, Abram stands in contrast to Noah. Whereas Noah is introduced as a "righteous" person (6:9), Abram is introduced simply as the son "of Terah" (11:27). So there is nothing to commend Abram to God when God calls him. After all, he comes from a pagan household. Moreover, he is an old man (12:4) who has spent his years experiencing nothing unusual but rather the brokenness of the curse. He has seen family members die. His wife is barren. And Haran, where he is living at the time, is an undesirable place. It may seem to Abram that his life has no promise. Nevertheless, God chooses him to receive the greatest promise in history. The calling of Abram is one of the weightiest moments between Eden and the cross. Yet as Moses records, God simply visits Abram—who is living in a land of idolatry—and chooses him on this simple basis: God's own favor and choice. This pattern will be repeated throughout the Old Testament (Exod 20:2; Deut 4:37; 7:6–8). While the doctrine of God's electing purposes strikes a blow at human pride, it lays bare the fact that God takes initiative to rescue undeserving people.

What is the nature of Abram's calling from God, and how does it relate to us today? The brokenness that comes from sin makes it difficult for us to have clarity on God's vision for our lives as believers, but Genesis 12 is a game changer in this regard. In the calling of Abram, we see God break through the brokenness to give us a helpful insight into his vision for our lives. First, the blessing of Abram begins with a *geographical* dimension as God calls him to a new place. We live in a mobile world where moving is common. So the danger is that a calling to a new land like what Abram experienced seems normal to us. But it wasn't normal during that time period. True, when God tells Abram to "go from your land" (v. 1), it is a calling to do just that. But it is also a call to leave everything behind—from his native people to his house to his heritage—for the sake of following God. As Hebrews 11:8 confirms, Abram walks by faith, not by sight, to an unknown future in an unknown place.

The New Testament helps us recognize there is even more going on with this calling to a new place than meets the eye in Genesis 12. When the martyr Stephen recounts this moment in Acts 7:4-5, he shows how the promise of a place and a people was never fulfilled during the time of Abram. Instead, the promise of a place only comes true through the son of Abraham, Jesus himself, who fulfills the covenant commitments and receives the covenant promise of a new place. What is this new place Jesus will receive in fulfillment of this calling on Abraham? Romans 4:13 explains that it is not ultimately limited to a parcel of land in Canaan but that Abraham would "inherit the world." What a stunning expansion of this promise of a place! The offspring of Abram will receive not only the land of Canaan but eventually the whole world. This promise of a new place finds its fulfillment in Christ through the restoration of Eden that arrives through the coming of a new creation. As a result, the gospel is a call to come home. God doesn't just promise to bring us into a new creation. He also brings a new creation into us (2 Cor 5:17). Like the prodigal who leaves a far country to return to his father's house, our heavenly Father welcomes us into a new place to belong through Jesus, the son of Abraham.

The Promise of a New People

Second, the blessing of Abram continues with a genealogical dimension as God calls him to a new people. In obedience to God's call, Abram and his entire household set out from Haran (Gen 12:4). The household of Abram includes his wife, his nephew Lot, and his servants and herdsmen. According to a later chapter, Abram's household numbers at least 318 men, besides women and children (14:14). Moreover, Lot is no poor relation tagging along but a wealthy individual with his own servants and herds (12:5).

Genesis 12:2 refers to a genealogical blessing linked to the call. God promises to make Abram "into a great nation." The language indicates not only that Abram will become a father but something like a king over a kingdom. Here, shortly after the Table of Nations in chapter 10, we see God calling Abram to establish a new kingdom, a "holy nation" (Exod 19:6). These will be people for God's own "possession," which is a theme that carries throughout the New Testament (1 Pet 2:9).

In a previous chapter, we saw that the people of Babylon failed in their attempts to make their own name great (Gen 11:4). But here God gives a promise to Abram to "make [his] name great" (12:2). The same verse supplies the why. God will make Abram's name great not so that he can turn inward in pride (like the tower builders) but outward in humility by being "a blessing" to others.

In verse 7, in a new scene set within the boundaries of Canaan, the text reveals that Abram doesn't just experience the promise of God but also the presence of God. With this first appearance of God made to a man since the fall, a biblical pattern is set in place: the presence of God brings the promise of God. He says, "To your offspring I will give this land." The term translated *offspring* is the exact same word used in the first messianic promise in Genesis 3:15.

But God's latest promise, with its exciting link to what God said to Eve, comes with a problem. How can Abram's offspring inherit the place where he stands when he has no offspring? After all, Abram is already seventy-five when he leaves Haran, and his wife is barren. Well, in another twenty-five years a son, Isaac, will be born to this couple.

But Galatians 3:16 provides the real answer to Abram's conundrum as it quotes Genesis 12:7: "Now the promises were spoken to Abraham and to his seed. He does not say 'and to seeds,' as though referring to many, but referring to one, 'and to your seed,' who is Christ." Who is the offspring in view within the promise, then? Ultimately, not Isaac or his son Jacob or any other mere human from Israel. Why? Because they failed to keep the covenant commitments. Perfect, sinless Jesus Christ, descended from Abraham, is the offspring intended here. One day soon, he will enter the promised land of salvation and usher a new people into a new creation.

The Promise of a New Purpose

Third, God's blessing of Abram culminates with a *generational* dimension as the Lord calls him to a new purpose. What is it? That "all the peoples on earth will be blessed through [him]" (12:3). The nations need a blessing because they are under the curse linked to the fall that happened in Eden. Within the promise of a global blessing is a call to a global mission. God is commissioning Abram and his offspring to advance his kingdom purposes in the world.

In verse 8, Abram celebrates his amazing encounter with God by building an altar for worship. Knowledge of God's purpose for him combines with the experience of God's presence to empower this expression of Abram's praise. This moment establishes another biblical pattern that continues through the construction of the tabernacle and the temple to mark the faithfulness of God toward his people.

What God speaks to Abram in Genesis 12:3 radiates down through the ages to Christ followers, the people of God today. The apostle Paul's explanation is helpful here:

> *Now the Scripture saw in advance that God would justify the Gentiles by faith and proclaimed the gospel ahead of time to Abraham, saying, 'All the nations will be blessed through you.' Consequently, those who have faith are blessed with Abraham, who had faith.* (Gal 3:8-9)

So Paul points out that when God speaks to Abram about a blessing coming to the nations through him, he is not only calling him to a new purpose. He is actually proclaiming the gospel, far in advance of Jesus's arrival on the world stage. The gift of grace God offers humanity through the death and resurrection of this descendant of Abraham is the way all the nations are blessed, as individuals from all over the world are made right with God through faith.

This reframing of Genesis 12 by Paul in Galatians 3 has everything to do with the purpose God has called us believers to live out today. The Great Commission of Matthew 28:18-20 is grounded in this Genesis 12 promise that the nations will be blessed through the offspring of Abraham. All of us who are Abraham's spiritual offspring in Christ get to share the good news about him, thus joining in the mission of being a blessing to the world.

The calling of Abram is a paradigm for God's calling on our own lives. A new place; a new people; a new purpose. This is the essence of God's calling to Abram. But it is also the essence of his kingdom. The kingdom of God, after all, is about God's people in God's place living for God's purpose. As sure as God is giving Abram a kingdom-sized calling in chapter 12 of Genesis, God has a kingdom-oriented calling for us. God calls us to a new *place* to belong; so we should ask ourselves the question, "Where can I make the most impact?" God calls us to a new *people* to invest in; so we should ask ourselves the question, "Whom can I make the most impact on?" God calls us to a new *purpose* to live out; so we should ask ourselves the question, "How can I make the most impact?" We will find our calling in Christ at the same place Abram did all those years ago: at the intersection of our place, our people, and our purpose.

The Testing of Abram and the Provision of God
GENESIS 12:10–14:16

Abram's is not a simple, happily-ever-after story. In fact, the giving of his calling is followed quickly by the testing of his calling. Abram immediately faces several big causes of concern. How he deals with them reinforces the truth that Abram was chosen not because of his perfection but because of God's grace. Nevertheless, in spite of the division and strife that arise from the actions of Abram, the protection and blessing of God remain evident, and the promise gets reaffirmed by a figure who points forward in a unique way to Jesus Christ. Generally speaking, the tests Abram faces represent what we might encounter as we seek to live out God's calling on our own lives.

Abram's Calling Is Tested by Adversity (12:10-20)

Just as Abram's obedience to God's calling gets underway, crisis comes. While we might assume God's calling would be followed by God's comfort, the next section of Genesis reveals that the calling of Abram is followed by several challenges each of us might still face today. The first challenge takes the form of adversity. In it the grandeur of Abram's calling collides with the hardship of Abram's circumstances: famine is sweeping the land of promise. There is not just a physical famine in Abram's new homeland; there is also a spiritual famine in Abram's new heart. Adversity tempts Abram to try to secure the blessing of God apart from the design of God. In fact, what happens in verse 10 is that the famine of food fuels anxiety leading to a famine of faith, resulting in Abram leaving Canaan behind. In going to Egypt, Abram seeks to meet his own needs through means of earthly protection rather than by asking for and expecting the eternal protection of God. Abram seeks protection not only from the danger of the famine but also from the danger of his own family. He asks Sarai to misrepresent their relationship (vv. 11-12). This theme of deception for the sake of self-protection shows up repeatedly in Genesis—from Adam to Abraham to Jacob to Joseph's brothers. Though God's promise of making Abram a father would naturally include his wife, Abram's fear leads him to see his spouse only as a risk to be managed, as a means to an end, as a matter of convenience rather than commitment. In different ways, that same temptation can show up in our relationships today. Adversity doesn't just test Abram's trust in God's protection but also his trust in God's provision. This particular inclusion in the narrative is important because just as Adam failed to protect Eve from the serpent's lies, Abram fails to protect Sarai from Egypt and and lies during the process.

For a moment, it seems as if Abram will have to receive the blessing God promised apart from God's prescribed design. Sarai is taken into Pharaoh's "household." But thinking him only her adored brother, the king treats "Abram well because of her" and greatly enriches him (vv. 14-16). In the end, however, this messy situation compromises Abram's reputation.

Nevertheless, the incident introduces another theme that's repeated in Scripture, that of pagan Egypt being a means of provision. Several times, in fact, the chosen people of God plunder these enemies of God because of the providence of God (Exod 12:36). Egypt serves this way again in chapter 43, when Joseph's brothers (descendants of Abraham) face another famine and Egypt meets their needs. It also happens in the time of the exodus, when the whole infant nation of Israel leaves their enslavement in Egypt to head back toward the promised land. Adversity compromises Abram's authenticity. Abram believed the path to the good life was through his own deception rather than God's design. The same danger faces us today. We are pulled to pretend for our provision.

Starting in Genesis 12:17, in fact, the text foreshadows that coming time of the exodus when another pharaoh will experience the many plagues on Egypt.

At the root of Abram's travel to Egypt and the deception he initiates there is doubt. But even though Abram doesn't trust in God's plan, at least not yet in a way that drives his decision making, he still receives the protection and provision he seeks. Why? Because in spite of him, God remains faithful to his promises. Though things might have turned out far differently for Abram once the truth about Sarai came out, Pharaoh just sends Abram away with "all he [has]" (v. 20).

Throughout history, humanity has repeatedly failed testing by adversity as Abram did. And he is certainly not the only believer to do so. But the New Testament shows us a profound parallel with what happens in Genesis 12. It suggests a day is coming when failure to walk by faith will no longer be the norm. When Jesus's life is in danger because Herod seeks to kill Jewish babies, his family doesn't flee *from* God's protection by escaping to Egypt on their own initiative. Rather, they flee *to* God's protection in Egypt out of obedience to his stated will (Matt 2:13-15).

Just as God calls his son Abram out of Egypt in Genesis 12, God also calls his son Israel out of Egypt in the exodus. Ultimately, God calls his Son Jesus out of Egypt as a fulfillment of the promise in Hosea 11 that is built on the pattern that begins here in Genesis 12. But the test of adversity is not the only challenge Abram faces.

Abram's Calling Is Tested by Abundance (13)

The second challenge to Abram's calling comes in the form of abundance. At this point, Abram is "very rich in livestock, silver, and gold" (v. 2). If adversity tests a calling through anxiety, abundance tests a calling through apathy. Yet Abram does better this round. He responds to having abundance not with complacency but with renewed commitment as he heads back toward his home and resumes his worship of

God. Though Abram abandoned his altar in adversity, he comes back to it in abundance. Though he turned away from God in crisis, he now calls "on the name of the LORD" in commitment (v. 4).

Abundance, however, tests not only Abram's commitment but also his character. When tensions between Abram and Lot's family arise because of Abram's newfound riches, his improving character is on display as he selflessly gives Lot the first choice of where to settle in the land (vv. 8-9).

In what may be an echo of 3:6, Lot looks out and chooses a section beyond the new place God to which God has called his uncle. Therefore, while Abram's selflessness in this instance suggests an effort to walk by faith even in the midst of abundance, Lot walks by sight. Whereas Lot had been living near "Bethel" (13:3), he now moves "his tent near Sodom" (v. 12). He moves from the doorstep of the place that means "house of God" to the doorstep of the place history associates with great sin (v. 13). Abundance, it seems, leads Lot to put himself in grave spiritual danger.

Meanwhile, Abram settles down "in the land of Canaan" (v. 12). This implies he is choosing to still trust the promises of God even as he begins to experience evidence of the blessing of God. At this point God renews his promise (vv. 14-15). Then God gives a fresh sense of the scope of his commitment to Abram in verse 16 as he declares, "I will make your offspring like the dust of the earth." In 2:7 God uses dust for the formation of humanity that begins with Adam. Now God uses dust to help describe the fruitfulness of a new humanity that officially begins with Abram.

In 13:17, God tells Abram to "get up and walk around the land" promised to him. This foreshadows the way Jesus, the ultimate son of Abraham, walked the face of this earth that he would inherit by fulfilling the promise. His coming fuels our hope and can help us withstand testing, whether we find ourselves in a valley of adversity or on a mountaintop of abundance. This passage shows us both can create a test for our dedication to God's calling. Adversity can fuel anxiety that tests our trust in God's calling. Abundance can fuel apathy that tests our commitment to God's calling.

Abram's Calling Is Tested by Attack (14:1-16)

The third challenge to Abram's calling involves an attack. Genesis 14 marks a sobering occasion since it is the Bible's first mention of a military battle. But it also marks a positive turning point in Abram's life.

In Genesis 12 Abram flees the promised land in search of protection and provision in a way that makes him appear cowardly and faithless. By contrast, here in Genesis 14 Abram leaves the promised land briefly in the role of a conquering warrior who is living out God's calling. In his response to injustice committed against his kin, Abram displays deep commitment to his calling.

This passage shows that though the Tower of Babylon itself fell, the prideful spirit of Babylon was not eradicated. In fact, James 4:1-2 reveals that the underlying factor shaping every conflict, whether an ancient battle like this one or the spiritual battles we face today, is not just a war involving people. It's a spiritual war of passions. In some ways, the military battle raging around Abram in Genesis 14 helps us make sense of the spiritual battles we face today (Eph 6:11-12). We believers, after all, face an enemy who is far more dangerous than "Chedorlaomer," a regional ruler of Abram's day (Gen 14:4). Our enemy is the "ruler of the power of the air" (Eph 2:2).

The military war outlined in Genesis 14:1-7 leads to a standoff resulting in looting and kidnapping. Lot, in fact, is the first prisoner of war mentioned in the Bible. He is taken when the marauding kings defeat those of Sodom and Gomorrah. Not content with their victory, they seek to disrupt the area's economy (v. 11). This first recorded act of plundering brings to mind John 10:10, where Jesus declares, "A thief comes only to steal and kill and destroy." Jesus is warning us that Satan does not just persuade us to sin through deception, but he also plunders us after we sin through accusation. He steals our joy, kills our hope, and destroys our witness. It seems, then, that the marauders' actions share commonalties with the way the devil operates.

When Lot is taken captive (Gen 14:12), it is not just a threat to the future of Abram's family but a threat to the future of Abram's calling. How was it that Lot, nephew of the wealthy Abram, found himself in this situation? Because by this point Lot had moved from living "near Sodom" (13:12) to living "in Sodom" (14:12). He had already become a slave to sin before he ever became a prisoner of war.

The attack tests Abram's calling as soon as he learns from an escaped captive that Lot is now a prisoner of war (v. 13). We might expect Abram to respond to this news with contempt: "I gave that guy the first choice of the land, so he will just have to endure the consequences of his decision." Yet Abram instead responds with compassion. Not with passivity but with pursuit. Not with resentment but with the intent to rescue his wayward family members from enemies (v. 20).

Abram's conquest establishes a pattern of kingdom warfare in which God brings about an unlikely victory over an undefeated enemy through an unexpected deliverer for an undeserving people. In the storyline of Scripture, in fact, the kingdom of Israel advances through a series of unlikely victories, including the exodus and the fall of Jericho, and through the involvement of unexpected deliverers like Gideon, Elijah, and David. In the New Testament, this pattern of kingdom warfare culminates in the work of Christ. No enemy was ever more undefeated than death. No victory was ever more unlikely than what happened at the cross and tomb. And considering his being born into a poor family and lack of military or political connection, no deliverer was more unexpected than Jesus. Nevertheless, this son of Abraham follows the way of Abram, leaving the comfort of God's place to go on a rescue mission for God's people so he can restore them to God's purpose. In fact, Abram's rescuing Lot from the enemies of God in Genesis 14 anticipates the son of Abraham's rescuing humanity from the ultimate enemy of God in Acts 2.

Genesis 14 is the end of the story for Chedorlaomer, king of Elam, and his band of rulers from Mesopotamia, yet it does not mark the end of the story for their kinsmen and descendants. At Pentecost, Peter shares the gospel for the first time to people from many nations. Acts 2:9 says these included "Parthians, Medes, Elamites; *those who live in Mesopotamia,* in Judea and Cappadocia, Pontus and Asia" (emphasis added). So, in his first recorded proclamation of the gospel, Peter speaks about the offspring of Abraham to a group that might well have included the offspring of Chedorlaomer. If so, the descendants of the defeated king of Elam are privileged to hear about the undefeated King of the universe and his loving rescue efforts on their behalf. Abram's rescue from the enemies of God in Genesis 14 anticipates the ultimate son of Abraham's rescue for the enemies of God in Acts 2.

The Blessing of Melchizedek and the Favor of God
GENESIS 14:17-24

To some, the end of Genesis 14 is an obscure passage sharing a pointless story. There is a temptation to overlook it because one of the most important passages in the whole Old Testament is coming up next in Genesis 15, where God makes a covenant with Abram. But here in chapter 14 we come face-to-face with one of the most mysterious yet significant figures in biblical history, Melchizedek. This passage answers several questions about this shadowy figure who prefigures the person of Christ.

So, first, *what type of king is Melchizedek?* Genesis 14:18 introduces him as the "king of Salem," but then the Bible never speaks about him again for hundreds of years. When it does, it helps reveal more about what type of king he is. Psalm 110:1-4 is David's reflection on Genesis 14 as he anticipates a future Messiah. The most quoted psalm in the New Testament, in fact, is Psalm 110. It gives a window into the nature of Melchizedek's kingship: he is a purposeful king (110:1), a powerful king (110:2), and a priestly king (110:4). Abram's brief encounter with Melchizedek in Genesis 14 anticipates the coming of the son of Abraham as the fulfillment of this type of kingship. That reality is seen even more clearly in Hebrews 7:1-3. The passage clarifies Melchizedek's identity, noting his name both means he is the "king of righteousness" and his location in "Salem" (which would become Jerusalem) means he is the "king of peace" (Heb 7:2; cf. Isa 9:6-7). It also confirms his purpose: "resembling the Son of God, he remains a priest forever" (Heb 7:3). When Melchizedek comes to Abram, he feeds Abram "bread and wine" (Gen 14:18). Later, the true King of Israel who is the "great high priest" will serve his disciples a meal— the bread of his body and "the cup" of his blood (Heb 4:14; cf. Luke 22:19-20). Hebrews tells us it is not that Jesus resembles Melchizedek but that Melchizedek resembles Jesus in this convergence of the roles of priest and king.

Second, *what type of priest is Melchizedek?* Genesis 14:18 notes that Melchizedek was "priest to God Most High." This is the first reference to a priest in the Bible, and it predates the Levitical priesthood of Israel. Hebrews 7:22-25 shows us humanity needs a priest not from the line of Levi but in the pattern of Melchizedek. That chapter reveals how Melchizedek points ahead to a better priest, Jesus Christ, who offers "a better covenant" (Heb 7:22). Other priests couldn't deliver on the promises of God because they failed in their own lives. But Jesus provides a guarantee for what God will do through the new covenant. Jesus Christ is a better priest who "holds his priesthood permanently" (Heb 7:23-24). One problem with Israel's priests, by contrast, is that death prevents them from continuing in the role. But Jesus continues forever through the power of an indestructible life and offers a perfect, ongoing sacrifice. Jesus Christ is a better priest who even offers a better hope. Our great high priest not only stands in our place through redemption but also makes our case through intercession. The result is a better hope rooted in a deeper peace because "he is able to save completely those who come to God through him" (Heb 7:25).

Third, *what type of blessing does Melchizedek bring?* The pattern of the Old Testament is for a superior to bless one who is inferior. Since Abram is one of the most significant figures in the Old Testament, it is shocking that he receives the blessing from this mysterious king (Gen 14:19-20). Nevertheless, Melchizedek mediates between God and Abram as he pronounces a blessing on Abram in the name of God. Just as Melchizedek mediates between God and Abram, Christ stands before the Father and mediates on behalf of his people (1 Tim 2:5). Hebrews 6:19-20 unpacks how this king in Genesis 14 points to a new and better Melchizedek who brings not an earthly blessing but an eternal one. In Jesus we have an "anchor for the soul, firm and secure" because he is the priest-king who has secured the blessing of God's promise for us. The path to peace does not come from the absence of problems but from the presence of his promise.

Fourth, *what type of response does Melchizedek deserve?* In Genesis 14:20 we find the first instance of a tithe offering in the Bible. Abram tithes to Melchizedek not because he demands it but because he deserves it. He gives Melchizedek a tenth of everything from his first and best, not as a complacent giver but as a "cheerful" one (2 Cor 9:7). This pattern of giving should be true for us today. Our commitment to the ultimate King should lead to our investment in the kingdom. The New Testament model of giving urges us to sacrifice our time, our talents, and our treasure for the sake of the gospel.

When we embrace the way of the kingdom, it should drive us to invest in the work of the kingdom. This passage points ahead to the reality that Jesus is the new and better Melchizedek, who is both the perfect King who defeats our enemies through his unstoppable power and the perfect priest who delivers us from our sin through his infinite mercy. And as Abram journeys from calling to crisis to commitment, this section of Genesis confirms a pattern of him walking by faith.

Reflect and Discuss

1. There is no clear explanation for why Abram, rather than another man, receives God's particular blessing. In the same way, Christians are undeserving of the favor and blessing of God extended to them. How should we react to this undeserved favor?

2. Abram dies before the fulfillment of what God promises him in Genesis 12. What does it mean to trust in a promise that is in the future and that you may not see fulfilled?

3. Abram sets out without any clear understanding of where he is headed. How is this an exercise of faith? What does faith look like in more everyday decisions?

4. When Abram faces the test of adversity, he attempts to use deception to secure the blessing of God. How do Christians find themselves "helping" God similarly? What does this passage suggest about our attempts to bring about God's promises on our own terms?

5. Paul shows us that all of creation is promised in Christ to the believer (Rom 4:13). What does the land promised to Abram have to do with that promise? How can trusting this promise help protect Christians from the lures of this current, fallen world?

6. Lot moves from being "near" Sodom (13:12) to "in Sodom" (14:12). What warning do you take from this?

7. Are Christians called to total separation from the world and sin? Explain why or why not.

8. When Abram faces the test of attack, he responds as a victorious warrior ruler who defeats his enemies under the power of God. How does this foreshadow the conquering King Jesus, both at his incarnation and at his second coming?

9. Melchizedek, the priest-king of Salem, anticipates Jesus, the future Priest-King of Jerusalem. Briefly explain how this is so.

10. Melchizedek is used as a type for Christ by later New Testament authors (Heb 7:4-10). How does the blessing Melchizedek gives to Abram in Genesis 14:19-20 foreshadow the blessing Christ gives to his people?

The Covenant with Abraham

GENESIS 15–17

Main Idea: The calling of Abram in Genesis 12 is followed by the covenant with Abram in Genesis 15, the crisis of Abram in Genesis 16, and the confirmation of Abram in Genesis 17. The heart of Abram's story reveals the heart of God for his covenant people in that God speaks, he sees, and he seals.

I.   **The Covenant with Abram and the God Who Speaks (15)**
   A.   The covenant and Abram's saving faith (15:1-6)
   B.   The covenant and God's sovereign faithfulness (15:7-21)
II. **The Crisis of Abram and the God Who Sees (16)**
   A.   Hardship happens when we resist the plan of God (16:1-6).
   B.   Healing happens when we experience the presence of God (16:7-16).
III. **The Confirmation of Abraham and the God Who Seals (17)**
   A.   The shape of the covenant (17:1-8)
   B.   The sign of the covenant (17:9-14)
   C.   The son of the covenant (17:15-26)

This section of Genesis is pivotal to the storyline of Scripture. It is a linchpin, a turning point, a hinge moment. Abram receives the covenant promise of God and responds in faith. But the length of time between the promise and its fulfillment causes Abram and Sarai to begin to doubt that the promise will ever come to pass. God repeatedly reminds them of the promise he already made, however. He continuously points back to what he has accomplished, and this is the foundation for trusting what he will do in the future. Nevertheless, because the timeline of God is not that of Abram and his wife, they attempt to help God along. The decision of Abram and Sarai results in strife and tension within the family of Abram that will continue for centuries afterward. It reminds us that our attempts to create the promises of God through our own means and plans are never successful.

The promises made to Abram and Sarai lead to a picture of what faith in the waiting looks like. Just as Abram looked forward to a coming child and the promised blessings of God, we look forward to the return of Christ and the fulfillment of all the blessings of which Christ is the initial down payment. The need to wait and trust in God was as much a struggle for Abram as it is for us. We should remember, however, that some of Abram's actions ultimately led to problems for him later in life.

The section ends with the arrival of the promised child, Isaac, and the sealing of the covenant with the ritual of circumcision. In this way, Abram is looking not only to the immediate child but also to the future child of promise. Both are born not as a natural result but through the working of the Spirit of God—the present child to a ninety-year-old woman, the future child to a virgin. This is to show that the promises of God come not through natural means but through the supernatural working of his Spirit.

The Covenant with Abram and the God Who Speaks
GENESIS 15

That Abram has questions concerning God's promises should assure all believers. Although he is presented throughout Scripture as the paragon of faith, Abram felt much uncertainty about just how the promises would be accomplished. But rather than condemning Abram's questions, God responds with further assurance that he will accomplish all that he has promised. As God speaks and seals this word of covenant, it reveals Abram's saving faith and God's sovereign faithfulness.

The Covenant and Abram's Saving Faith (15:1-6)

The story of Abram shows that all believers are faced with a choice when they find themselves in the waiting room of life, when they note the gap between their expectations and experience, between God's promised rewards and their present reality. The question is, Will the believer respond with fear or faith? What we find in Genesis 15 is that Abram, though he has deep concerns, shows us the four marks of saving faith.

The first mark of saving faith is *dependence*. Saving faith depends on the protection of God. Verse 1 is the first instance in the Bible where God appears "in a vision." What's at the heart of this visitation? God wants Abram to realize he is his "shield." That is, God himself is Abram's protection. If even this celebrated chosen one of God who just won a stunning military victory needs to hear that God is his shield and that his security and future are thus not all up to him, then we do too. Rather than relying on self, saving faith depends on God as our Savior.

The second mark of saving faith is *desire*. Saving faith desires the provision of God. When Abram responds to God's vision of protection, it is not with an exclamation point but a question mark: "GOD, what can you give me, since I am childless and the heir of my house is Eliezer of Damascus?" (v. 2). At first glance, this seems like an expression of doubt. But Paul explains this about Abram:

> He did not waver in unbelief at God's promise but was strengthened in his faith and gave glory to God, because he was fully convinced that what God had promised, he was also able to do. (Rom 4:20-21)

Thus, Abram's question is not evidence of unbelieving doubt but speaks of his unwavering desire for God to accomplish what he said. In fact, in verse 3 Abram seems to be ready to accept that God's promises may come true in an unconventional sense. How does God respond in Genesis 15:4? God meets Abram's desire with a more detailed promise involving the provision of a biological son. This second mark of saving faith doesn't just depend on God as our Savior but desires for God to be our Lord—the one who sees our desires and provides for them one way or another as he sees fit.

The third mark of saving faith is *delight*. Saving faith delights in the promises of God. Abram has embraced by faith the promise made in Genesis 12 to make him a great nation. That's why he headed out from Haran and settled his tents in Canaan. Now, as he looks to the heavens in Genesis 15:5, he can anticipate it with the help of a stunning illustration. When God explains to Abram the significance of the countless stars, it takes his eyes off the wounds of the past, the weariness of the present, and the worries of the future. Just imagine Abram's awe as he looks up at the heavens and hears, "Your offspring will be that numerous" (v. 5). The essence of saving faith is that it delights in the promises of God. For us today, saving faith recognizes that Jesus is not just the Savior we need and the Lord we want but also the treasure we seek. Abram's view of the crystal-clear starry sky reminds us that the clearer our sight of the promises of God, the greater our delight in the promises of God should be.

The fourth mark of saving faith is *decision*. Saving faith decides to embrace and follow the plan of God. Abram shows us that the final mark of saving faith is when our dependence, our desire, and our delight drive us to a decision to trust the plan of God for our lives. And when Abram believes the Lord in this sense, God credits "it to him as righteousness" (v. 6). This one phrase helps us make sense of the purpose of the Bible and God's overarching plan for us.

In fact, Romans 4:22-25 shows that Abram's faith is a model for saving faith. Specifically, Paul states, "Now 'it was credited to him' was not written for Abraham alone, but also for us. It will be credited to us who believe in him who raised Jesus our Lord from the dead" (Rom 4:23-24). Romans 4 confirms what Genesis 15 clarifies: our righteousness doesn't depend on our behavior but our beliefs; it doesn't depend on our fruit but our faith. (After all, Abram was not righteous on his own: he turned away from God during the famine and turned away from his wife in Egypt.) When we decide to trust in Jesus as our Savior, Lord, and treasure, it changes everything for us. He takes our sin, and we receive his righteousness. He takes our guilt, and we receive his grace. He takes our shame, and we receive his salvation. Abram's decision to follow the plan of God reveals that the gift of saving faith is not based on what we do but on what God has done for us.

The Covenant and God's Sovereign Faithfulness (15:7-21)

In Genesis 15:7, the focus of the text shifts from Abram's saving faith to God's sovereign faithfulness. It pivots from Abram's conviction to God's covenant. What is a covenant? It is a foundational promise from God rooted in his own character and the certainty of his commitments. One of the most remarkable things about the 9/11 Memorial & Museum in New York City is that the whole museum is underground, allowing visitors to see the architectural and structural elements that established the foundation for the construction. In a sense, the biblical covenants function in a similar way: they provide the architectural and structural foundations that sustain the storyline of Scripture. The covenant with Abram in Genesis 15 builds on the calling of Abram in Genesis 12 to display God's sovereign faithfulness rooted in God's people living out God's purpose in God's chosen place.

In God's sovereign faithfulness, he establishes a covenant involving "this land," that is, the land of Canaan where Abram resides (v. 7). But even though Abram has unwavering faith, he still has questions about his uncertain future: "How can I know that I will possess it?" (v. 8).

After all, he does not own a square inch of soil within Canaan. So, while Abram's faith is unwavering, he remains unsure about how this promise too will be fulfilled.

This should give hope to the believer in Christ who has questions. The Lord does not condemn Abram's questions, nor does he say Abram is no longer righteous for asking them. How does God respond to Abram's questions about possessing the new place? With the shedding of blood (vv. 9-11). Sacrifice is foundational to the cutting of a covenant. And this particular sacrifice anticipates the coming of Christ, who establishes a new covenant through his death and resurrection. Through his death, the spotless "Lamb" of God "takes away the sin of the world" (John 1:29). And as the bodies of animals are torn in two in this scene involving covenant with Abram, the curtain in the temple is torn in two in the one involving Jesus (Matt 27:51). As a result of the new covenant, Jesus will one day welcome all who believe in him into the promised new creation (cf. Rev 21–22).

Here, in God's sovereign faithfulness, he is establishing a covenant created for a *new people*. Echoes from the garden of Eden scenes are present in this passage. To begin with, "a deep sleep came over Abram" (v. 12). Both in Genesis 2:21 and here, a deep sleep is used in reference to the bringing about of new people—the first of these, of course, is a new bride. Here, however, a whole new tribe is in view. In addition, the word "offspring" in 15:13 is the same term used in Genesis 3:15 in the first promise of salvation in the Bible, showing continuity between these promises. But this covenantal promise of a new people doesn't just look back to God's sovereign faithfulness in the past. It also looks forward to his commitment to faithfulness in the future. Verses 13-16, after all, paint a picture of future trials for God's people. They will be sojourners and slaves who face hundreds of years of difficulty. Nevertheless, there is hope in the midst of hardship. According to 15:14, the trials faced by God's people will be overcome by the deliverance provided by God's faithfulness.

In God's sovereign faithfulness, he establishes a covenant centered on a *new purpose*. In verses 17-21 we encounter one of the most bizarre moments in the Bible. After the animals are sacrificed and their corpses are spread out, a "smoking fire pot" and "flaming torch" pass through them. What is going on? The cloud of smoke and the pillar of fire, as evidenced in later books of the Old Testament, represent the presence of God (Num 9:15-23). And in ancient times it was common for those in a promise to walk between animals split in two as a symbol of what should happen if one of the partners failed to keep the covenant. But critical here is that only God walks between the animals because he is the one making the commitment. He is putting his character and his commitment on the line.

Why is this reality important? The one who participates in the making of covenant determines the purpose of the covenant. Since God is the one who makes the promise, he gets to determine Abram's purpose. That same concept holds true with regard to the new covenant, established by the death and resurrection of God's Son. We are called to a purpose of faithfulness on the basis of the shed blood of Jesus and the fire of the Holy Spirit within us.

The Crisis of Abram and the God Who Sees

GENESIS 16

If Genesis 15 describes God as the Lord who speaks, chapter 16 describes God as the Lord who sees. God not only sees the broken, in fact, but brings comfort. This passage is filled with difficult topics: infertility, infidelity, abuse, and abandonment. Their presence helps us see how we should respond in the midst of hardships of our own. The passage explains that God sees us in our hardship and can give us hope in spite of it, as well as healing.

The root of much of the hardship experienced in this section of Genesis is the impatience of Abram and Sarai as they wait on the promises of God. We too often find that when our desires cause us to pursue a different direction from God's design, that alternate direction will lead to destruction. The fundamental problem of this passage is that sometimes the people of God try to pursue the promise of God apart from the plan of God.

Hardship Happens When We Resist the Plan of God (16:1-6)

The Bible doesn't sugarcoat the fact that the saints still sin at times. Genesis 16, tucked away between the creation of the covenant in Genesis 15 and the confirmation of the covenant in Genesis 17, provides an excellent example of this. At first, it seems like a detour or a distraction to the narrative of Abram. God's man Abram has been in the promised land for a decade by this point. He has survived famines and wars. But now he and his wife come face-to-face with the most dangerous challenges we all experience: uncertainty, impatience, confusion, and desperation. Tragically, the great faith evidenced in Genesis 15 is followed by the sad tale of a great fall in Genesis 16 as the pair tries to fulfill the promise of God apart from the plan of God. Doing so inevitably leads to pain.

This passage reveals several aspects of the hardship that happens when we resist the plan of God for our lives. First, hardship comes through *broken trust*. Sarai is struggling with infertility. But the deeper issue is not Sarai's broken body but her broken trust in God (v. 2). Sarai isn't just doubting God's promises. She is also blaming God for her problems. In her mind, he is not just withholding what is good but also causing what is bad.

Second, hardship comes through *broken vows* as Abram agrees to go along with Sarai's plan (v. 2). Like his forefather Adam in Eden, Abram thus abandons his leadership over his family and capitulates to his wife's unhealthy desire. In what happens here through verse 4, there also are echoes of Genesis 12. In Egypt, Abram pretended Sarai was not his wife. Now Sarai wants Abram to pretend that she is not his only wife. In another echo of events back in Eden, Abram "listened to the voice of Sarai," signaling that her disobedience to God's design leads to his own disobedience (v. 2 ESV). A broken timeline leads to broken trust which leads to broken vows. As a result, it leads to broken hearts, broken bodies, and ultimately a broken family.

Third, hardship comes through *broken relationships*. After Hagar becomes pregnant, the text shows how broken trust leads to broken choices that result in broken relationships (vv. 4-5). Corruption breeds contempt which breeds conflict which breeds condemnation. Hagar's pride combines with Sarai's pity and Abram's passivity to bring about the destruction of the moment.

Fourth, hardship comes through *broken people*. Abram gives Hagar back to Sarai for condemnation (v. 6). Imagine Hagar's situation. As a servant with few rights, she is pressured into being a solution to her mistress's problem. As a result, she doesn't just witness Sarai's brokenness over her infertility anymore. Now she experiences the results of that brokenness within herself. It is not too much to say that Hagar is the victim of both sex trafficking and domestic violence. And if Abram is guilty of using her body, Sarai is guilty of crushing her soul. So she flees. She would rather be anywhere, even the wilderness, than here. That is how broken she is. When the people of God fail to trust the plan of God, hardship results.

Healing Happens When We Experience the Presence of God (16:7-16)

Genesis 16 doesn't show us only the path to hardship but also the path to healing. Healing happens when we receive the promise of God through the presence of God.

By verse 7, Hagar is a single mom-to-be stranded in the wilderness. Her situation is reflective of the reality in which many of us find ourselves. She feels alone, vulnerable, and is making her way through a valley of despair. Because of the sinful actions of others, she finds herself suffering and far from help or hope. Or so it seems.

Some may be wondering like Hagar: Is there any hope? This passage shows several dimensions to the path of healing after hardship.

Precisely where we find Hagar in 16:7 is important. "The spring on the way to Shur" is near her native Egypt. As many of us are wired to do in times of trouble, then, she starts heading back toward what was home once things go awry. But even being back in her old home will not offer her the help she needs. Hagar needs the presence of God. Indeed, who appears to her but "the angel of the Lord" (vv. 7-14)?

While some believe this to be an angelic figure like Michael or Gabriel, many scholars equate an encounter with the angel of the Lord with an appearance of God himself. How the visitor speaks to Hagar and how she responds to him support the theory (vv. 10,13). The technical term for this is a Christophany—an appearance of the Son of God before he took on flesh as Jesus. If this is indeed a Christophany, then this scene is a preview of John 4:1-26 where Jesus meets with another woman at a well. In both cases, the *presence of God* brings a woman healing after hardship.

The angel of the Lord seeks out Hagar with a pair of questions in 16:8 that every one of us needs to personalize in our pain. In verse 8 he asks, "Hagar, slave of Sarai, where have you come from and where are you going?" In other words, he asks her a question about direction and destiny. A question about her trials but also her trajectory. When the presence of God brings us face-to-face with our past and our purpose, we are better positioned to find healing.

In what happens next, we see that healing after hardship also comes through the *provision of God*. But even so, healing does not always come easily. Surprisingly, the angel of the Lord instructs Hagar, "Go back to your mistress and submit to her authority" (v. 9). This command is not intended to encourage survivors to return and submit to their abusers. Instead, it is establishing a pattern in Scripture in which God reveals that future suffering can be the pathway to future blessing. Later, this pattern is at work in the lives of Isaac, Jacob, Joseph, Moses, David, and ultimately Jesus himself. Hagar's healing after hardship will come through God's provision of protection when she returns back.

Also important to Hagar's healing is a promise, which is a subtle indicator that one of the ways God brings healing after hardship is by helping us see how good can arise from the bad experiences in our lives. He does exactly that for Hagar as she receives the promise of mothering a multitude of "offspring," beginning with "Ishmael," whose name reminds her that the Lord himself "has heard [her] cry of affliction" (vv. 10-11). Nevertheless, attached to the promise is a preview of the future conflict God's chosen people will face (v. 12). It indicates that Abram's failure in a moment, and the related injustice against Hagar, will lead to generations of conflict for their progeny.

Finally, within the section we see that healing after hardship comes through the *providence of God*. Imagine for a moment Hagar's fear as she obediently switches course to return to Abram and Sarai. Yet that "Abram named his son . . . Ishmael" indicates that at some point following her arrival, she boldly tells him exactly what happened out near the spring of Shur. And he believes her (v. 15). Thus, Hagar's return to Abram leads to Abram's return to God. But the providence of God brings healing for Hagar even before that reunification with the household for which she works. Remember, when first we met Hagar in the narrative (16:2), the woman was so lowly that Sarai would not even refer to her by name. Yet this one whose mistress acted as if she had no name is the one who gives God a new name. In fact, Hagar is the only person in the Old Testament to do so. What is it? In 16:13, she "named the LORD who spoke to her: 'You are El-roi,' for she said, 'In this place, have I actually seen the one who sees me?'" In their sin, Abram and Sarai see Hagar only for what she might do. Yet God sees her for who she is. They use her, but God sees her and provides her with a hopeful future.

Likewise, God in his providence sees us in our pain and sends his Son to save us. This one that Isaiah 53:3-5 describes as the Suffering Servant meets us in our sin and suffering to bring hope after hardship. Jesus still sees. Jesus still helps. Jesus still heals.

The Confirmation of Abraham and the God Who Seals
GENESIS 17

If Genesis 15 reveals the God who speaks and Genesis 16 reveals the God who sees, then Genesis 17 reveals the God who seals. The covenant with Abram culminates in the confirmation of Abram as the text jumps thirteen years ahead from the previous chapter. Here God not only gives to Abram the covenant—for a third time—but a new name: Abraham. God also institutes circumcision, a sign that will become a hallmark of the Jewish faith, before promising the imminent arrival of the child through whom all the promises of God will start to come to pass.

If we can understand the significance of the sealing of this covenant promise, it will transform how we pursue Jesus in our lives.

The Shape of the Covenant (17:1-8)

Though it marks Abram's third covenantal moment with the Lord, Genesis 17 gives us the clearest account of God's covenant with him. That is part of why this chapter is referenced more than two dozen times in the New Testament. It brings God's covenant commitment to Abram to a culmination. This occurs when Abram is "ninety-nine years old" (v. 1).

Thirteen years have passed since the events recorded in the Bible's previous chapter. But there is still no child for Abram and Sarai. While Abram was already seventy-five years old when God promised he would be a great nation (12:2-4), the only child born to him thus far is Ishmael. And every time Abram sees that teenager, he is surely reminded of his own failure to trust the promise of God.

After Abram's sinful failure in Genesis 16, in fact, we might expect God to resist Abram in anger. Instead, he keeps pursuing Abram in love by renewing the covenant. God begins by announcing himself: "I am God Almighty" (17:1). This is a proclamation of God's presence and his character. It parallels his coming introduction to the promise to Jacob, Abram's grandson, in 35:11. As Exodus 6:3 makes clear, however, there is an important distinction between the way God reveals himself to Abram and then later to the people of Israel. To Abram he reveals himself as God Almighty but not yet as Yahweh, "the LORD."

God follows this introduction with the instruction that Abram is to "live in [his] presence and be blameless" (Gen 17:1). These two commands are incumbent on all God's people, past and present. Believers are to live with awareness of the presence of God and stand before him in holiness (Rom 12:1; Eph 1:4). The character of God that shapes the covenant is the foundation for reshaping one's character.

Genesis 17:2 reminds the reader that proof of God's covenant with Abram will involve God multiplying him "greatly." This third round of covenantal promises connects back to the original covenant commitment in Genesis 1:28 where Adam is told to multiply. In fact, the text is presenting Abram as a new Adam who will be fruitful and multiply and fill the earth, just as the original progenitor of humanity was intended to do. Perhaps realizing this, the one who had previously fallen on his face in wrongdoing now falls "facedown" before God in worship (v. 3). He will do this again after the promise of the imminent birth of Isaac (v. 17).

God gives six aspects of the covenant, beginning in verse 4. First, God presents Abram with a *new purpose*—he will be "the father of many nations." This role will begin to play out throughout the rest of the book of Genesis, where his descendants become patriarchs of different nations (25:1-6,12-18). But in Romans 4:16 Paul will expand on the idea, making clear that Abram was never intended to be the father of *only* many biological descendants. Always on God's mind were his spiritual descendants from the many nations, too. With regard to believers in Christ, Paul writes,

> "This *is why the promise is by faith, so that it may be according to grace, to guarantee it to* all the descendants—*not only to those to the one who is of the law but also to those who are of Abraham's faith.* [Abram] *is* the father of us all." (Rom 4:16; emphasis added)

What is Paul saying? Not just that many nations will come from Abram but also that many nations will come with him in the gospel of Jesus Christ. Abraham is the father of all those who place their faith in Jesus Christ. The promise comes to him by faith, so that through Jesus, the ultimate biological offspring of Abram, believers of every nationality, that is, the figurative offspring of Abram, are welcomed into the family of God according to grace.

Second, God presents Abram with a *new name.* Abraham (Gen 17:5).
In the original language the name *Abraham* sounds like the combina-
tion of the words for "father" and "many." This shift in names marks the
covenantal moment in which Abraham finds himself. The new name is
picked up by Paul again in the aforementioned passage of Romans. Of
him, Paul writes,

> *As it is written: I have made you the father of many nations—in the
> presence of the God in whom he believed, the one who gives life to the
> dead and calls things into existence that do not exist. [Abraham]
> believed, hoping against hope, so that he became the father of many
> nations according to what had been spoken: So will your descendants
> be.* (Rom 4:17-18)

Abraham's new name is intimately connected to his new purpose. Paul
credits the man's faith as the basis for the new role that leads to his
new name.

Third, God presents Abraham with the promise of a *new people.*
Genesis 17:6 speaks of how God will increase Abraham's family: God will
make him "extremely fruitful" and cause "nations and kings" to come
from him. For one thing, God will establish his new people in a global
kingdom. This verse extends the covenantal promise to be fruitful and
multiply from Genesis 1 in several ways. To begin with, it speaks to the
prolific fruitfulness of Abraham. Abraham's descendants will be as num-
berless as the stars or grains of sand (22:17). In addition, Abraham will
not only be fruitful but will also produce whole countries and leaders.
The apostle Paul notes that Abraham was strengthened in his faithfulness
when God spoke this to him (Rom 4:19-22). The writer of Hebrews confirms that from Abraham came innumerable descendants (Heb 11:12).

Fourth, God presents Abraham with the promise of a *new commitment.* Genesis 17:7 speaks of the "permanent covenant" God is making to
be not just Abraham's God but also "God of [his] offspring after [him]."
This is the same kind of language God uses in the Noahic covenant
(9:6). And this is not a temporary commitment. It is an everlasting covenant for all generations. The author of Hebrews will use the language
of the personal God in 11:16 where he says, "God is not ashamed to be
called their God." Just as the Lord promises to Abraham that he will be
his God, the author of Hebrews points out that for people of faith in the
Old Testament, God is not ashamed to be their God. Why? Because they

are seeking a "city" that "he has prepared" for them, a city that will be the culmination of the everlasting covenant made with Abraham.

Fifth, God presents Abraham with the promise of a *new place*. Verse 8 is the promise of God to provide the land of Canaan as an eternal possession. Abraham had sojourned through many lands for almost twenty-five years. There is now a promise that one day he and his offspring will have the land where he currently stands as their own. Forever. The promise of land is mentioned by the author of Hebrews as a matter that helps evidence Abraham's faith (Heb 11:8-10). Abraham leaves a place of inheritance and goes to a place of instability because he trusts this faithful God. He speaks of how Abraham believes God will ultimately provide for him in the future a "city that has foundations" and "whose architect and builder is God" (Heb 11:10). While the modern reader knows the outcome of Abraham's story, Abraham was stepping out into the unknown. He was abandoning comfort and stability by leaving Haran. But throughout his relocation, he was driven by a motivation that God would provide all that he had promised. All along, his expectation of a new place in the future transformed what he was willing to do in the present.

Finally, God presents Abraham with a *new hope*. Verse 8 speaks of Abraham's "future offspring." The text has already established that Abraham can expect a child and that nations are to arise from him (15:4-5; 17:3-4). But who is *this* "future offspring"? Galatians 3:16 confirms it is the long-expected Messiah. There Paul writes,

> *Now the promises were spoken to Abraham and to his seed. He does not say "and to seeds," as though referring to many, but referring to one, "and to your seed," who is Christ.*

In part, then, Jesus makes his way to the cross, defeats Satan, sin, and death, and is raised so that he might fulfill the covenant commitments given to Abraham and receive the covenant blessings promised to Abraham. This is what Paul is describing in Romans 4:20-25. The faith credited to Abraham was not just for Abraham alone but also for us. The coming Messiah would be the true, faithful offspring of Abraham. He would fulfill the covenant and receive its blessings. That's why Paul highlights how this covenant with Abraham foreshadows the promise established by Abraham's ultimate offspring in the new covenant when Jesus "was delivered up for our trespasses and raised for our justification" (Rom 4:25). Even in the covenant promised to Abraham in

Genesis 17, the seed of a new covenant that would come in Abraham's offspring is present.

The Sign of the Covenant (17:9-14)

Throughout Scripture, a covenant often comes with a sign. When God made a covenant with Adam, he was given Eve. When God made a covenant with Noah, he was given a rainbow. Now, when God makes a covenant with Abraham, he is given circumcision.

Why did God choose to seal the covenant in this way? First, circumcision reveals the nature of the covenant, which is linked to a promise that originated back in Genesis 3:15—the seed of the woman will crush the head of the serpent. The sign of this Abrahamic covenant thus involves the seed-generating organ of men. Paul declares, however, that circumcision doesn't just reveal the nature of the promise but also the nature of faith. Of Abraham he writes,

> And he received the sign of circumcision as a seal of the righteousness that he had by faith, while still uncircumcised. This was to make him the father of all who believe but are not circumcised, so that righteousness may be credited to them also. (Rom 4:11)

So the physical marking of circumcision was intended to serve as a daily reminder of the spiritual marking of faith. But this faith was not just for Abraham. It is for all who trust in Christ.

The process of circumcision signals the purpose of circumcision. What is the *process* of circumcision? It involves the cutting away of the "foreskin" (Gen 17:11). According to verses 12-14, circumcision is intended to happen on a male's eighth day of life as a sign of new creation and his participation in the covenant. It is not just for Abraham's biological line but also for foreigners brought into the "household" of God's covenant people (v. 13). Those who fail to follow the sign of circumcision will be "cut off" from the covenant (v. 14) through their sin.

What is the *purpose* of circumcision? As circumcision marks out the people of God, it also anticipates what God is going to do in Christ through the cross. When Jesus is circumcised on the eighth day (Luke 2:21), it is an indication that the new creation is dawning. The death of Jesus is the fulfillment of this covenant sign. On the cross, he is crucified naked in a public display of one who has been cut off from his people.

He is carried outside the gates of the city and separated from God. He is literally bearing the weight of the curse of God for you and for me. Jesus takes the punishment of the covenant so we can receive the promise of the covenant. The sign of physical circumcision thus points ahead to a deeper spiritual reality. What starts with a physical marking of the flesh in Genesis 17:11 points ahead to the need for a spiritual marking (Deut 30:6). This is why Paul says that, for new covenant believers, "true circumcision is not something visible in the flesh" but instead "circumcision is of the heart" (Rom 2:28-29). For the believer who is under the new covenant established at the death and resurrection of Jesus, it is not a physical circumcision but rather one of the heart that is required. Physical circumcision is disgusting, messy, and intimate. But this is necessary in that it helps us see that our sin is just the same: disgusting, messy, and intimate. Only a circumcision of our hearts, a cutting away of sin, can set us free. When we are united to Christ by faith, his circumcision becomes our circumcision, both the physical circumcision he experienced on the eighth day and the figurative circumcision he experienced on the cross (Col 2:11-12). Paul takes a hard line against those who would require circumcision from the new Gentile converts. Why? Because to require circumcision is to say that the individual does not share the identity of Christ (Gal 2:11-14).

For the church, baptism replaces circumcision. It is a visible, outward sign of one's participation in the new covenant. When a new believer goes under the water of baptism, he or she is acknowledging having once been cut off from the covenant due to personal sin. But when he or she is lifted out of the waters, that is a symbol of being raised to walk in the newness of life offered those who believe Jesus has conquered the grave. Baptism does not determine our place in the family of God. Rather, it displays our place in the family of God.

The Son of the Covenant (17:15-26)

The covenant with Abraham culminates in the first gender reveal party in recorded history. Before the big announcement, Abraham's wife receives a new name, Sarah, which means "princess." From her will come a royal lineage because she will help produce nations and kings (v. 15). Here, in fact, we find a repeated theme of the covenant and kingdom. The future promises have a royal component to them (v. 16; 35:11; 49:10). Sarah receives a promise of blessing: she will have a son and a legacy. The promise that she will produce kings and nations builds on the Genesis 3:15 promise. The royal lineage that starts with Sarah will eventually focus into a coming son of King David. The New Testament highlights Jesus as the royal Messiah.

How does Abraham respond to hearing, "I will give you a son by [Sarah]" (17:16)? Abraham's response is both to fall "facedown" in worship and to laugh (v. 17). Abraham is filled with a joyful amazement in God's goodness, despite their advanced age. Nevertheless, he wonders aloud about Ishmael being "acceptable" (v. 18), which would seem an easier solution to the promises getting fulfilled than he and Sarah parenting an infant in their advanced life season. However, as Paul makes clear in Romans 4:19, Abraham sees the weakness of his body without being shaken in his faith. Abraham's laughter is not a sign of unbelief. Rather, it is a sign of faithful surprise and amazement at the overwhelming goodness of God. Abraham trusts in his provision.

The promise of this new son is closely connected to the name of this new son. The child to be born is to be called Isaac, which means "he laughs" (v. 19). And as sure as Abraham laughed over news of his coming, Sarah will also laugh in the next chapter when she hears for herself that she will conceive and give birth before a year has passed (18:12).

However, God is faithful to keep his promises, and a child is born. God next affirms the covenant to be not just with Abraham or his immediate descendant, Isaac, but for all descendants. Just as with Abraham, God will extend his promised blessing to Isaac as a "permanent covenant with his future offspring" (17:19).

Yet Isaac is not the only son of Abraham who receives the blessing of God in this passage. Abraham's suggestion of Ishmael as a possible alternative leads God to tell Abraham of the blessings ahead for Ishmael. Though Ishmael does not receive the promise of the everlasting covenant, he still receives a blessing from the Lord. The blessings of Isaac and Ishmael, in fact, parallel each other (v. 20; cf. 26:4). Both are told to be fruitful and multiply. From Ishmael will come "twelve tribal leaders," like the twelve tribal leaders that come from Jacob (17:20). Both are promised that they will be "a great nation" (v. 20). Nevertheless, in that aforementioned pattern that shows up repeatedly in Genesis, God chooses the younger brother instead of the older brother to fulfill the royal promise started in Genesis 3:15.

After this encounter, God withdraws or ascends from Abraham (17:22). This language is like what appears in God's encounter with Jacob after he renames him Israel and blesses him (35:13).

The confirmation of the covenant with Abraham culminates in the commitment of Abraham and his household as they undergo circumcision as a covenant sign (17:23-27).

Reflect and Discuss

1. When Abraham questions the ability of God to give a child, is it a cry about whether God can do what he said? Why or why not? Why does waiting often cause us to doubt God's ability?
2. Abraham's belief or faith is counted as righteousness. So, what is faith? Why is it essential for salvation?
3. Even as Abraham is filled with faith, he still has questions. What does this reveal about the relationship between faith and honest questions? Does faith mean there is no room for questioning God?
4. The covenant made with Abraham will be essential for Israel throughout the Old Testament. What is the nature of a covenant, and how does this specific covenant reveal the character of God?
5. Abram and Sarai's actions with Hagar result in Ishmael, who is not the promised child. In what way do your own actions betray the belief that God's promises can come through the works of the flesh rather than the Spirit?
6. Sarai's actions toward Hagar are abusive and a transgression of her authority over Hagar. So, how can we make sense of the angel's command for Hagar to return and submit to Sarai's authority?
7. The covenant God makes with Abraham in Genesis 17 comes with the covenant sign of circumcision. How does this sign point ahead to Jesus? What is now the sign of the new covenant for the people of God?
8. The covenant made with Abraham includes a promise of a judgment and a blessing. Why are the two often found together in Scripture? Can God's blessing come apart from judgment?
9. Both Abram and Sarai are given new names that reflect their new identities under the covenant. What is the significance of these new names?
10. Though Ishmael will not be the inheritor of the blessing, God will bless him for Abraham's sake. What might this suggest for those who are outside the new covenant?

The Judgment of Sodom and the Rescue of Life

GENESIS 18–19

Main Idea: God sends judgment against Sodom and Gomorrah in a way that sets a pattern for how he handles future sinful rebellion. But first, he demonstrates his covenant faithfulness by promising to provide offspring to Sarah and then by rescuing Lot from the fires of judgment.

I. **Abraham and the Promise of Life (18)**
    A. Abraham and the protection of life (18:1-8)
    B. Abraham and the provision of life (18:9-21)
    C. Abraham and the prayer for life (18:22-33)
II. **The Judgment of Sodom and the Rescue of Lot (19)**
    A. Lot and the value of life (19:1-11)
    B. Lot and the rescue of life (19:12-22)
    C. Lot and the judgment of life (19:23-29)
    D. Lot and the "preservation" of life (19:30-38)

The Lord often works in mysterious ways. In contrast to what God does with Abraham in this section, God does not always reveal his plans to his people. Yet he is always at work.

With echoes of the Abrahamic promise earlier in the Genesis narrative, God's actions here are based on past promises to the patriarch. God declares again that Abraham will "become a great and powerful nation" and that "all the nations of the earth will be blessed through him." This language in 18:18 closely parallels New Testament descriptions by both Peter (Acts 3:25) and Paul (Gal 3:8) of how the Abrahamic covenant ultimately finds its fulfillment in Jesus. Nevertheless, God connects Abraham's calling with his character and his covenant. God chooses Abraham the individual for a twofold purpose. First, so that he will walk in holiness by "doing what is right and just" (18:19). Second, so that he might contribute to fulfilling the covenant promises. Calling and character are the foundations for covenant, which is exactly why the New Testament demonstrates how Jesus is called by the Father and walks in sinless integrity on his path to securing the covenant promises of God that were made to Abraham.

In his prior descriptions of Sodom, Moses has already acknowledged that "the men of Sodom were evil, sinning immensely against
the LORD" (13:13). In this way, Sodom serves as a local and renewed
manifestation of the pervasive evil that characterized the earth before
the flood. In a sense, what happens at Sodom is in some ways reflective
of the Tower of Babylon incident (11:5). For instance, the Lord came
down to witness the builders' wickedness firsthand. He takes an up-close
look at the state of things in Sodom, too. At Babylon prideful humans
attempted to equal God through their wickedness. At Sodom humanity
seeks to escape God through their wickedness. Moreover, in the same
way that there was an outcry from the blood of Abel because of Cain's
sin (4:10), there is now an "outcry" regarding the iniquities of Sodom
and Gomorrah, whose "sin is extremely serious" (18:20).

What is the nature of their sin? Given the Genesis narrative, most
assume it is sexual sin and debauchery. But the Bible portrays it more
holistically elsewhere. Ezekiel 16:48-50, for instance, tells us that it is
twofold. First, in their pride the citizens there refuse to use their privileged position as a platform to provide for the poor (Ezek 16:49).
Pride causesd Sodom to turn inward in self-protection for their needs
to the neglect of the poor. Second, their pride manifests itself in that
they "[do] detestable acts before [God]" (Ezek 16:50). Thus, pride
also causes them to turn outward in self-provision for their flesh to the
neglect of God's coming law (Jude 7).

Sodom and Gomorrah are the incarnation of much of what is said
at the start of Romans. In their pride, their hearts are "darkened" as
they claim "to be wise" (Rom 1:21-22). Through their actions, they
suppress the truth of God "by their unrighteousness" (Rom 1:18). As
a result, God gives them over to their "disgraceful passions," with alarming results (Rom 1:26). Like all unrepentant sinners, those in Sodom
and Gomorrah "deserve to die" (Rom 1:32). The judgment of these cities thus serves as a warning to all about the consequences of sin.

Abraham and the Promise of Life
GENESIS 18

Now that God has confirmed the covenant with Abraham through the
sign of circumcision, the story of Genesis begins to advance. Before God
judged the earth through the flood, he prepared to preserve Noah. In a
similar way, before God judges Sodom and Gomorrah through fire, he

first prepares to preserve Abraham. Ultimately, the covenantal protection of God delivers his chosen one from the judgment of God.

Abraham and the Protection of Life (18:1-8)

After the circumcision of the males in Abraham's household, he is found resting near "his tent" (v. 1). The story that follows is a case of Abraham's desire to protect life in every way possible. When he sees "three men" approach, Abraham does not ignore or greet them with skepticism. Rather, he welcomes them. He not only sees them, but he eagerly runs toward them (v. 2). Based on this reaction, it seems as if he recognizes that this is the Lord accompanied by two angelic beings. Indeed, as he approaches them, he bows in deep honor or worship (v. 2). He brings them to his house and offers them protection from both the elements and the untamed wilderness around them. If there was ever a time that Abraham might have felt justified to selfishly serve his own needs, it would be in this moment as he and his family recover from enacting the sign of the covenant. Yet, instead of doing so, he focuses on the needs of others.

His actions may also speak to what becomes apparent later in the narrative: Abraham desires to protect life. In urging the guests to rest in his tent's shade, he offers them protection from the elements. Abraham doesn't just see their needs; he also serves their needs. Abraham's protection is more than an offer of comfort, however. He also extends refreshment in the form of water to wash their feet and nourishment. Abraham serves swiftly, sacrificially, and selflessly (vv. 6-8). His actions are an example of how God has called us to show hospitality (Rom 12:13; 1 Pet 4:9).

It is significant that Abraham selects a "tender, choice calf" for his guests (v. 7). It means he is sacrificially providing them with a meal from the best of his herd. Rather than presenting them with the household's leftovers, he has fresh food prepared for the visitors (vv. 6-8). Moreover, this wealthy man with servants of his own *serves* the guests while declining to partake himself (v. 8).

Some people might read this passage and think, *Sure, it is obvious that Abraham would sacrificially serve their needs because this is God himself and several angels.* If we ever had the chance to serve God as Abraham does in this passage, we would do it in the same swift, sacrificial, and selfless way. But, in the parable of the sheep and goats, Jesus seeks to transform our perspective on the topic of hospitality (Matt 25:34-40).

With the parable, Jesus essentially declares that we are all in the same situation as Abraham when it comes to how we should treat those with whom our paths cross. No matter who they are. In it, he says, "Truly I tell you, whatever you did for one of the least of these brothers and sisters of mine, you did for me" (Matt 25:40). The lesson here is that when we serve the needs of those around us, when we care for the vulnerable in our communities, when we stand for life at every stage from the womb to the tomb, we are actually serving God himself.

Abraham and the Provision of Life (18:9-21)

Next the passage touches on the provision of life offered Abraham by God. It begins as the most prominent visitor asks Sarah's whereabouts (v. 9). It climaxes in his giving of a general timetable for Isaac's arrival (v. 10). This moment of divine announcement foreshadows coming promises to Zechariah and Mary involving the upcoming births of John the Baptist and Jesus; these sons will advance the promises of God, too (Luke 1:30-33).

Meanwhile, at the entrance to the tent and likely thinking herself unnoticed, Sarah responds to the news of when she is to give birth with laughter (vv. 10,12). Unlike Abraham's laughter of delight in the promise of God, Sarah's laughter seems to involve disbelief in the ability of God. The resulting question the divine visitor asks is just as relevant today as it was then: "Is anything impossible for the LORD?" (v. 14).

Just as Abraham and Sarah felt there was no way God would provide for them, Christians may find themselves harboring doubts about God's abilities too. Perhaps because we long for healing involving a cancer diagnosis or because it seems a prodigal son is unlikely to return. But the reply the Lord gave to Sarah's incredulity is essentially the same response given by Jesus to his followers: "With man this is impossible, but with God all things are possible" (Matt 19:26). The apostle Paul will ask a similar rhetorical question about separating us from the love of God (Rom 8:31-39). Nothing is too large, too complicated for God to accomplish. We do well to remember that.

Before the heavenly company departs from Abraham's sight entirely, the Lord reveals to Abraham that he's come in part to take a closer look at the state of things in wicked Sodom (vv. 17,20-21). In sharing this, the Lord helps highlight the significance of Abraham as his chosen servant and steward of the covenant promise. After all, he reaffirms the covenant yet again in verse 18. Still, the most significant statement in this segment is verse 19. The Lord says of Abraham,

> *For I have chosen him so that he will command his children and his house after him to keep the way of the LORD by doing what is right and just. This is how the LORD will fulfill to Abraham what he promised him.*

These verses designate what is to characterize the conduct of the people of God: righteousness and justice. Moreover, the passage connects their faithfulness in the way of the Lord to the fulfillment of his promises. God has pledged that he will fulfill this covenant regardless of any human effort, but here he reiterates the responsibility of his people to live faithfully before him. Sadly, what the storyline of Scripture later reveals is that none of Abraham's offspring are perfectly faithful to these covenantal expectations until the ultimate son of Abraham arrives. Jesus Christ lives a sinless life of righteousness and justice that enables the Lord to "fulfill to Abraham what he promised him." Then, in a recapitulation of Eden and the Tower of Babylon (3:8; 11:5), the Lord goes down to see the depths of Sodom's sin.

Abraham and the Prayer for Life (18:22-33)

Once Abraham understands the plan of God, it drives him to plead for the protection of life. When most people encounter the story of Sodom, they focus on the judgment of God. But this portion of the passage also highlights the patience of God. God shows patience not because he is weak but because he is willing for sinners like the Sodomites to turn from darkness to light through "repentance" and faith (2 Pet 3:9).

Here Abraham examines the integrity of God's impending actions. Throughout the Bible is a recurring concern about the justice of God that Abraham articulates by asking, "Will you really sweep away the righteous with the wicked?" (Gen 18:23). Is Abraham testing the character of God? Is he pressuring him through persistence? Whatever the motivation for his interrogation, Abraham appeals to God's righteousness as the means to challenge his actions. As Abraham offers what is the first prayer of petition recorded in the Bible, he is serving as a righteous mediator pleading for the salvation of sinners. This prefigures the work of his greatest son, Jesus, who is the ultimate mediator between God and man (1 Tim 2:5). Jesus, however, doesn't just plead for the salvation of sinners; he also purchases the salvation of sinners.

That Abraham appeals to God's character as the basis for preserving any righteous persons in Sodom is apparent when he asserts, "You could not possibly that!" (v. 25). Just imagine the passionate pleading in his posture, facial expression, and tone. The same is apparent when he asks the rhetorical question, "Won't the Judge of the whole earth do what is just?" (v. 25). In this way, Abraham agrees that God not only has the authority to judge Sodom but also has the responsibility to judge Sodom justly (Deut 32:4). The implication of God's response is easy to miss but important to process. Rather than saying, "If I find fifty righteous, I will spare those fifty," he implies a substitutionary deliverance: if he finds fifty righteous, then he will "spare the whole place for their sake" (v. 26). This foreshadows the work of Jesus on the cross: the perfect righteousness of one has the ability to cover over the unrighteousness of others in a way that spares them from God's wrath (Matt 5:13; Jas 5:20).

At this point in the text, an ongoing negotiation ensues in which Abraham appeals to the Lord and receives his assent not to destroy the city if there are fifty, then forty-five, then forty, then thirty, then twenty, and ultimately ten righteous people in the city. Abraham's approach brings to mind Jesus's future parable of the persistent widow (Luke 18:1-8). Sometimes, persistence ensures the alignment of conduct with character.

Embedded in Abraham's approach is also both a right view of God and a right view of man. He recognizes that God is "Judge of the whole earth" and does "what is just" (v. 25). Repeatedly, he appeals to the kindness and mercy of God to "not be angry" with his requests. But Abraham also acknowledges a right view of humanity in his reluctance to press for increasing accommodations. Also, echoing the creation account in Genesis, Abraham humbly acknowledges the frailty of humanity since he is "dust and ashes" (v. 27). This right view of God and man facilitates a right request from Abraham, and this formula holds true throughout the New Testament as it describes the proper pattern of prayer and petition (Matt 7:7-9; 1 John 5:14-15).

At the culmination of this interchange, God agrees to spare the city if only "ten" righteous people are found in it (Gen 18:33). As the text soon reveals, however, there are not even ten righteous inhabitants remaining in Sodom or Gomorrah. This is significant not only for those cities but also because it subtly draws attention to a global problem outlined in the book of Romans. It says, "There is no one righteous, not even one" (Rom 3:10; echoing Ps 14:1-3). And since that is true, the judgment Sodom faces is a reminder of the judgment due against all those who are unrighteous. Abraham seemed hopeful that perhaps ten righteous people would be found in the city. You would imagine he would have been even more optimistic if it was a global quest in which there only needed to be ten righteous people among billions of humans living today. However, the Bible is clear that, apart from Christ, all of us have fallen short of the glory of God and fail to exhibit the righteousness required for right regard before him.

The Judgment of Sodom and the Rescue of Lot

GENESIS 19

What are some of the most shocking accounts of sin recorded in the Bible? Judas betraying Jesus and David choosing adultery with Bathsheba immediately come to mind. Nevertheless, some of the most glaring accounts of sins in the Bible are right here in Genesis. Adam and Eve eating forbidden fruit; only one generation out of the garden, Cain murdering his brother Abel; and even the overwhelming sinfulness of humanity in Noah's day before the flood. But there is perhaps no more glaring tale of sin in the Bible than this multilayered account of what was happening in Sodom and Gomorrah. And that makes it an excellent backdrop for displaying the judgment of God against sin while tempering it with news of the deliverance of Lot and his family (cf. 2 Pet 2:6-10).

Lot and the Value of Life (19:1-11)

As chapter 19 advances the Genesis storyline, two angels appear at Sodom's gates. Abraham's nephew Lot, sitting nearby, rises and bows in an act of humility that contrasts the pride that permeates the city in which he lives. Hospitably, he pleads with them to stay at his house and to allow him to care for their needs (v. 3). Through this act, Lot literally fulfills Hebrews 13:2: "Don't neglect to show hospitality, for by doing this some have welcomed angels as guests without knowing it."

After a feast is served to the guests at Lot's home, a crowd surrounds it. In fact, the "whole population" of the men of Sodom encompass it (Gen 19:4). Many of these are no doubt men Lot would recognize. This universal appearance of the townsmen indicates their total complicity with the evil permeating their city. All by itself, this suggests the angels will not, in fact, find ten righteous people in Sodom. Whereas Lot seeks out the travelers to serve them humbly as Abraham did, the men of Sodom seek out these travelers only to violate and use them sexually. The men's stated desire to "have sex with them" suggests a nefarious desire for erotic satisfaction (v. 5). This falls in line with God's description of Sodom in the book of Ezekiel: "They were haughty and did detestable acts before me" (Ezek 16:50).

Lot's quick response, "Don't do this evil, my brothers" (v. 7), suggests this type of behavior is neither new to Lot nor something he condones. Indeed, Peter explains of Lot, "Day by day, his righteous soul was tormented by the lawless deeds he saw and heard" (2 Pet 2:8). In other words, the Sodomites' actions on this night are no surprising departure from their normal behavior. They are a reflection of a culture that has given itself over to the power of sin.

Tragically, while Lot doesn't agree to their demands, he doesn't resist their desires. Instead, he offers a cowardly, wicked compromise. Rather than allow his invited guests to be thrown to the mob outside his home, Lot instead proffers his virgin daughters (v. 8). One can only imagine how the daughters felt, assuming they overheard this conversation. Regardless, the offer does nothing to appease the mob, who simply criticizes Lot as being nothing more than an outsider who "came here as an alien" and now is "acting like a judge" before threatening to harm him along with the visitors (v. 9). Lot, it seems, lives in a cancel culture even more vicious than our own. This city rejects any outside standard for correcting their conduct, whether from Lot or from the Lord.

We, too, live in a society giving itself over to the power of sin. How do I know this is so? For one, because it celebrates sexual activity that violates God's design, and thus the land is filled with the survivors of sexual violence. While it is tempting to respond to that revelation by saying, "At least things aren't so bad here that we have all the men in our society busting down hotel doors to sexually violate strangers," consider that our own culture does much the same thing more subtly and anonymously. We may not show up at someone's physical doorstep, but many show up at someone's digital doorstep through the use of pornography. Many have become like the men of Sodom yelling, "[S]end them out!" so they can violate strangers via images on the screen. The spirit of Sodom indeed lives on behind every pornographic Internet search. That same power of sin holds sway in many of us today. That's why some of us are enslaved to pornography. The danger is that you might become like Lot: you have lived in this culture for so long and you have figured out how to hide your sin so well that it is tormenting your righteous soul (2 Pet 2:8).

Yet God in his kindness can save us even from ourselves if we turn to him in faith and repentance. When, in verses 9-10, the hordes of Sodom press forward to break down the door to Lot's house, the angels step in and strike all the men with blindness. First, they were figuratively blind with temptation by their wicked desires. Now, they are literally blind because of their wicked desires. The fact that those who were blinded included "both young and old" suggests that this act of judgment and accountability came to all who were involved. This halts the fulfillment of their wicked desires because now they are "unable to find the entrance" (v. 11). Despite their blindness, the mob relentlessly seeks to satisfy its wicked desires. What a trenchant reminder of the strength of the temptations that tug at every human heart throughout history. What happens to the men of Sodom in this scene parallels Paul's claim about how Satan blinds people through temptation and sin. He writes, "[T]he god of this age has blinded the minds of the unbelievers to keep them from seeing the light of the gospel of the glory of Christ, who is the image of God" (2 Cor 4:4). So, in striking the men blind physically, God is making obvious what is already true of them spiritually.

Lot and the Rescue of Life (19:12-22)

Sodom's sin has reached its day of judgment. Nevertheless, the patience of God creates an opportunity for rescue before his wrath falls. The angels warn Lot to gather his family and escape the city (v. 12). And as they do, they at last acknowledge the purpose for their arrival: "[T]he LORD has sent us to destroy" Sodom and Gomorrah (v. 13). This call to escape near the beginning of the Bible foreshadows similar instructions at its conclusion when the following directions are given in Revelation. The Lord says, "Come out of her, my people, so that you will not share in her sins" (Rev 18:4).

That Lot's family doesn't believe what the angels claim is evident in that his sons-in-law "thought he was joking" (Gen 19:14). Perhaps this reaction mirrors the skepticism Noah surely experienced while building the ark. In any event, it seems that as in the days of the flood, here rescue seems unnecessary to many people until it's too late to escape.

Amazing in this passage is the fact that despite the urgency of the angels, Lot hesitates to evacuate his family. The night of the angels' feast has passed, and though "daybreak" has arrived, Lot must be prompted to move (v. 15). Why? It seems that even though he anticipates the impending judgment, it is difficult for him to abandon the familiar and follow God by faith. There is, in fact, something about fallen humanity that makes us hesitate to trust in the deliverance of God when it means we must flee the comfort of our sinful surroundings to see it.

Eventually, the angels grab Lot's hand and bring him and his family outside of the city "because of the LORD's compassion for him" (v. 16). Yet rather than running as instructed, Lot attempts to negotiate the terms of God's mercy. Instead of escaping to the hills as commanded, he pleads with the angels to allow him to "flee to" a nearby town instead (vv. 18-20). How often are Christians pulled toward doing the same thing? We are tempted not only to linger in our sinful surroundings rather than to flee in submission to our Savior but also to negotiate the terms of our surrender to God's mercy.

The New Testament makes clear that this rescue of Lot is a foretaste of what he does for those of us who are found in Christ. One beauty of God's rescue is that he doesn't just command us to escape judgment on our own. As with Lot, he takes reluctant refugees by the hand and patiently guides us out of the zone of judgment because he is merciful to us. The angels urge Lot and his family, "Don't look back and don't stop anywhere on the plain! Run to the mountains, or you will be swept away!" (v. 17; cf. Matt 24:16-18). Similarly, everyone in Christ is called to not look back or stop during their faith journey (Luke 9:62).

As the apostle Peter writes, if God "rescued righteous Lot," then that means he "knows how to rescue the godly from trials and to keep the unrighteous under punishment for the day of judgment" (2 Pet 2:7-9). In our compromised culture, we Christians may sometimes identify with Lot, who was surrounded by sin, oppressed, coerced toward compromise, and—barring intervention—doomed to be swept away in judgment along with the wicked. But the gospel infuses believers with a promise of protection on this point. The Lord will sustain the godly through their trials. But he will also hold the unrighteous accountable in judgment, just as he did in Sodom.

Lot and the Judgment of Life (19:23-29)

Like the flood of Noah's day, the judgment against Sodom and Gomorrah follows a pattern for judgment seen throughout the Bible. There are several characteristic features of this paradigm. First, God's judgment is *warranted by sinful rebellion*. Sodom faces judgment because the "outcry against its people is so great before the LORD" due to their sin (v. 13). Romans 6:23 teaches that "the wages of sin is death." And in his justice, God holds humanity accountable for their sin. This is what happens to the citizens of Sodom and Gomorrah, but it is appointed for everyone who is outside of Christ (Heb 9:27).

Second, God's judgment is *carried out by God himself*. As the sun rises heralding the day of judgment, "the LORD rain[s] on Sodom and Gomorrah burning sulfur from the LORD" (v. 24). This description makes unmistakable the active role God plays in this judgment when it states both that "the LORD . . . rained burning sulfur" and that it was "from the LORD." God carries out judgment himself, even at the cross of Christ. He pours out the cup of his wrath on the Son (Isa 51:17; Matt 26:39; Rev 14:9-10). As a result, God made Jesus, "who did not know sin to be sin for us, so that in him we might become the righteousness of God" (2 Cor 5:21).

Third, God's judgment is *comprehensive in scope*. No one remaining in these two cities escapes his wrath because only Lot was found to be righteous (see 2 Pet 2:7), and he was taken out. Because "all have sinned and fall short of the glory of God" (Rom 3:23), this judgment is a warning for all sinners who find themselves outside of Christ. God's judgment at Sodom, in fact, is often used as a model for future judgment of the wicked (Deut 29:23; Ps 11:6; Isa 13:19). What happens there is a foretaste of what God will do to the nations in judgment for their sin (Zeph 2:9). Sodom is even a foretaste of what God will do to his people to bring them to repentance (Amos 4:11). As Jude 7 points out, Sodom and Gomorrah "serve as an example by undergoing the punishment of eternal fire."

Fourth, God's judgment is *universal in nature*. When God's judgment comes against Sodom and Gomorrah, it is a complete destruction in which God "demolished these cities, the entire plain, all the inhabitants of the cities, and whatever grew on the ground" (v. 25). What happens at Sodom is thus a prelude to the pattern of warfare God's people would carry out against their enemies in the conquest of Canaan, in which Israel is told, "[C]ompletely destroy them. Make no treaty with them and show them no mercy" (Deut 7:2). The universal nature of God's judgment, however, helps bring attention to his equally expansive offer of grace. Jesus himself becomes "the atoning sacrifice for our sins, and not only for ours, but also for those of the whole world" (1 John 2:2).

Fifth, as I've touched on already, God's judgment *anticipates his future eschatological judgment.* When Abraham looks over the destroyed valley and sees that the "smoke [is] going up from the land like the smoke of a furnace" (v. 28), those fumes are a foretaste of future judgment (Matt 10:15; 11:24). As Luke 17:29-30 declares, "[O]n the day Lot left Sodom, fire and sulfur rained from heaven and destroyed them all. It will be like that on the day the Son of Man is revealed." When writing of the final judgment in the book of Revelation, John repeatedly draws on the imagery of Sodom when describing the eschatological end of God's enemies (Rev 19:20; 21:8-10).

Sixth, God's judgment is *rooted in his covenant faithfulness.* At Sodom, judgment and mercy meet because of God's faithfulness to his covenant promises. Just as God remembered Noah after the judgment of the flood (8:1), so too God "remembered Abraham and brought Lot out of the middle of the upheaval" (19:29). God fulfills his covenant commitments by preserving the righteous from judgment.

At Calvary, however, Jesus receives God's judgment on the cross as he takes on the sins of his people. Nevertheless, on the third day, the Messiah experiences God's rescue in the resurrection as God vindicates him as the true and faithful son of Abraham who receives the blessings of the covenant.

The shocking thing about the judgment of Sodom and Gomorrah is not that God actively holds humanity accountable for their sin through judgment. The shocking thing is not even that God seems to select Sodom and Gomorrah arbitrarily when there were likely other cities living in debauchery at the time. Instead, the shocking thing about the judgment of Sodom and Gomorrah is that, in his mercy, God has chosen to spare so much of humanity from the same fate, since we all deserve it due to sin. The destruction of Sodom reminds us of God's justice in holding people accountable for their sins. But it also reveals his mercy as he rescues Lot as a foretaste of the covenant faithfulness experienced by all those who unite themselves to Christ by faith.

Lot and the "Preservation" of Life (19:30-38)

After the judgment of Sodom and Gomorrah, Lot and his daughters find themselves in a desperate situation. Even though Lot lobbied for Zoar to be saved so that he could reside there, he is now too "afraid to live" in this small city that was spared (v. 30). Why? Perhaps he fears another brimstone deluge will strike. Perhaps he and the girls worry locals will associate them with the incident and do them harm. While the text does not tell us the answer, it does indicate they prefer living in a cave to staying in Zoar.

Lot's daughters in particular have endured a tumultuous time. First, they possibly overheard their father offer them up as sexual objects to the marauding crowd, who were seeking to violate angels. Second, their future husbands had laughed at Lot's warning to flee and thus got left behind and destroyed (v. 14). Third, they left everything they owned to escape their home. All their friends and neighbors, as well as their father's livelihood and possessions, were destroyed by sulfuric showers. And finally, they lost their mother, who turned into a pillar of salt for disobeying God (v. 26). It is unlikely they had a chance to say goodbye to her. Now, isolated in a cave with few provisions for the present and no obvious prospects for the future, they grow anxious.

What happens next indicates that even though Lot's daughters had been taken out of Sodom, the sinful spirit of Sodom had not been taken out of them. In their despair over finding themselves in such a difficult situation, they make a desperate decision. Rather than choose to trust their father's Lord to provide the miracle of life in his own way and timing, they seek to take care of their desires according to their own devices. They take turns getting Lot drunk and sleeping with him so that they might "preserve [their] father's line" (v. 35).

This is the low point in the Genesis story. At work in this disturbing story is a pattern in which people bypass God's design for producing offspring by pursuing prohibited methods for procreation. The drift away from sexual expression being limited to only husband and wife shows up in the lives of the patriarchs as they take concubines (16:1-15) and multiple wives (29:30–30:24). But in Genesis, the matter reaches its lowest point with this act of incestuous sexual violence. It is a perversion of God's design for sexuality. Paul condemns a similar type of sexual anarchy in his first letter to the Corinthians (1 Cor 5:1). Nevertheless,

Lot's daughters carry out the same kind of assault on their father that he'd been willing to let the mob do to them.

At first, it seems odd that Lot's two daughters can't trust God to provide for their futures. After all, they have just witnessed the Lord rescue them from the fiery judgment of their own city. But even though God saved them in the past, they refuse to trust him with their future. Unfortunately, that same lack of trust in spite of God's track record of faithfulness shows up repeatedly in the lives of people in the Bible and often shows up in our own decisions as well. This lack of trust undergirds Israel's creation of the golden calf (Exod 32), David's illicit census (2 Sam 24), and Peter's three denials (Luke 22:54-62). As stated in a previous chapter, doubt drives disobedience.

This story of the illicit actions of Lot's daughters is not just a random, inconsequential part of the Genesis narrative. The offspring from this connection in the cave will give rise to two people groups who end up plaguing God's people in the future. Moab fathers the Moabites (v. 37), and Ben-ammi becomes the patriarch of the Ammonites (v. 38). Later, as Israel ventures toward the promised land, God initially protects the land of the Moabites and the Ammonites from their conquest (Deut 2:9,19), but they are later defeated by David (2 Sam 8:2), and they continued to rebel against Israel (2 Kgs 1:1).

More importantly, however, one illicit offspring conceived in the events of Genesis 19 connects directly to God's grand story of redemption. Though brought forth through iniquity, Lot's son Moab becomes the ancestor to a young woman named Ruth (Ruth 1:4). This Moabite woman faithfully follows the Lord's will into a relationship with Boaz of Judah and ultimately becomes the great-grandmother of King David (Ruth 4:21-22). So the rebellion of Lot's family produces a son, whose clan would eventually raise up a Moabite woman, whose lineage would produce a messianic Son. That Son would be the one to destroy the power of sinful rebellion that ensnared Lot's daughters in Genesis 19 and grips each one of us who are outside of Christ. The cave of Moab's conception, therefore, points ahead to the tomb of the Messiah's resurrection. God works through the brokenness of what happened in the cave to prepare the way for the one who rescues us from our own brokenness.

Reflect and Discuss

1. What does Abraham's hospitality have to do with his respect for life? How do Christians evidence this in their generosity and hospitality to strangers?

2. If we are honest, are there things we think are too difficult for God to accomplish? Since nothing is too difficult for God to accomplish, how do we undermine this belief by our actions?

3. Abraham is able to question God and receive an answer. What does this reveal about God, in terms of our honest questions and doubts?

4. Abraham's question—"Will you really sweep away the righteous with the wicked?"—speaks of his faith in God's just character. What light does this shed on his actions toward Sodom and Gomorrah?

5. God's answer is that he will spare the entire city if there are a few righteous people inside of it. What does this reveal about God's grace and mercy?

6. What do the actions of Lot regarding his daughters when the mob surrounds his house indicate about the righteousness of even this one whom the angels were sent to save before the destruction of Sodom?

7. Lot pleads with the angels as he flees Sodom. In what ways do Christians try to negotiate their own deliverance by God?

8. God is active in the judgment against Sodom and Gomorrah. He is also active in the judgment of Christ for sin on the cross. What does this reveal about the holiness of God and his attitude toward sin?

9. Lot's wife is punished for her disobedience to the command of the angels. Why do you think she looked back? What things in your life would cause you to hesitate if God's angels told you to flee?

10. The incestuous relationship between Lot and his daughters is a story that should cause sorrow. However, God uses it in the larger story of redemption when a descendant of Moab (Ruth) will become an ancestor of King David and eventually of Jesus. What does this show about God's ability to use even the most broken situations for the goal of glorifying his Son?

A Faith That Works

GENESIS 20–22

Main Idea: This section of Genesis marks a turning point in the life of Abraham. In it, he faces a choice between fear and faith. He faces a choice between the child of the flesh and the child of the promise. He even faces a choice for his son between life and death. As he faces the ultimate test regarding the sacrifice of his son Isaac, he exemplifies his faith through total obedience to the commands of God.

I. **The God Who Protects and the Same Old Schemes (20)**
   A. The fear of Abraham (20:1-2)
   B. The protection of God (20:3-18)
II. **The God Who Gives and the Birth of the Child (21)**
   A. The birth of Isaac (21:1-7)
   B. The dismissal of Hagar and Ishmael (21:8-21)
   C. The covenant of Abraham with Abimelech (21:22-33)
III. **The God Who Demands and the Faith of Abraham (22)**
   A. The command of God (22:1-6)
   B. The obedience of Abraham (22:7-12)
   C. The substitution for Isaac (22:13-19)
   D. The future wife of Isaac (22:20-24)

By this point in the narrative, one might expect Abraham's faith to start being evidenced by a string of consistent right actions and good decisions. Unfortunately, the opposite happens in chapter 20. And this causes new problems for his family. As he comes into the land of Abimelech, his old trend toward deceit endangers the promises of God as well as the people of the land. By fearing the nations more than trusting in the God who is his shield (15:1), Abraham continues to try to help God achieve the promise through the means of the flesh. However, God continually intervenes to protect the seed and his promise to Abraham and Sarah. The promises are realized in an initial way with the birth of Isaac, the child of the covenant (21:1-3).

With Isaac's birth, it is made clear who will be Abraham's heir. But the ongoing tension between Sarah and Hagar illustrates the manner in which the promise will be obtained (21:8-10). Hagar, in fact, represents the attempt to force the promise through the means of the flesh. Meanwhile, Sarah represents the supernatural fulfillment of the promises of God. However, even in this struggle is the seed of the future reality that those outside the promise will be grafted in. Just as God hears Hagar in the wilderness, God will hear the Gentiles in their spiritual wilderness.

Finally, in the most memorable moment of Abraham's life, Abraham exercises total obedience to God in his willingness to sacrifice the promised child. This obedience evidences his now unwavering faith. And it points forward to a future sacrifice that ultimately will fulfill all the promises of God. Abraham's obedience is received by God, and then a reiteration of the blessing on Abraham is given. God continually sets before Abraham the truth of the promise. This secures and builds up his faith.

The God Who Protects and the Same Old Schemes
GENESIS 20

For the second time Abraham deceives another powerful man about his relationship to Sarah. This deception is indicative of Abraham's relationship with both his wife and the surrounding nations. Although promised a land and a child through his bride, Abraham's actions to protect himself threaten their fulfillment. Nevertheless, God is faithful. He protects Sarah and ensures that the promise is brought to fruition.

The Fear of Abraham (20:1-2)

In chapter 20 comes news of another encounter between Abraham and the nations. The country in view is Philistia. There are two things to notice in this specific exchange. First is how Abraham acts in his relationship with his wife. Second is how he acts toward Abimelech, here representative of both his own land and the nations in general. In both cases, Abraham's actions are dishonorable. And were it not for the intervention of God, they would work against the promised fulfillment for which Abraham longs.

When Abraham lies about his wife, Sarah, he dishonors her. Moreover, his action ends up forcing her to lie about the nature of their relationship, too (v. 13). At the same time, Abraham is refusing to be associated with her. Considering the pattern in Genesis 1 and 2, this is no small problem. The unwillingness of Abraham to admit Sarah's relationship to him shows that he is more concerned about whatever threat nations and their kings might pose to him personally than he is about her.

In fact, when called out for his deception, Abraham hides behind the claim that there is "absolutely no fear of God in this place" (20:11). Yet the irony is that it is actually his fear of people that motivated his decision. He claims to be protecting his wife—noting this scheme is not entirely untruthful because she technically is his sister (v.12). Nevertheless, in this second betrayal of his duty as a husband and related twists of truth, Abraham has fallen back on an old scheme to protect himself. He thus shows fear and cowardice before the foreign ruler Abimelech.

The relationship of Abraham with the nations is the second thing to note in this passage. Abraham has been told that "all the peoples on earth will be blessed through [him]" (12:3). However, in this instance, Abraham's interactions with the nations lead to a curse, not a blessing (20:3). Moreover, while God has promised to raise up kings from Abraham, he lives in fear of the existing kings around him rather than operating confidently in light of what God says. The actions of Abraham here thus betray the fact that he is more fearful of the nations than he is faithful to God's promise. This is especially unusual considering what God said to Abraham in 15:1: "Do not be afraid. . . . I am your shield."

The Protection of God (20:3-18)

Since Abraham's deception places the promise of God in danger, God intervenes. First, "in a dream" God gives Abimelech a direct warning that to continue a relationship with Sarah will result in his death (v. 3). At the same time, God is causing every woman in the king's harem to be barren "on account of Sarah" (v. 18). God rebukes Abimelech and prevents him from touching Sarah (v. 6; cf. Ps 105:14-15). The text makes clear that Sarah has no extramarital relations with Abimelech (v. 16; cf. Ps 105:14-15). This is a critical detail because it means there can be no question that the father of her child is anyone other than Abraham.

Abraham's actions dishonor his wife. In contrast to the way her frightened husband misuses her, this foreign king treats Sarah with respect. Even God agrees that the man took her under his roof "with a clear conscience" (v. 6). Moreover, Abimelech graciously responds with great generosity toward her deceptive husband by giving him gifts when the truth becomes known (v. 14). Further, he gives a large sum of silver as a sign that she has not been violated (v. 16). Abraham is willing to have his wife become a member of Abimelech's harem to protect his own life. Abimelech is willing to be defrauded to show the innocence of this woman. In these actions is a rebuke of the statement made by Abraham that "there is . . . no fear of God in this place" (v. 11). Abraham is the one who does not fully fear God or honor his commands.

In all of these events, God is not just protecting Sarah. He is extending grace to Abimelech. But more importantly, he is protecting the ultimate offspring he promised to Abraham. Despite Abraham's fear for his life and lack of trust, God is ensuring his promises will be fulfilled.

God honors Sarah because of the promised child. This commitment is endangered if she is a member of Abimelech's harem, so God supernaturally prevents this from hindering his promises. God's specific actions involving the women of Abimelech's household in this narrative are important (vv. 17-18). Why? Because they underscore God's power over fertility. He has control over the wombs of Abimelech's wife and female slaves, thus helping to prove that he maintains power over Sarah's. Just as he closes the wombs of these women and then opens them again in response to Abraham's prayer, he will open the closed womb of the ninety-year-old Sarah to give her the promised child in the next chapter.

The God Who Gives and the Birth of the Child
GENESIS 21

Will the promises of God come through the child of the slave or the child of Sarah? The birth of Isaac resolves this question as it marks the arrival of the promised child of Abraham and Sarah. This is, finally, the realization of the initial fulfillment of God's covenant commitment. But it further exacerbates the tension between Hagar (and her son Ishmael) and Sarah.

The Birth of Isaac (21:1-7)

The long-awaited arrival of Isaac is presented in a rather summary fashion. The Lord visits Sarah and does what he promised through her union with Abraham. She conceives the child, delivers Isaac, and little more is said (vv. 1-3). The name of the baby means "laughter." Sarah says that God has brought laughter to her and that others will laugh with her (v. 6). They will do so because she has conceived at an incredibly advanced age. So advanced that it seems impossible. Sarah says that this impossible act has happened precisely because God has kept his promise at the "appointed time" (v. 2).

This idea of laughter resulting from the fulfillment of the covenant points not just toward his people laughing. It also points to the way God "laughs" over his enemies as he keeps his covenant through the ultimate son of Abraham (Pss 2:4-6; 59:8). God laughs precisely because he brings about his promise despite the impossibility of the odds.

The Dismissal of Hagar and Ishmael (21:8-21)

Sarah is not the only one who laughs at the birth of her son. By the time Isaac is weaned, Abraham's son Ishmael is also laughing. At Isaac. And not in delight over his half brother but in derision (vv. 8-9). Sarah responds to his mocking by seeking to throw Hagar and Ishmael out into the wilderness again (v. 10). She doesn't just want to send them away. She wants them driven out to die alone.

To his credit, Abraham is hurt at the thought of such a fate for his first son. He finds it "very distressing" (v. 11). But God, knowing that the separation will not lead to the pair's death, tells him to "listen to" Sarah. Why? Because in spite of Sarah's wicked reaction, Abraham's line—that is, the promised line—will "be traced through Isaac" (v. 12). As if to assure Abraham he is not knowingly sending them out to their deaths, however, God promises to protect "the slave's son" and bring forth "a nation" from Ishmael because he is Abraham's child (v. 13). Nevertheless, going forward there can be no confusion about which is the child of promise. Abraham's attempt to obtain the promise through the means of the flesh is obscuring the work of God. Therefore, Hagar and Ishmael are sent out (v. 14).

Paul recognizes the significance of this moment in the book of Galatians. From his own perspective, after Christ's first coming, death, and resurrection, he sees that there is more going on here than simply curbing a volatile domestic dispute about inheritance rights. Rather, the matter of Hagar and Sarah and their sons figuratively represent two covenants (Gal 4:24). Ishmael, the son of Hagar, represents the then-yet-to-come Mosaic covenant from Mount Sinai that was associated with the law that binds its children in lifelong slavery to sin (Rom 6:20). In contrast, Isaac, the promised son of Sarah, figuratively represents the Abrahamic covenant that was associated with a promise. Jesus sets believers free from slavery to sin by making us children of promise (Gal 4:28; 5:1).

God uses the evil actions and wicked spirit of Sarah to help bring about the inheritance for Isaac. The inheritance her son receives will lead down the line to Jacob and the people of Israel, culminating in the Lord Jesus Christ. While this does not commend the actions of Sarah, it does point ahead to a crucial theme that reappears at the end of Genesis. What one person means for evil, God means for good (50:20).

God does not leave the exiled woman and boy alone in the wilderness. Rather, just as he promised Abraham, he protects Hagar and her son. Back in Genesis 16:11 Hagar was instructed to name this boy Ishmael because the Lord listened to her affliction. Now, the God who listens is the one who hears the cries of the young man whose name means "God listens" (21:17). Back in Genesis 16:13 Hagar declared that the Lord is a God who sees her. Now, in her desperation, the Lord again proves he sees her in her trouble and opens her eyes to see his provision of water (21:19). In all this God demonstrates that through the seed of Abraham all the nations will be blessed; God will even hear the cries of the Gentiles (who, like Ishmael, are not Isaac's descendants) and care for them.

The Covenant of Abraham with Abimelech (21:22-33)

As life moves forward for Hagar and Ishmael, Abraham continues living in the land of Abimelech. When Abimelech and "the commander of his army" approach his camp, the patriarch likely experiences some anxiety (v. 22). After all, the last time he interacted with Abimelech, Abraham deceived him and endangered the health of his kingdom (vv. 2-3). But while their former interaction centered on deception, this second meeting will see the two men agree to live peaceably. They establish a covenant with each other that Abimelech calls on Abraham not to break (21:23).

Interestingly, the foundation for this covenant is the loyalty and friendship extended by Abimelech to Abraham. Despite the deception of Abraham, the leader had remained kind to him and gave him gifts of livestock (20:14). Abimelech recognizes that God is with Abraham and therefore seeks a covenant with him to ensure their continued good relations. Another ruler called Abimelech will use this same rationale when he creates a covenant with Abraham's son Isaac (26:26-33).

This particular covenant reflects two of the central concerns of all tribes in this period: water and warfare. Every tribe, after all, would naturally seek both provision and protection in a hostile landscape. This becomes obvious in the striking of the covenant, because as soon as it is complete, Abraham brings a complaint about the unfair seizure of "[a] well" (21:25). To his credit, Abimelech does not appear to have any knowledge of the act. So after the concern is addressed, Abraham gives Abimelech sheep and cattle as a sign that seals the covenant between them (v. 27). He is returning the kindness Abimelech showed him in their first encounter.

The place where this covenant is made is "Beer-sheba" (v. 31). In the original language "Beer-sheba" means "the well of the oath," or "the well of the seven," reflecting the number of animals given to Abimelech to seal the covenant. After the oath is made and things are formalized, Abimelech and his army commander leave satisfied. Interestingly, when Isaac later restores this well where the covenant was made (26:33), he also restores the name of the area. The well (and the name) are signs of the lasting nature of the covenant made between Abimelech and Abraham.

Following Abimelech's departure, Abraham plants "a tamarisk tree." He then calls "on the name of" Yahweh, the everlasting God (v. 33). The covenant Abraham cut with Abimelech, then, may remind him of the covenant made with him by God. It may also remind him of the covenant faithfulness of Yahweh. Whatever the reason, he breaks out in worship to "the Everlasting God" (v. 33). This mirrors his actions after the initial covenant in 12:8.

The theme of God as "the LORD, the everlasting God" recurs throughout redemptive history. The psalmist writes, "Before the mountains were born, before you gave birth to the earth and the world, from eternity to eternity, you are God" (Ps 90:2). The writer of Hebrews says, "Jesus Christ is the same yesterday, today, and forever" (Heb 13:8). God does not just make an everlasting covenant with Abraham, then. He too is everlasting. God existed before all creation. He is the same yesterday, today, and forever. There is a consistency in the eternal nature of who God is. For this reason, the covenant with Abraham is a permanent covenant in part because its author is not just faithful but eternal.

The God Who Demands and the Faith of Abraham
GENESIS 22

God's demand for Abraham to sacrifice Isaac opens one of the most complicated passages in Scripture. With the death of Isaac, after all, would go the hope of the promise. Nevertheless, at this point Abraham remains unwavering in faith and sets out to obey the hard command.

In the end, God's provision of a substitute for Isaac points to the future work of Christ. And Abraham's forward-looking faith leading to his obedience serves as an example of how Christians should act as they anticipate the ultimate fulfillment of God's promises.

The Command of God (22:1-6)

This is one of the most troubling passages in Scripture, partially because it seems one-half of an extreme contradiction. God commands Abraham to sacrifice his son. Yet God will later command the Israelites to wipe out the peoples of Canaan who practice child sacrifices, which he "hates" and finds "detestable" (Deut 12:31; 18:9-12). So, why is it acceptable for God to command such a thing in this instance? One answer is found in Genesis 22:1: "God tested Abraham." Even before he tells this particular narrative, then, Moses assures the reader that what he or she is about to read is just a test.

Any parent understands the anxiety and questions that God's command here no doubt brought to Abraham's heart. But consider how much more overwhelming it would seem if you were as old as he and the life of the long-promised child of the covenant was on the line. Regardless, God tells Abraham to override the affection and love he has for his son in light of the authority of God.

To his credit, Abraham believes God has the right to do this. This serves as evidence that he is adopting the same type of sentiment advocated by Jesus when he tells the disciples that they must "hate" father, mother, wife, and even their own lives if they want to be his followers (Luke 14:26). It is the same type of sentiment Jesus desires to hear when he restores Peter by asking him, "Do you love me more than these?" (John 21:15). For the believer, the natural affections of this life must be secondary to love for God and obedience to him and to the cause of Christ. This is exactly what God is saying to Abraham: *Do you love me more than this? Do you believe me more than this?*

The command is also troubling because it appears to jeopardize the very thing promised to Abraham. God is telling him to kill the promised child through whom all the blessings and promises of God are to come! If Abraham sacrifices this son, he is not just killing the child; barring a miracle, he is cutting off all hope for the promise (Heb 11:17). Yet he is willing to do it. Why? Because he believes God can still bring about the promise somehow.

Abraham has repented of his actions with Hagar. There is no try-ing to help God here. The reason he has such obedience is found in Hebrews 11. According to the writer of that book, Abraham believes that if God could give him the child in his old age, then God can also "raise someone from the dead" (Heb 11:19). God is saying to Abraham here that he can and will turn every part of the curse of Genesis 3 back. Even death cannot hold back the promise of God. Here God is declar-ing that he is Lord and Destroyer of death, and that the covenant is stronger than death (Heb 2:14-15). This scene thus points to the Sunday morning when God will raise Christ from the dead and conquer death. Abraham's faith that God can raise his son from the dead points ahead to our faith in the one whom God has since raised from the dead.

The Obedience of Abraham (22:7-12)

The faith of Abraham is proven by the actions of Abraham. He is not acting so that God will reward him for obedience. And the point here is not what he is doing but that what he is doing reveals what he believes. For the same reason Jesus will tell those who listen to his teaching to examine their values and priorities in order to evaluate their faith (cf. Matt 6:25-34; 7:21-23). The individual who refuses to give up money, home, or family for the sake of Christ's kingdom is refusing to believe that he or she will receive more than the value of that loss in the king-dom of God. He or she may be trusting in personal ability to achieve the blessings of God. By contrast, as Abraham builds the altar, binds his son, and brandishes his knife, he shows through his actions that he is walk-ing by faith and not by sight (Gen 22:9-10). His actions are proof that he now trusts in God, not himself, to accomplish what God has promised.

Later, in his letter James draws from this passage when he discusses the theme of obedience. For James, the faith of Abraham is not found in the emotions Abraham experiences. Instead, his difficult actions at the altar reveal that Abraham's "faith was active together with his works, and by works, faith was made complete" (Jas 2:22). Indeed, in this act Abraham evidences the faith commended in Genesis 15:6 (Jas 2:23). Faith is at work as he sharpens the knife, arranges the wood, and binds Isaac.

This idea that true faith shows up through action leads Paul to define the Christian life as a "fight" or "race" (2 Tim 4:7) calling for significant effort (Phil 3:12). Faith is expressed through action in the face of the impossible. Nevertheless, according to the author of Hebrews, faith acts and perseveres because it does not focus on the things that are seen but on the things that are unseen (Heb 11:1).

In Genesis 21:11-12, at the last moment before the knife falls, God halts Abraham. He has passed this difficult test of his faith. The chosen one, who has repeatedly chosen fear over faith by disobeying God in various ways, now chooses faith over fear in obedience to God.

The Substitution for Isaac (22:13-19)

The death of Isaac is averted because God provides a substitute. God gives to Abraham "a ram," which is then sacrificed, and God accepts that death in place of Isaac's (v. 13). This matter of God's providing a substitutionary sacrifice is one of the clearest biblical foreshadowings of Christ and what he would come to do. After all, in the narrative a loving father offers up his "only son" in a sense, who willingly walks toward his own death (v. 2). And how would that death occur? It involved his being strapped to wood and would culminate in his being slain. The wood Isaac carries is a figurative picture of Christ's cross (v. 6). The substitutionary death of the ram, though, points to the substitutionary death of Christ (2 Cor 5:21). Even the location of the sacrifice, "the land of Moriah," is significant (Gen 22:2). It is the future location of the temple, where the sacrificial system will be used for generations (2 Chr 3:1). Yet at the death of Christ, this sacrificial system will find its fulfillment as the Lamb of God becomes "one sacrifice for sins forever" (Heb 10:12). Jesus comes as a new Isaac—the one and only Son of God who is actually sacrificed on the mountain. As Abraham proves his love for God throughout this story, so too does the Father prove his love for sinners by not withholding his Son from us (Rom 5:8).

In Genesis 22:15-18, "the angel of the Lord" reaffirms the promise of the covenant. The first time he calls to Abraham from heaven it is to tell him to stop the sacrifice. Now, the second time the angel of the

Lord calls to Abraham from heaven it is to tell him the covenant will continue. Again, we see the same dimensions of the covenant as before: it still involves a *new people* in a *new place* living out a *new purpose.* This people related to Abraham will be more numerous than "the stars of the sky" and individual grains of "sand of the seashore." Their place will be secured as they "possess the city gates of their enemies." Their purpose relates to Abraham's obedience to the covenant: "And all the nations of the earth will be blessed by your offspring because you have obeyed my command" (vv. 17-18).

Abraham's life as the first of God's covenant people is bookended by two tests. In the first test, Abraham experiences the calling of God in Genesis 12 to leave behind his homeland to pursue the promises of God. But now, in this final test after God provides the promised son of the covenant, Abraham faces the most difficult choice of his life. Regardless, in both cases, he faithfully obeys.

The Future Wife of Isaac (22:20-24)

The genealogy that concludes chapter 22 resembles most genealogies in Genesis. However, it has two peculiarities that make it distinct and explain its inclusion. First, this genealogy is not narrated by Moses. Rather, the text says that "Abraham was told" what is found here, signifying a messenger related this particular genealogy to Abraham (v. 20). So there is a level of personalization at play here that makes this genealogy distinct. More importantly, unlike most genealogies in the Bible, this one culminates in the birth of a daughter, not a son. This daughter is "Rebekah" (v. 23). Many lineages in the Bible highlight only male descendants because sons received inheritance and perpetuated a family's line. Thus, sons are presented as more significant than daughters in most cases. However, this list includes and culminates in mention of Rebekah. She would become the wife of Isaac and mother of Jacob, also called Israel, father of the twelve tribes of Israel. By including these genealogies, Moses is showing how God is faithful to keep his covenant promise of protecting the bloodline through which the Messiah would come.

Reflect and Discuss

1. Why is Abraham's deception of Abimelech especially problematic in relation to Sarah? What does this matter reveal about Abraham's marriage and trust of God?

2. When Abraham lies to Abimelech, he misrepresents the character of God to the nations. How might Christians do that today?
3. Why does Moses make clear that Abimelech has no sexual relations with Sarah? What is at stake if the child is not Abraham's?
4. Unlike Abraham, Abimelech shows his respect for Sarah by giving a gift of silver as a pledge that she has not engaged in an illicit relationship. What does this gift and effort to protect Sarah's reputation suggest about the value of women?
5. The birth of Isaac is presented matter-of-factly. What does this reveal about Moses's belief in the power of God?
6. The actions of Sarah toward Hagar and Ishmael are some of the most problematic in Scripture. How are Christians to make sense of them?
7. God does not abandon Hagar and her son. After all, he is the God who sees and the God who hears. What should the fact that God responds to the cries of the oppressed lead Christians to do?
8. Abraham's willingness to sacrifice Isaac contradicts the natural parental impulse. Christians, however, are to hold all things as secondary to the promise and cause of Christ. What areas are especially hard for you to treat as secondary to his authority?
9. Abraham's willingness also contradicts the promise of God. How can blessing come through death? In what other ways has God used tragedy and death as a means of providing blessing?
10. A sacrificial substitute for Isaac is provided by God. How does this episode foreshadow God's future provision of a perfect sacrifice for his people?

A Funeral and a Wedding

GENESIS 23–24

Main Idea: Here the Genesis narrative begins to transition from Abraham to the next generation. By chronicling Sarah's death and the marriage of Isaac, the text shows the promises made to Abraham do not stop with him or his immediate descendants.

I. **Abraham and a Burial Plot (23)**
   A. Abraham sojourns in the land of Canaan (23:1-6).
   B. Abraham owns land in Canaan (23:7-20).
II. **Abraham's Servant and a Bridal Journey (24)**
   A. A servant sent for a bride (24:1-14)
   B. A woman drawing water at a well (24:15-32)
   C. A servant recounting God's providence (24:33-49)
   D. A bride for a promised son (24:50-67)

Genesis 23 and 24 mark a turning point as the book's narrative begins to shift beyond Abraham. This transition to a focus on his son is completed in Genesis 25 with Abraham's death. Genesis 23 tells the story of the burial of Sarah in a way that signals, for the first time, that God has begun to keep his promise to provide Abraham's offspring with establishment in the land of Canaan. In one of the longest narratives in Genesis, chapter 24 demonstrates God's providence as he guides Abraham's servant in finding a suitable wife for Isaac. Through the marriage of Isaac to Rebekah, we see God further his promise to provide numerous offspring to Abraham.

Abraham and a Burial Plot

GENESIS 23

A day arrives when Abraham the sojourner must secure a burial place for his deceased wife Sarah (vv. 2-3). When he takes possession of the area that becomes her burial plot (and later the resting place of many others in his family), it is a partial fulfillment of the land promise made many years earlier. God, in fact, brings to fulfillment both the promises of *land* and increasing *lineage* in chapter 24.

Abraham Sojourns in the Land of Canaan (23:1-6)

Genesis 23 opens with the death of a matriarch, Sarah. She is the only woman in the Genesis narrative whose lifespan is given, "127 years" (v. 1). When Moses takes the time to note her age, he is recognizing the special place she holds in the redemptive story of the people of God. Sarah is the wife of Abraham and mother of all the children of Israel. Though Abraham was sorrowful at the barrenness of Sarah, his sorrow turned to joy with the birth of Isaac. Yet with Sarah's death, Abraham's joy has turned once again to mourning and weeping (v. 2).

Abraham approaches the Hethites, in whose land he resides, to request a plot in which to bury Sarah's body. Specifically, he desires a certain cave. He begins negotiations with them by highlighting that he is a foreign resident among them (v. 3; cf. 17:8). Typically, foreign residents were not entitled to purchase land, thus placing Abraham in a significant bind. He is old. His wife is dead. And he has neither place to bury her nor right to do so because he is a sojourner.

The theme of the sojourner recurs throughout the Bible. Later, when God is explaining how the Israelites will possess the land as their own, he reminds them that they will nevertheless remain "temporary residents" in it since Canaan ultimately is his (Lev 25:23). Later than that, when David prays to the Lord, he recognizes that the nation has indeed come to be filled with "temporary residents" (1 Chr 29:14-19; Ps 39:12). But the author of Hebrews sheds light on the *redemptive* dimension of Abraham's sojourning. He writes,

> *By faith [Abraham] stayed as a foreigner in the land of promise, living in tents as did Isaac and Jacob, coheirs of the same promise. For he was looking forward to the city that has foundations, whose architect and builder is God.*
>
> *By faith even Sarah herself, when she was unable to have children, received power to conceive offspring, even though she was past the age, since she considered that the one who had promised was faithful. Therefore, from one man—in fact, from one as good as dead—came offspring as numerous as the stars of the sky and as innumerable as the grains of sand along the seashore.*
>
> *These all died in faith, although they had not received the things that were promised. But they saw them from a distance, greeted them, and confessed that they were foreigners and temporary residents on earth.* (Heb 11:9-13)

The author of Hebrews thus recognizes the importance of the sojourner theme for Abraham and his offspring. Their recognition that they were foreigners and temporary residents did not just have to do with their status in the land of Canaan. But in fact, as Hebrews 11:13 says, they "confessed that they were foreigners and temporary residents on earth" itself. They knew that *this earth* in its current fallen state was not their ultimate home and that God had given them a greater promise than just ownership over a portion of it—even if they did not fully understand how such a promise would be realized.

The sojourner theme carries into the New Testament. The Gospels present Jesus as a sojourner, nomadic and transient. In fact, Jesus says this about himself: "Foxes have dens, and birds of the sky have nests, but the Son of Man has no place to lay his head" (Luke 9:58-59). Thus Jesus too recognizes himself as a temporary sojourner during his time on the earth, which is in line with the way the author of Hebrews describes Abraham and his other offspring. Like Abraham, Jesus had no official place to call his home. Nevertheless, Jesus calls us to follow him.

In light of this, it should not surprise us when we see the Bible presenting the church in sojourning terms. What Abraham literally experienced in Canaan, we now experience on earth in a figurative sense. First Peter 2:11 says, "Dear friends, I urge you as strangers and exiles to abstain from sinful desires that wage war against the soul." In other words, Peter teaches that we believers are temporary residents—sojourners—here on earth. And the fact that we are should fuel our ongoing fight against temptation. By recognizing that we are not at home in this current world but that home is yet ahead of us, we are helped in the work of resisting the works of the devil that wage war against us.

In response to Abraham's request, the Hethites recognize his special distinction as a person of God. In fact, they declare that he is "a prince of God" (v. 6). This suggests they recognize his special chosen status before the Creator. They thus offer unexpected accommodation and hospitality, telling him to choose the best burial place and that it will not be refused him. In humble response to their hospitality, Abraham bows down before the Hethites (v. 7). Although they have just elevated him by recognizing him as a prince, he lowers himself in appreciation of the kindness he receives from them.

Abraham Owns Land in Canaan (23:7-20)

In response to the Hethites' generosity, Abraham requests permission to buy the cave belonging to a man named Ephron. It turns out that Ephron is willing to give the cave and the land around it to him because of his great respect for Abraham (v. 11). However, Abraham insists on buying it at full price in the sight of the local leaders (v. 13). This scene helps highlight two major themes that will be important throughout the rest of Scripture.

The first theme is that of death being tempered by hope. Abraham's actions here secure a burial plot (a sad thing) but also ensure that there is no doubt about his ownership of this particular slice of Canaan (a happy, hope-filled development). Abraham pays for the property and takes legal possession of it in front of the leaders who sit at the gates of the city, the place where business transactions are normally conducted (vv. 16-18; cf. Ruth 4:1). As a result of this agreement, the burial site can continue to be used by his family. And in the future it will also house his body, as well as the bodies of Isaac, Rebekah, Jacob, and Leah (Gen 49:29-32; 50:4-14). Even to the point of death, these particular people lived in hope and assurance that God would keep his promises to his people (Heb 11:13). After all, by leading Abraham to purchase the cave, God had already started to make good on his promise to give him the promised land.

This theme of hope in spite of death should be amplified for believers living on the resurrection side of the cross. After all, though Jesus died a criminal's death, he conquered the grave and defeated death itself (2 Tim 1:10). Those of us who follow Jesus should have no fear of death. As the author of Hebrews declares,

> Now since the children have flesh and blood in common, Jesus also shared in these, so that through his death he might destroy the one holding the power of death—that is, the devil—and free those who were held in slavery all their lives by the fear of death. (Heb 2:14-15)

Just as Sarah and Abraham died in hope, we too can know that even death will not prevent the fulfillment of God's salvation promises to us.

The second biblical theme arising in this section is promised-land ownership itself. With the fair purchase of the parcel by Abraham, there is no doubt about who owns it. Much of what leads Abraham to refuse Ephron's offer of a gift is that he wants to avoid any possible dispute over rights arising in later years (Gen 22:13). The promise of the land made to him back in Genesis 12:1, then, finds its initial fulfillment here. While this is but a cave and field, it nevertheless serves as a down payment on the promise that God will give the whole area to Abraham and his descendants one day. Thus, a place of burial shows that the covenant is still alive. Possession of a land that God intends people to have remains a prominent theme throughout the Bible. In the beginning in 1:28, for instance, God commands Adam and Eve to be fruitful, multiply, and "fill the earth." Adam and Eve initially possessed even Eden, which was the throne room of the kingdom of God. But when sin fractured their relationship with God, the couple was cast out of the garden and lost the best of the land. In a similar way his chosen people are later removed from the land of promise due to Israel's sin and rebellion.

The idea of the "promised land" first comes into view in 12:1, when God initially calls Abraham (Acts 7:3). For a long time, this promise of land receives only incremental fulfillment. Until the conquest of Canaan recorded in Joshua. Referring to the end of the conquest, Joshua 21:43-45 says,

> So the LORD gave Israel all the land he had sworn to give their fathers, and they took possession of it and settled there. The LORD gave them rest on every side according to all he had sworn to their ancestors. None of their enemies were able to stand against them, for the LORD handed over all their enemies to them. None of the good promises the LORD had made to the house of Israel failed. Everything was fulfilled.

Later, under the rule of King Solomon, Israel's possession of the land was expanded to its broadest point: "Solomon ruled . . . from the Euphrates River to the land of the Philistines and as far as the border of Egypt" (1 Kgs 4:21; cf. Gen 15:18-21). Through Solomon's reign, the land belonging to God's people reached its widest geographical boundaries. And for a short time, it may have seemed as if the land promise had been realized to its fullest potential.

Israel, however, soon engages in a grievous pattern of sin culminating in exile. Thus, God removes his people from the land of promise as an act of judgment (2 Kgs 24:14). Yet despite the exile God offers a prophecy of restoration in Isaiah 51:3:

For the LORD *will comfort Zion;*
he will comfort her waste places,
and he will make her wilderness like Eden,
and her desert like the garden of the LORD.
Joy and gladness will be found in her,
thanksgiving and melodious song.

Just as Israel was longing for the promised restoration of the land during the exile, they were also awaiting the promised Messiah who would come and rescue them from their enemies.

When Jesus enters redemptive history, the Bible's theme of land possession is reframed in Matthew 5:5. Jesus says, "Blessed are the humble, for they will inherit the earth." In that statement Jesus expands the promised land far beyond the scope of even Solomon's reign to encompass the entire planet. The fact that it applies to more than just the people group descended from Abraham in the traditional sense is suggested in the Great Commission as Jesus tasks his followers with making "disciples of all nations" (Matt 28:19). In Christ, the Bible's promises about the faithful inheriting land will come true for all who trust in him. As Paul declares in Romans 4:13,

For the promise to Abraham or to his descendants that he would inherit
the world was not through the law, but through the righteousness that
comes by faith.

Here Paul echoes Jesus in his recognition that the promise of a new place does not simply involve a parcel of land in the Middle East but the entire world. And its ultimate fulfillment is linked to faith in Jesus, the ultimate Son of Abraham.

The author of Hebrews 11:8 says,

By faith Abraham, when he was called, obeyed and set out for a place
that he was going to receive as an inheritance. He went out, even
though he did not know where he was going.

This statement provides continuity between this passage in Genesis 23 and its ultimate fulfillment in Christ as described by Paul in Romans 4. This connection is strengthened by Revelation 21:1-2, where John describes the coming of a new heaven and a new earth featuring the holy city—the new Jerusalem (cf. 2 Pet 3:13)—where God and redeemed humanity will dwell in harmony. As momentous as it is, then, Genesis 23 is but the initial fulfillment of the promise God made to Abraham in 12:1. However, this further develops a major motif that saturates the storyline of Scripture—the promise of a new place.

Abraham's Servant and a Bridal Journey

GENESIS 24

Genesis 24 provides one of the most extensive and detailed love stories in the Bible. But unlike a Hallmark Channel film intended to document the unique circumstances leading to the unlikely marriage of Isaac and Rebekah, this chapter is loaded with evidence that beneath the surface, God is working yet again to bring the Abrahamic promise to fruition.

A Servant Sent for a Bride (24:1-14)

After acknowledging Sarah's interment (23:19), Moses turns his attention back to Abraham and matters involving the next generation. As if to emphasize the latter's significance, he writes, "Abraham was now old, getting on in years" (24:1). Indeed, by this point Abraham the patriarch has lived a long life and been blessed by God in many ways (v. 2; cf. 13:2). But though the word *blessed* appears repeatedly throughout this chapter (vv. 1,27,31,35,48,60), there is one particular blessing Abraham lacks. He has not yet been blessed with grandchildren to continue his line. In fact, Isaac does not even have a wife.

Yet you can see Abraham's deepened trust in God's covenant faithfulness because Abraham does not take matters into his own hands recklessly as he once did with Hagar. Rather, Abraham calls a trusted servant of his household and sends him on a mission to find a suitable wife for Isaac. This task is urgent because Sarah is dead and Abraham is old. Again Abraham is left to wonder how God will fulfill his promise if Isaac does not have a wife.

Abraham requires his servant to swear an oath that he will seek a wife for Isaac not among the local "Canaanites" but from Abraham's relatives in his native homeland (vv. 2-4).

This situation, too, speaks to a repeated theme of the Bible. The people of God are not to marry outsiders. This is not a matter of ethnicity but of faith and unbelief. Deuteronomy provides clarity when it says,

> You must not intermarry with them, and you must not give your
> daughters to their sons or take their daughters for your sons, because they
> will turn your sons away from me to worship other gods. (Deut 7:3-4)

The Lord knows, and the Bible later affirms, that when his people inter-marry with outsiders they are often led astray. For one thing, when peo-ple accommodate the worship of false gods, they also easily forsake their call to holy obedience to the Lord alone. And even should they avoid committing outright idolatry personally, believers who marry unbeliev-ers set any children that might come of their unions up for confusion with relation to spiritual matters.

As Abraham continues to give instructions to his servant, he has in mind the promise given in Genesis 12:1. In fact, he connects the ser-vant's current mission with God's past promises, telling the man to trust the guidance of the angel he is sure God will send to help in these pro-ceedings (24:7-8). Abraham knows that God has promised the land not only to him but to his "offspring" (v. 7). And it is time for the blessing to pass to Isaac so he can forward it along as well. This is why Abraham takes such care to instruct his servant.

Eventually, however, the blessing on Abraham finds its way to the people of God as a whole. In Galatians 3:16 Paul helps Christians rec-ognize that they are included in the promise made to Abraham when he writes,

> Now the promises were spoken to Abraham and to his seed. He does not say "and to seeds," as though referring to many, but referring to one, "and to your seed," who is Christ.

So, in a sense, Genesis 24 is part of our own story because of our union with Jesus that comes by faith. His coming as a human infant, after all, is tied to these proceedings.

Throughout his instructions to the servant, and especially in verse 7, Abraham repeatedly points to the power and authority of "the Lord." Abraham recognizes God's authority by calling him this and recognizes God's sovereignty by pointing out that he is "God of heaven and God of earth" (v. 3; cf. 2 Chr 36:33; Ezra 1:2). Abraham also recog-nizes God's providence when he recounts how God "took [him] from [his] father's house and from [his] native land" (v. 7; cf. 12:1). He rec-ognizes God's revelation when he declares that God "spoke to [him] and swore to [him]" (cf. 15:1-5). Further, Abraham recognizes God's promises when he quotes him as saying, "I will give this land to your offspring" (cf. 12:7; 15:18; Exod 32:13-14). He also recognizes God's protection when he tells the servant, "He will send his angel before you" (cf. Exod 23:20).

After taking "an oath," the servant departs with ten camels and many goods for the future bride's family (24:9). Little information is provided about his journey, but the servant eventually arrives at a well in the country of Nahor, Abraham's brother. In God's providence he arrives at the time when women come "to draw water" (v. 11). While Scripture is full of instances in which important moments happen at water wells, this is possibly the most significant encounter at a well in the Bible because of its important place in the redemptive trajectory of the Old Testament. While at the well, the servant offers a prayer for success and the favor of God because of his covenant with Abraham (v. 12). The servant even prays with specificity: "Let the girl [who does as I ask and more] be the one you have appointed for your servant Isaac" (v. 14). This, in fact, is the first recorded prayer for guidance in the Bible. Soon, the specificity of his prayer leads to the visibility of God's answer.

A Woman Drawing Water at a Well (24:15-32)

Beginning in verse 15, God starts to answer the servant's prayer before he has even finished offering it (cf. Isa 65:24). The text describes Rebekah, the woman he sees, as "very beautiful" (Gen 24:16). Right away the servant hopes that this particular virgin may be the one. He approaches her and asks for water from her jug, which shows he is alert for the sign requested in verse 14.

As if on cue, Rebekah consents and then speaks of her intent to draw water for his camels as well (vv. 18-21). When Rebekah finishes this task, she is probably surprised when the servant shows his gratitude by giving her gold jewelry. But this paves the way for his next request of even more hospitality in the form of a place to sleep for the night (vv. 22-23). When Rebekah confirms that he is welcome and also reveals her identity as Abraham's niece, he responds with joyful worship (vv. 24-26; cf. Exod 4:31).

The servant worships because he recognizes that God "has not withheld his kindness and faithfulness from [his] master" (v. 27; cf. Ruth 2:20; Ezra 9:9; Neh 9:17). His recognition of God's covenant faithfulness overflows into worship. This action is significant because, as the psalmist shows, God's covenant faithfulness really extends to the whole people of God. Indeed, "[the Lord] has remembered his love and faithfulness to the house of Israel; all the ends of the earth have seen our God's victory" (Ps 98:3).

In God's providence he has supplied a wife for Isaac from the people of Abraham, and the servant rightly credits the Lord for leading him on the journey. God not only supplies his provision but also offers his presence on the journey. In this scene we see yet again that, when it comes to his covenant people, God is with them and for them. This will be a recurring theme in the time of the exodus when God leads his people out of Egypt (Exod 13:21). And later it will be apparent that God is with us and for us, his church, as well (Matt 28:20; Phil 4:19).

After her unusual encounter, Rebekah hurries home to tell her family about what has happened (v. 28). What comes next marks the introduction of "Laban," Rebekah's brother, who will figure more prominently in the life of Isaac's son Jacob. Laban sees "the ring and bracelets" on her wrists and is likely gripped with greed (vv. 29-30; cf. 30:27). He at least immediately recognizes the servant's material riches and assumes he is blessed. He runs right out to him, declaring, "Come, you who are blessed by the LORD" (vv. 29,31; cf. 26:29). The servant is then led to the home and given water for his feet and straw for his camels. Yet in spite of all the excitement, he is almost certainly filled with tension as he prepares to make his request for Rebekah to become Isaac's wife.

A Servant Recounting God's Providence (24:33-49)

In the longest speech in Genesis, the servant attempts to convince Rebekah's family that they should allow their daughter to be taken to a foreign land to marry a man they do not know. To gain their trust and ease concerns, he offers several important pieces of information. First, he establishes that he is "Abraham's servant" (v. 34). That's a name they recognize. He clarifies that Abraham has been blessed with wealth by God and that "he has become rich" (v. 35). Moreover, he assures them that the potential groom Isaac is not old but was born to Sarah later in life (v. 36). He also confirms that Abraham has given a substantial inheritance to Isaac (v. 36). Then he shares about how he is under an oath from Abraham to find a wife from among Abraham's people, not the Canaanites (vv. 37-38). After that, he appeals to the providence of the Lord by telling them of Abraham's assurance that God would send his angel and make the "journey a success" (v. 40). The servant concludes his speech by recounting the providential encounter at the well and then asking for an immediate answer to his petition (vv. 42-49).

When the servant recounts Abraham's words, "the LORD before whom I have walked" (v. 40), he brings up a theme that reappears throughout the Bible. The theme of walking with the Lord, in fact, begins in Genesis as Adam and Eve walk with God in the garden of Eden (3:8). Later, Enoch is described as one who "walked with God" (5:24). So is Noah (6:9). Two implications lie at the root of this concept of walking with God. The first is *intimacy*. Those who walk with God are connected to him. The second is *accountability*. Those who walk with God are seen by him and held accountable for their actions (17:1; 1 Kgs 2:4; 8:23; 2 Kgs 20:3; Ps 116:9).

Although people were intended to walk with God in intimacy and accountability, we see instead that they often run from him, as did their ancestors Adam and Eve after the fall (Rom 8:5-8). However, Jesus is presented in Scripture as the faithful Adam who walks blamelessly with God in perfect intimacy and total accountability and makes it possible for those who trust in his death and resurrection on their behalf to "have boldness and confident access [to God] through faith in him" (Eph 3:12). In light of this amazing gift, it should be no surprise when we believers are called to "walk" in a manner "worthy" of the gospel (Eph 4:1; Phil 1:27; Col 1:10). Just as the servant himself chose to walk before the Lord in intimacy and accountability in Genesis 24, Christians are called to do the same by the power of the Spirit.

A Bride for a Promised Son (24:50-67)

Bethuel—Rebekah's father—and Laban respond to what the servant shares by affirming that the recent development in her life is "from the LORD" (v. 50). In other words, Rebekah's family recognizes God's providence and embraces it. They say that they "have no choice in the matter," or more literally, "We cannot say to you anything bad or good" (v. 50; cf. 31:24). They consent to allow Rebekah to "be a wife" for Isaac according to the Lord's revealed will (Gen 24:51). Again, the response of the servant is to worship before offering additional gifts to Rebekah's family (vv. 52-53).

The next morning when the servant attempts to leave immediately to complete his mission, however, the family delays him. Though Rebekah was present to hear all that the servant said about why he'd come and they've already given permission, they want to know Rebekah consents to the plan. This does not seem to be a righteous action. Laban and his family have already agreed to send her. Even so, Rebekah agrees to go with Abraham's servant, and together the two depart. But the minor delay foreshadows the larger problems that will occur later between a son of Rebekah and Isaac and this branch of the family tree.

Rebekah's obedience to the will of God in this narrative brings to mind Mary's response to Gabriel when the angel appears to her announcing the impending birth of the Messiah (Luke 1:38). Because of Rebekah's willingness, the family sends Rebekah off not just with her personal nurse but with a blessing of fruitfulness and victory that echoes previous blessings (v. 59-60; cf. 17:6; 22:17). It too foreshadows the future. As the servant walked by faith to find Rebekah, she now walks by faith toward a new place and a new people.

The description of Rebekah meeting Isaac seems lifted from a romantic movie. When Rebekah sees Isaac for the first time, she gets off her camel, and she takes her veil and covers herself (vv. 64-65). Likely with a mixture of excitement and uncertainty, Isaac takes Rebekah as his wife. With God's help, the servant has brought them together, and Rebekah becomes a comfort to Isaac after Sarah's death (v. 67).

It can be tempting to assume the primary focus of this text is the exemplary characters and actions within the narrative. We might focus on marriage or the call to faithful obedience, too. Or on powerful prayers and sacrificial service. But all of these are secondary matters. Genesis 23 and 24 provide a story of God's providence and his faithfulness to his promises. They were written to help demonstrate the remarkable things God did to raise up the offspring of the woman who will crush the head of the serpent.

Abraham's servant, whose name we do not know, didn't realize the crucial role he was playing in redemptive history since he could not see the full picture from his vantage point. But his task was much bigger than just finding a bride for Isaac. Ultimately, he was playing a small part in the greater story of Christ's coming and finding a beautiful bride of his own. The church.

Reflect and Discuss

1. Sarah is remembered as the mother of the promised child. Name other biblical women remembered for playing a unique role in the story of Christianity. Make sure to briefly identify their roles.

2. For much of his life, Abraham lives as a sojourner. The whole Bible continues this sojourning theme. What difference can it make to recognize that we Christians are sojourners and strangers in this life (1 Pet 2:11)?

3. Why does Abraham insist on buying Ephron's land rather than accepting it as a gift?

4. The death of Sarah and her burial are not without hope (Heb 11:13). Explain why. What hope do Christians have in spite of death?

5. How does the task of the servant reflect Abraham's faith in the promise? How does his search for a wife for Isaac help to further that promise's fulfillment?

6. Meetings at wells are significant in the Bible. Why is this one of such central importance to the storyline of Scripture and redemptive history?

7. How does the servant's story to Rebekah's family reveal the theme of God's faithfulness in Abraham's life?

8. The response of the servant to Laban and Bethuel's agreement is worship. Why is worship an appropriate response?

9. Rebekah is a comfort to Isaac after his mother's death. Why are husbands and wives to care for each other through the trials of life? What does it mean to be a comfort to one's spouse?

10. This servant who has helped ensure the line of the promise goes unnamed. What does this suggest about our own roles in the story of redemption? Why can we serve wholeheartedly, even without recognition?

Sinful Appetites and Sovereign Blessings

GENESIS 25:1–27:40

Main Idea: God continues to bring about the promised blessing even after the death of Abraham. He blesses Abraham's descendants, Isaac and Jacob, not because of their own merit but because of his covenant faithfulness. The continued favor of God is brought about by trusting in the promise given to Abraham that will ultimately be fulfilled in Christ.

I.   **The Descendants of Abraham and the Struggle with Appetites (25)**
   A. Abraham's children bury their father (25:1-18).
   B. Isaac's children struggle in the womb (25:19-26).
   C. Esau's appetites reject the inheritance (25:27-34).
II. **The Child of Abraham and the Unruled Appetite (26:1-33)**
   A. Isaac's appetites and the deception of Abimelech (26:1-25)
   B. Isaac's covenant and friendship with Abraham (26:26-33)
III. **Jacob's Deception and the Stolen Blessing (26:34–27:40)**
   A. Jacob's deception of Isaac (26:34–27:25)
   B. Isaac's blessing of Jacob (27:26-29)
   C. Isaac's "blessing" for Esau (27:30-40)

These chapters conclude the Abrahamic narrative as the text turns toward the life of Abraham's son, Isaac. Although Abraham has multiple children, Isaac receives the inheritance and blessings and thus holds brief preeminence in the story. In this section Moses highlights the special relationship the children of promise have with God. Nevertheless, God's promise to remember Abraham's other descendants also receives attention. For instance, from Abraham's second wife, Keturah, come children who will be patriarchs of mighty and prominent nations: Midian and Sheba. Also, the faithfulness of God toward Ishmael is revealed when the promises made in Genesis 17 are fulfilled in the genealogy included here, marking the end of Abraham's life. Still, the focus of the text is primarily the turn toward Isaac as the father of Jacob and Esau and thus the channel through whom the blessings of God continue.

In the inclusion of Jacob and Esau in the narrative, the ongoing struggle against sinful appetites is again on display. Both Esau and his father, in fact, are repeatedly characterized as being ruled by their appetites, specifically their love of food. They are also shown to trust not in God's promise but in their own power and physical ability. However, God is shown to work against these desires of the flesh when he chooses to favor the younger stay-at-home twin over Esau, Isaac's favorite. While Jacob is in no way a person of integrity either, as exhibited by the fact that his name means "deceiver," God's choice makes clear that the promise will not be accomplished through the ways and means that are acceptable to the world. Rather, it will be done according to his plan.

Tragically, the reliance of Isaac and Esau on the flesh rather than on the power of God leads them to despise the promise. Neither man values the promise or trusts in God to accomplish his plan. Isaac, after all, repeats the embarrassing failure of his own father by deceiving a nation about his relationship to his wife. Esau cares so little about it that he trades claim to the divine inheritance for a bowl of stew. In the New Testament, he is cited as an example of those who do not esteem the promise and consequently cut themselves off from the person of Christ (Heb 12:16-17).

Despite all this sinfulness and evil behavior, God proves able to bring his plans to fruition. In fact, in his providence God chooses to work through the sinful actions and behaviors of Isaac, Rebekah, Jacob, and Esau to advance his promise to Abraham of a coming offspring who will bless many nations. This should give the Christian hope that, in spite of wicked circumstances and sinful behaviors, God's overarching plan is not thwarted. Even the sinful actions of those who crucified Jesus, after all, were used to bring about the salvation of the people of God. God is repeatedly responding to the actions of humanity and bringing about the blessing of Christ.

The Descendants of Abraham and the Struggle with Appetites
GENESIS 25

As the section on Abraham closes, the narrative moves to his immediate descendants, son Isaac and grandson Jacob.

Abraham's Children Bury Their Father (25:1-18)

For many, the opening of Genesis 25 comes as a surprise. Why? It introduces readers to a second wife of Abraham, Keturah. The text does not specify whether Abraham took her as a wife before or after Sarah's death. But according to what's said in verse 6 and a later genealogy, she may have been a concubine to Abraham prior to their marriage (1 Chr 1:32-33). Regardless, verses 2-4 describe something shocking: aged Abraham fathered six sons through her. The list of names here is important because later sections of the Old Testament will include mentions of Midian and Sheba, two nations arising from two of Keturah's sons. The Midianites, in fact, feature prominently in the story of Israel during their time in Canaan. They are usually a source of trouble for the tribes (Judg 6:3). The name Sheba will reemerge during the time of Solomon when "the queen of Sheba" appears to Solomon to test his wisdom and then give him praise and gifts (1 Kgs 10:10).

Beginning in verse 5, Isaac is the one son through whom the covenantal blessings flow. And although all his half brothers are mentioned, they don't receive the inheritance Sarah's son receives. While Abraham gives the other descendants "gifts," his giving "everything [else] he owned to Isaac" makes clear that the blessings of the future covenant will move through Isaac to future generations (v. 5). So too does the fact that the other descendants are sent "to the land of the East," away from Isaac (v. 6). Moses is making a clear distinction between the one through whom the blessings flow and all others. There can be no ambiguity on this point.

After the giving of the inheritance, Abraham's death is described in verse 8 by four characteristics. The text describes his death as "his last breath," a phrase pointing back to the creation of Adam when God "breathed" into those made in his image (2:7). This same description will be used of both Isaac (35:29) and Jacob (49:33). Also, verse 8 says that Abraham died at a "good old age." This suggests a fullness of life, just as God had promised him (15:15). Further, he is described as "old and contented," an allusion to the joy that comes uniquely through the faith and faithfulness of Abraham. Last, it is said that Abraham is "gathered to his people." Yet while Abraham joins his forefathers in death, his descendants will spread widely throughout the world and be as plentiful as the stars in the sky. In time, his burial plot will be shared with Isaac and Jacob (49:31; 50:13).

At this point in the narrative, though, God blesses Isaac after the death of his father, and the focus of Genesis moves away from Abraham to this heir of promise (25:11). But before the text turns to Isaac completely, it presents a genealogy of Ishmael and his descendants (vv. 12-18). Though the covenant and blessings flow through Isaac, God promised to "bless" this son of Abraham too (17:20). Ishmael's descendants include twelve men who become leaders of their own clans. And as the angel of the Lord also prophesied (16:12), Ishmael "stay[s] near all his relatives" (25:18). Though the covenant and blessings flow through Isaac, Moses confirms the faithfulness of God toward Ishmael, fulfilling the promises God made to Hagar about him.

Isaac's Children Struggle in the Womb (25:19-26)

A situation arises in the life of Rebekah that mirrors the one faced by her mother-in-law, Sarah. Just as Sarah had been barren (11:30), Rebekah finds herself childless. Again, then, the promise of many descendants coming from the line of Abraham seems in danger because of infertility, a struggle that will continue to plague the lives of the patriarchs. In this case, Rebekah's husband cries out to God on her behalf and asks that she be able to conceive. God is "receptive" to the prayer of Isaac, and Rebekah conceives not one baby but two (25:21).

Infertility continues to be a difficult burden today. It can persist for many reasons, and sadly, some who long to conceive will only do so after prolonged periods of waiting, while others may never experience such blessings. The Bible holds forth no specific promise for women or families longing for biological children yet struggling with infertility, but it does point again and again to the goodness and mercy of God. And it proves that the Lord can send children to a couple who supposedly can't conceive. Christian couples experiencing difficulties of this nature, however, must remember that ultimately their hope is not found in bearing children. It is instead found in the perfect provision of God, who sees and hears his people—especially in our longing, waiting, and suffering. God not only hears our prayers, but he is always faithful to answer them according to his will, sometimes in ways that defy our hopes and expectations. A couple experiencing the hardship of the infertility burden should be shown sensitivity and be reminded of God's love.

In verse 22, Moses refers to the "children inside [Rebekah]." Though not yet born, then, they are neither merely potential children nor biological tissue. They are two people with personalities who have been "remarkably and wondrously made" (Ps 139:14). That Moses describes the twins as struggling within the womb of Rebekah, in fact, contributes to a big-picture truth about these boys that's already beginning to make itself known: the pair will struggle to get along. Thus Moses, as do other writers of Scripture, speaks clearly about the personhood and personalities of children within the womb. From the moment of conception, each baby is of great worth. Being made in God's image, they possess inherent dignity and value. They are therefore worthy of protection.

Rebekah, feeling her sons jostle one another inside her, questions why it is happening (v. 22). The Lord replies with the revelation that it is not just two children but the progenitors of two rival nations who struggle within her (v. 23). So the promise God made to Abraham that nations will come from him is being fulfilled in part through Rebekah (17:4-5). From Esau will come the Edomites, and from Jacob will come Israel. God's answer to the prayer of Isaac has not only brought about the birth of a child but also the birth of two distinct people groups.

The differences in the two children become apparent almost as soon as they debut. Moses notes that when the first son, Esau, is born, he is covered in red hair (v. 25). Esau is a primal and powerful individual; he literally looks like an animal. The distinctive firstborn, Esau, would seem to be the obvious choice to be the founder of a nation. He has great physical power. He is a skilled hunter, a man of the outdoors. Nevertheless, this powerful individual is not the person God has chosen to advance the lineage of the promised son. Rebekah knows this upon his delivery because, prior to it, God tells her that the younger child will rule over the older (v. 23).

The prophet Malachi points back to distinctions between the two brothers when speaking of the favor of God over Israel, Jacob's descendants (Mal 1:1-5). God tells them through Malachi that he favored the younger child (their forefather) over the older child (Esau). But the New Testament explains that God did so before the twins were even born. The apostle Paul specifically uses the example of Jacob and Esau to answer the question of whether God is partial in bestowing favor and blessing (Rom 9:6-16). In doing so, Paul explains what is happening in Genesis 25. He writes,

[T]hough [Rebekah's] sons had not been born yet or done anything good or bad, so that God's purpose according to election might stand— not from works but from the one who calls—she was told, "The older will serve the younger." As it is written: "I have loved Jacob, but I have hated Esau." (Rom 9:11-13)

In this way, Paul shows that the promise to Abraham comes through Jacob not because of the merit of Jacob but because of God's own sovereign decree and electing purpose. Jacob therefore has no reason to boast about this election, nor do his descendants. In fact, Jacob, whose name means "deceiver," is shown to be a person who could never earn the favor of God any better than Esau could.

For the Christian, this should give both warning and hope. The warning comes from the reality that there is nothing we can do on our own to earn God's favor or secure his blessing. The blessing of God is not due to any merit or desirable traits in our lives. Therefore, it is a gift to be cherished. So, how does this bring us hope? Because it reminds us that the election of God is based on the will of God facilitated through the grace of God in Christ. As we realize we did not earn the blessing of God extended to us through Christ, we start to realize that we cannot revoke it either (Eph 1:3-6). God will always remain faithful to that promise.

Esau's Appetites Reject the Inheritance (25:27-34)

As Moses describes Isaac and Jacob as opposites, it sets up a struggle for the inheritance. Esau is described as an "expert hunter, an outdoorsman," while Jacob is "a quiet man who stay[s] at home." Parents Isaac and Rebekah, having different preferences too, each favor a different child. In the end their favoritism pits the children against each other to a greater extent. Isaac prefers Esau because he likes to eat the food Esau brings him. So, in contrast to where Jesus commends the gift-giving ability of fathers in the Gospels (Luke 11:11-13), Isaac is the receiver of gifts rather than the giver. Isaac receives from Esau, so he loves him (Gen 25:28). In a sense, then, Esau earns the love of his father Isaac. Meanwhile, Rebekah spends more time with Jacob and favors him.

The tension between the brothers mounts as the text explains how Esau gives up his birthright, that is, the inheritance that would usually belong to Esau by right of his being the firstborn. When he returns home from hunting one day, Esau is exhausted. His appetite is strong, and the scent and sight of a meal in process are compelling. Jacob is preparing a red-colored stew or soup—which is likely a meal Jacob learned to prepare from his mother during his extensive time alongside her in the family's home. Esau expresses his desire for the soup, and Jacob, recognizing his brother's vulnerable condition, offers a bowlful in exchange for Esau's birthright (v. 31). The birthright was the inheritance that was Esau's by right as the firstborn son. Esau, with minimal thought, foolishly gives away his birthright for one meal. Moses comments on his foolishness this way: "So Esau despised his birthright" (v. 34).

Esau's despising the birthright resurfaces in the New Testament as a warning. The writer of Hebrews will point to this moment as an example of the danger of the appetites of the flesh. His evidence that Esau is an "immoral" and "irreverent" person is what happens here in Genesis 25 (Heb 12:16). Hebrews warns us not to follow our appetites through the sin cycle to this same pattern of foolish disobedience. The path of the flesh indulges the appetites, whereas the way of the Spirit governs them wisely (Gal 5:16-26). Esau is ruled by his own appetites and desires to the point that he doesn't even esteem his birthright. He just gives it up in favor of gratifying his pressing appetites. The New Testament warns us that, apart from Christ, all of us do the same thing.

When Esau's actions are contrasted with the example of Jesus, the rejection of the birthright becomes even more objectionable. Jesus faces a temptation similar to the stew incident while in the wilderness. When he is both tired and extremely hungry, he is offered a meal by Satan. But to meet his appetite in this way will cost him his inheritance. Getting him to do that is at the heart of Satan's words in Matthew 4:3. In essence, he says, "If you are the sinless Messiah, create for yourself a meal and satisfy your appetite." Christ refuses to do so, not because he believes eating is sinful but because he believes the inheritance ahead is more important than immediate gratification.

When Esau despises the birthright, he personally eliminates himself from inheriting the promises of God. By cutting off his hunger, he cuts himself off from the blessing that will ultimately come through Jesus, the greatest Son of Abraham. Similarly, we too must decide whether to gratify the appetites of the flesh by persisting in unbelief or rule over them in faith because of the value of the inheritance promised us in Christ (Phil 3:7-9).

The Child of Abraham and the Unruled Appetite
GENESIS 26:1-33

This chapter steps away from the introduction to Jacob and Esau to focus on a particular incident involving their parents. What we see in it is that while wise children can discern whether their parents' actions are something to emulate or to avoid and act accordingly, Isaac repeats a particularly poor action of his father in dealing with the surrounding nations. In the incident Isaac, like Abraham, decides to deceive and lie about his relationship with his own wife. Why? For the same reason as his father—to try to protect and ensure the continuation of the promise. Nevertheless, in spite of the deception and Isaac's lack of character, God remains faithful and blesses this heir of the promise. God remains committed to bringing to completion the blessing and promise of Jesus.

Isaac's Appetites and the Deception of Abimelech (26:1-25)

This scene shares parallels with stories from the previous generation (chaps. 12 and 20). Just as in Abraham's day, it opens when there is a "famine in the land" (v. 1; 12:10). Unlike his father, however, Isaac refuses to "go down to Egypt" to provide for himself in crisis (v. 2). Why? Because God's command not to enter Egypt is built on a reminder of his covenant. The covenantal language given to Isaac mirrors the promises already given to Abraham. When God says, "I will give all these lands to you," there is the promise of a place. When God says, "I will make your offspring as numerous as the stars of the sky," there is the promise of a new people. When God says that "all the nations of the earth will be blessed by your offspring," there is the promise of a new purpose (vv. 3-4). God reaffirms his covenant for the next generation.

Nevertheless, after Isaac receives the same covenantal promises as Abraham, he soon responds to circumstances with the same fearful disobedience Abraham evidenced. Isaac settles in Gerar, now ruled by another king named Abimelech, with much the same anxiety his father had when he was there. He worries the local men might kill him because of the beauty of his wife (v. 7). Therefore, he starts spreading among this Abimelech's people the same lie his father Abraham told about Sarah in the time of a previous Abimelech. Isaac claims his wife is merely his sister (v. 7; cf. 20:2).

Things grow tense after Abimelech himself sees "Isaac caressing his wife Rebekah"—expressing the natural and holy desire that husbands and wives should have for each other (v. 8). "What have you done to us?" the leader asks him. "One of the people could have easily slept with your wife, and you would have brought guilt on us" (v. 10). Isaac's deception here demonstrates both a failure to protect his wife and that he does not trust God.

The Lord, however, continues to bless Abraham's family. Despite the deceptions perpetrated by Isaac, God causes him to reap a harvest one "hundred times" larger than "what was sown" (v. 12). In this action, God is not honoring the deception or the deceiver. Rather, he is honoring the promise made to Abraham—the promise that will find fulfillment in the person of Christ—and continuing his plans to bring it to completion. God can use even the evil actions of these patriarchs to prepare the way to conform the descendants of Abraham into the image of Christ. But God does not honor Isaac's deception. Instead, at Beer-sheba, God reaffirms the promise he made by saying to Isaac, "I will bless you and multiply your offspring *because of my servant Abraham*" (v. 24; emphasis added). Aware that the Lord is blessing him in spite of himself, Isaac is moved by the kindness of the Lord and builds an altar there, calling "on the name of the LORD" (v. 25). In doing so Isaac again follows a path similar to Abraham's. He shifts from fear to faith and from worry to worship.

Isaac's Covenant and Friendship with Abimelech (26:26-33)

Again in the book of Genesis, the text presents an encounter with an Abimelech that is full of uncertainty. In verse 16, Abimelech cast deceptive Isaac out because he saw him to be a threat to the stability of the kingdom. Now, the same man and his commander seek Isaac out. Upon meeting these men, Isaac interrogates them, inquiring what they want from him (vv. 26-27). The men declare that they know the Lord is "with" Isaac. Thus, they have come to make peace (vv. 28-29). As a previous Abimelech recognized that the Lord was with Abraham, this one and the commander of his army also recognize the same is true of Isaac. The men affirm a covenant signaling peace between the people of Isaac and those of Abimelech.

Abimelech pursues this covenant out of a desire for security. At first, he and his commander believed security would come from exiling Isaac.

However, they now realize that a covenant with him is the best way to ensure their own protection. The promise not to harm each other is based on the precedent that Abimelech dealt kindly with Isaac (v. 29), but it is built also on the record set by the covenant between a previous Abimelech and Abraham (21:22-34). Here these leaders of their respective people spell out the covenant, and it is confirmed with a celebration and oath (26:30-31).

Good news keeps coming for Isaac. After the covenant is sealed, Isaac receives word that water has been rediscovered at the well of Beersheba (vv. 32-33). It marks the very place where the covenant between Abraham and a different Abimelech formed (21:31). In the intervening years, however, the well was stopped up by the Philistines after Abraham's death (26:15). That water is rediscovered at the location at such a time connects the covenant of Abimelech with Isaac to the covenant of the king's predecessor with Abraham. Both are signs of the peace between Abraham and his line with Abimelech and his line, and they signal the continued blessings of God on his people.

Jacob's Deception and the Stolen Blessing
GENESIS 26:34–27:40

Jacob's deception of his father Isaac involves another indulgence of human appetites over the promises of God. At the behest of their mother, scheming Jacob steals the blessing from his older brother, Esau. There is nothing about Jacob that merits the blessing. Yet once again, the faithfulness of God is shown as God continues to uphold his word despite Jacob's deceitfulness. In this, God makes clear that even the sinful acts of his creatures will not thwart his plans to bring about the promise.

Jacob's Deception of Isaac (26:34–27:25)

As Isaac goes blind in his old age, he realizes that the time has come to pass his blessing to a son (27:1). As he prepares to bless his firstborn and favorite, Esau, Rebekah plots to deceive her husband to benefit her own favorite, Jacob (vv. 5-10). Unlike the previous episode in which Esau forfeited his birthright, this deception does not begin with Jacob. It is the idea of his mother. And just as Adam listened to Eve and was led astray, now Jacob listens to Rebekah as she entices him toward sin. Nevertheless, Jacob is fully complicit in this effort to deceive his father. Together, mother and son go to great lengths to carry out the plan. To mislead all of Isaac's senses, they place hairy animal skins on Jacob's arms, dress him in Esau's clothes, and prepare a feast of game they know Isaac will appreciate. Even Jacob's speech is part of the ruse as he goes so far as to invoke the blessing of God as the reason he returns so quickly with the food (v. 20). Previously, Jacob tricked his way into the inheritance (25:29-34), and now he is grasping for the Abrahamic blessing again through lies and manipulation.

Isaac's Blessing of Jacob (27:26-29)

When Isaac smells the clothes of his visitor, he believes Esau is before him and offers his blessing in ways that extend the covenantal promises that began with Abraham. First, Isaac offers the blessings of "abundance" and victory (vv. 28-29). But he also echoes the calling of Abraham in Genesis 12:3 when he asserts, "Those who curse you will be cursed, and those who bless you will be blessed" (27:29). Thus, in spite of the sin of Rebekah and Jacob, God is extending the blessing of Christ through this scheming son. The blessing Isaac pronounces over Jacob, after all, does not find its fulfillment in the person of Jacob. True, he is God's choice to receive the blessing in spite of his actions here (25:23; Rom 9:13). But the blessing itself is fulfilled in the person of Christ. It will not be Jacob who will see this blessing fulfilled to its full extent within his lifetime. Rather, the promise will be carried down through Jacob's line until it reaches its fulfillment in Jesus of Nazareth.

Moses, speaking under the influence of the Spirit of God, is telling the reader that Jacob is not the end. He is not the final son of the promise given to Abraham. In the few chapters that cover his life, Jacob tries to supplant his brother and deceives his father. Still, the promise is the critical piece in this story of deception. God is going to honor and keep the promise all the way through to the end in Jesus. An angel will say to Mary that her son will have a great name and will rule "over the house of Jacob" in a kingdom that will have no end (Luke 1:33), which is a reference back to this blessing. So while the promise is given to Jacob, the promise is more importantly given to Jesus. God is faithful to keep that promise.

Isaac's "Blessing" for Esau (27:30-40)

When Esau returns, he and Isaac quickly discover the treachery of Jacob. Esau desperately pleads for the same blessing (v. 34). When Isaac denies his request, Esau realizes that Jacob has now cheated him out of both his birthright and his blessing. Esau's frantic appeal for a blessing in spite of this does not result in the same blessing Isaac gave Jacob. Rather Isaac's blessing is a declaration that Esau will continue down the path he has chosen. Esau is told that he will live and die by his sword (v. 40). Thus, the physical power and prowess Esau is so proud of will characterize his life, but his will be a life of futility. God knocks him from his position of power. God declares that the promise will come through Jacob because Esau despised his inheritance. Jacob's line, and not Esau's, will be blessed because Esau despised his inheritance. Through Jacob, the promise will continue.

We should remember that the promise is preeminent for the lives of the children of Abraham. The key to walking in a manner worthy of the gospel is to keep our eyes fixed on Christ, the ultimate offspring of Abraham, and believe that honoring Jesus is worth resisting our sinful appetites. The alternative is to repeat the sin of Esau. Deceived by the pull of his own appetites, he lost sight of the preeminence of the promise. Likewise, we can be tempted to indulge the passions of the flesh (Heb 11:16-17). However, those who do so, rather than being led by the Spirit, ultimately find themselves in the same place as Esau: weeping and hopelessly seeking the restoration of an inheritance we despised (Heb 12:16-17). Still, this portion of Genesis shows that fallen humanity cannot thwart the sovereign blessings of God.

Reflect and Discuss

1. Why does Abraham give the inheritance to Isaac only? What does this reveal about the plans of God?
2. God was faithful to Abraham and made Ishmael a great nation as well as Isaac. However, Ishmael was not the child of promise. How should Christians consider the blessing of Ishmael?
3. Barrenness is a continual problem in the lives of the patriarchs. What makes it such a threat to the promise of the blessing in Abraham? How should Christians respond to infertility?

4. Moses speaks of "the children" in Rebekah's womb. How does this point to the personhood of these infants, even at this early stage in life?

5. The favor of God on Jacob instead of Esau can be a bit perplexing. However, it points us to the truth of the unmerited blessing and grace of God on his people. How are Christians to think of their own salvation in light of this reality?

6. When Esau despises his birthright, he essentially rejects the blessing and inheritance that come from the promise God made to Abraham. How has being ruled by his appetites cut Esau off from this blessing?

7. How does the fear of Isaac and Abraham create problems for their wives and the inhabitants of the land of Philistia? What spiritual lessons can we take from this?

8. Isaac and Rebekah reinforce the bad habits of their children. How can Christian parents help their own children avoid indulging their naturally sinful appetites?

9. Jacob steals the blessing through deception, yet God still honors the blessing. Is God honoring the theft? How are we to understand what God is doing here?

10. Esau is given a blessing that affirms his warlike and animalistic nature. Paul says in Romans 1 that God gave humanity over to their desires. So, how is this blessing in a sense also a curse for Esau?

Jacob's Stairway and the Tribes of Israel

GENESIS 27:41–30:24

Main Idea: The results of Jacob's deceptions force him to flee to his uncle's home. There he meets Rachel and Leah, both of whom become his wives. On the way there, Jacob experiences God in a powerful way through a dream that fundamentally transforms his perspective. Later, as a testament to the blessing of God on Jacob, God will give him sons who will become the future heads of the tribes of Israel, thus advancing the story of redemption to the birth of this people and their nation.

I. **Jacob Flees and Goes to Laban (27:41–28:9).**
    A. Jacob is sent to find a wife (27:41–28:5).
    B. Esau is left to take another wife (28:6-9).
II. **Jacob Dreams and Sees a Stairway (28:10-22).**
    A. Jacob and his blessed dream (28:10-15)
    B. Jacob and his fearful worship (28:16-17)
    C. Jacob and his holy vow (28:18-22)
III. **Jacob Works and Secures Two Brides (29:1-30).**
    A. Jacob is overcome with desire (29:1-19).
    B. Jacob is deceived by Laban (29:20-30).
IV. **Jacob Fathers the Twelve Tribes (29:31–30:24).**

Jacob's actions in the previous chapter force him to run for his life. Following the advice of his mother and father, Jacob travels to visit his Uncle Laban in Paddan-aram, both so that he might find protection and so that he might find a wife among his mother's family. In the flight from his home, Jacob leaves everything behind: his dwelling, possessions, birth family, and friends. He is alone—a rather inauspicious beginning for a man destined to father the twelve tribes of Israel. But events in Jacob's life soon take an unexpected turn through an unusual dream he has in the wilderness. In it, he learns he will be blessed by God. He will then go on to find a family of his own and possessions through his dealings with Laban. Ultimately, he receives two wives and eventually twelve sons, as well as many herds and flocks.

There are three things to notice in this section. First, the story of Jacob's journey to Haran is a testament to the faithfulness of God to provide and ensure the promise he made to Abraham. Jacob is in no way deserving of the blessing. But God has chosen to bless him, and no circumstance will stop the fulfillment of the promise. In fact, in the end the blessing comes through unlikely means: through the actions of the deceitful Laban who attempts to take advantage of Jacob. God's favor, however, turns each deception into a chance to further his own promise.

Second, this section reports on the birth of eleven of the twelve sons of Jacob—all but Benjamin. These children, born to two wives and two servants, will be the heads of the future tribes of Israel. Already, then, the promise made to Abraham to be the father of *many* nations is coming to fruition. From these twelve will spring a larger and larger number of people until they are an entire nation of Israelites who will eventually conquer the land of Canaan. Here God's continued work in bringing about the promised line and ensuring the coming of the ultimate promised seed reaches a new point in the history of redemption.

Finally, the treatment of Leah by her husband should give hope to the believer. Leah is ill-treated by Jacob and unloved, yet she becomes mother of six of the tribes, including two of the most important: that of Levi (the line of priests) and of Judah (the line of kings). Believers who read about Leah's difficult life should take heart that the challenges they face are part of God's providential plans, even if they are unaware of how everything fits together. Yet unlike Leah, Christians living today are able to see the fulfillment of many of God's promises in Christ and can take comfort in them.

Jacob Flees and Goes to Laban
GENESIS 27:41–28:9

This passage opens on the news that "Esau held a grudge against Jacob" over what happened at their father's bedside and planned to kill him (v. 41). Thus, Jacob must flee from his home and find a wife in a distant land. Throughout all that happens here, Moses shows us that Jacob is not a person we would expect to be the chosen recipient of God's blessings. This helps us grasp that it is only because of the promise made before his birth that Jacob will advance the line of the coming Messiah.

Jacob Is Sent to Find a Wife (27:41–28:5)

When Rebekah hears of Esau's determination to get revenge, she tells Jacob to flee to her brother's home "for a few days" (vv. 42-44). And this time, she apparently seeks Isaac's support of her plan for this son because she speaks to him about the need to find Isaac a wife from somewhere outside the immediate vicinity (v. 46). What she says to her husband here does not speak well of Esau's choice of wives. Back in 26:35, Moses notes that these Hethite women that Esau married had "made life bitter for Isaac and Rebekah." But here Rebekah admits things have gotten so bad with these two brides that she is "sick of [her own] life because of [them]" (27:46). Isaac takes her concerns to heart and insists that Jacob not marry a local Canaanite woman but "marry one of the daughters of" his mother's brother instead (28:2).

Thus Jacob leaves with the blessing of both his father and his mother to go and seek a wife in the country of Laban. He is sent out with the full support of his father, who asks that "the blessing of Abraham" be given to Jacob and his "offspring" (28:4). Without a wife, there can be no seed of promise. The invocation of the blessing and mention of offspring is a request for God to continue the line of promise.

Esau Is Left to Take Another Wife (28:6-9)

Even though Esau knows Isaac sent Jacob to Paddan-aram, he does not follow him (v. 6). Instead, Esau attempts to make amends with his parents. He has despised the birthright and rejected the inheritance. He has been tricked out of the blessing and has married two women from Canaan whom his parents despise. Therefore, he tries to regain their favor by going and taking a wife from among his grandfather Abraham's other descendants. He chooses a "daughter of Ishmael." Keeping his former wives, he adds this bride to his family (v. 9). This, of course, will do nothing to ease tensions between him and his parents.

Nevertheless, from an outward standpoint, it seems at this part in the narrative that Esau is the twin who is most blessed. He remains in the promised land, while Jacob flees in exile. He has wives while Jacob is alone. He has wealth while Jacob is a homeless wanderer. For a moment, then, we see in Esau's life a glimpse of the puzzling "prosperity of the wicked" mentioned in Psalm 73:3. Nevertheless, the blessing will come through Jacob, even though such a thing would seem unlikely and counterintuitive at this time.

Jacob Dreams and Sees a Stairway
GENESIS 28:10-22

Both Jacob's vision of a stairway and his response set the stage for later Christian worship. The stairway between earth and heaven, for instance, will be realized in the person of Jesus, who is the true "gate" to heaven (John 10:9). Jacob's response, essentially reverential fear, sets the pattern for later individuals who enter the presence of God. God's declaration of blessing on him prepares the way for all his later actions toward Jacob.

Jacob and His Blessed Dream (28:10-15)

As Jacob journeys to Haran, he stops to sleep along the way. To do so, he uses a stone for a pillow. (Stones, of course, were no more comfortable as pillows then than now.) The importance of this night, however, is found not in Jacob's discomfort but in the dream. Jacob dreams of a "stairway" coming down from heaven with "angels" ascending and descending it (v. 12). Moreover, Jacob sees Yahweh "standing there beside him" (v. 13). The Canaanite nations and other religions of Jacob's day affirmed the concept of a temple or ziggurat reaching to the sky so that one could get the sense of going up to the heavens by climbing it. The Tower of Babylon is one such example (11:4). But in contrast to these earthly constructions made by human hands, what Jacob sees seems to come down from heaven itself. And it is not people he sees climbing up to heaven but angels who are trekking back and forth between earth and heaven.

Jacob's stairway dream is a reversal of the Tower of Babylon in another way. Instead of trying to make a way to God like his ancestors did at Babylon, Jacob merely witnesses the existence of the stairway and then experiences God standing alongside him. This dream transforms Jacob's perspective because it promises God's presence with him. The Lord directly reaffirms the promise of his presence as he gives Jacob a fresh blessing just after the dream (28:15).

Later, Jesus will pick up the dream's language and imagery of ascending and descending in the Gospels when he says, "Truly I tell you, you will see heaven opened and the angels of God ascending and descending on the Son of Man" (John 1:51). Thus Jesus uses this language to reveal to his disciples that he is the stairway or gate that goes between this world and heaven. In this way Jacob's stairway anticipates his coming offspring as the only way anyone can come to the Father (John 14:6). What Jacob sees in his vision is a foretaste of what will come to fruition in Jesus Christ.

What God speaks to Jacob in this section is a promise that Jacob will be the channel through which the blessing of Abraham and Isaac comes. In verses 13-14, in fact, this blessing for Jacob includes the three major dimensions that have shown up repeatedly in God's covenantal commitments: the promise of a *new place* ("I will give you and your offspring this land"), a *new people* ("Your offspring will be like the dust of the earth"), and a *new purpose* ("All the peoples of the earth will be blessed through you and your offspring"). This is important because Jacob received the blessing through theft and deception, making conniving and deceptive Jacob an unlikely person to be blessed. Nevertheless, God makes clear that he intends to bless this deceitful trickster over his brother. Why? Because of what was said by God before his birth: "[T]he older will serve the younger" (25:23). Jacob's sin and rebellion fall—unintentionally on his part—into the plan of God. Therefore, God ratifies what Isaac has done in giving the blessing. God is declaring that Isaac may not have fully known who he was blessing, but God knew, and God blesses Jacob despite his wickedness.

Jacob and His Fearful Worship (28:16-17)

When Jacob wakes from the dream, his response is terrified worship. In verse 17 he is afraid and says, "What an awesome place this is!" A pattern of fear will be repeated throughout the Bible at many points when God appears before his people. For example, Isaiah's vision of God's throne room leads him to lament, "Woe is me for I am ruined" (Isa 6:5). Jacob's reaction, then, is appropriate in the presence of God.

In modern times the reaction advocated in Old Testament accounts such as this one, however, can be glossed over by those who wish to downplay the idea of the fear of God. So often that phrase is qualified and tamed to make it palatable and comforting. The word "fear" is often replaced with "reverence" when stories such as this one are shared. But while reverence is an important attitude, its presence does not negate the fear such passages relate. Later, for example, Jacob will swear "by the Fear of his father Isaac" (31:53). Jacob does so because he recognizes that he is in the presence of God, and the proper response to that is fear. In fact, the term he uses in 28:17, "awesome," is another word that captures this idea of holy fear. Jacob is full of awe, full of reverent fear and wonder. This dream therefore marks a turning point in Jacob's life. Here Jacob begins to embody what the Proverbs declare to be true: "The fear of the LORD is the beginning of wisdom" (Prov 9:10).

Jacob's fear anticipates a significant moment in the lives of Jesus and his disciples, too. When the disciples witness the transfiguration, their response imitates his. Jacob witnesses a stairway and angels ascending and descending on it to God. The disciples see the stairway personified in Jesus, and he is revealed with two prophets of God standing next to him. At the sight, the disciples fall face down in fear (Matt 17:6). Additionally, the image Jacob uses of "the house of God" describes a meeting place between heaven and earth (Gen 28:17). This image will be realized in the person of Jesus. He is the temple, the house of God (John 2:18-22), as well as the gate (John 10:9). Jacob's experience with the presence of God in his dream drives him to the fear of the Lord and reverent worship. That same reality should be true for us today as we experience the presence of God through this ultimate son of Jacob.

Jacob and His Holy Vow (28:18-22)

On the morning following his dream, Jacob makes a vow accompanied by the setting up of a marker and a consecration of this place. He renames the place Bethel, or "house of God." The marker he erects will be replaced by an actual altar several years later (35:7).

In this scene, Jacob makes a conditional promise to God that reveals his uncertainty. He expresses that "if God" ensures his protection and provision on the journey, "then" the Lord will be his God (28:20-21). This implies he does not yet possess the faith Abraham had. Even though he has received great blessings and the promises made to Abraham, that is not enough for him to feel sure about this God. Thus Jacob, assured heir of the promise, declares that he will follow God only if God meets certain requirements. Nevertheless, the "tenth" (or tithe) he promises to God will later become a regular practice for the Israelite people who descend from him (v. 22; Deut 14:22).

The "stone" Jacob sets up and consecrates is to be the initial stone of a future sanctuary (28:22). The building of sanctuaries, in fact, will be an important practice for those who lead the people of God (e.g., Moses will build the tabernacle, and Solomon will build the temple).

Ultimately, this initial stone points forward to yet another future building. Just as Christ is the cornerstone on which the people of God are being built into a temple for God (1 Pet 2:1-10), here we see a future reality built on a past promise.

Jacob Works and Secures Two Brides
GENESIS 29:1-30

Jacob arrives at his Uncle Laban's home feeling so overcome with desire for the man's daughter Rachel that he seems willing to agree to any price to be her husband. Yet here Jacob the deceiver meets his match. Even so, the deceptive acts of Laban ultimately result in the emergence of the heads of the twelve tribes of Israel, furthering God's plan to create a new people for himself.

Jacob Is Overcome with Desire (29:1-19)

As Jacob goes on from Bethel, he eventually comes to a place with a well. This well is covered by a stone that requires multiple men to move (v. 3). It turns out that not only do the men who will move it know Jacob's Uncle Laban, but they point out to Jacob that Rachel, a shepherdess and Laban's daughter, is approaching the well at that moment with Laban's flocks (v. 9). Upon seeing her, Jacob does something impressive. He, seemingly with supernatural strength, single-handedly moves this large stone because he is so overcome with desire for this woman (v. 10). He then goes right up to her and kisses her and tells her who he is. Jacob is so captivated by Rachel that he soon promises to work "seven years for" her as a bride-price (v. 18).

At play in all this is a picture of holy desire between a man and his future wife. Jacob is so moved with desire that he is willing to do anything for this beautiful woman. Jacob is not interested in just any woman. He wants a specific woman. It is not that she meets some list of requirements that he possesses; he has a romantic attachment to this woman. And this kind of passionate, single-minded pursuit is celebrated throughout Scripture. The Song of Solomon, for instance, speaks of this kind of romantic attachment. The Bible shows that sexual attraction is a healthy part of romantic love, though that does not mean erotic desire is everlasting. Nevertheless, this "earthly" love (*eros*) can be beautiful and is praiseworthy when joined together with sacrificial and "heavenly" love (*agape*). Christians should beware of the tendency of cultures to define love solely in terms of physical and erotic attachment. This can lead to a continual searching for some kind of "feeling" easily mistaken for love. But prudent awareness is not dismissal.

In the Gospel of John, the idea of an important encounter happening at a well appears again. There Jesus has a discussion with a woman from Samaria. In the Genesis story, Jacob is on a journey and rests at a well. Likewise in John, Jesus is traveling from Judea to Galilee and stops to rest in Samaria at Jacob's well (John 4:6). The Samaritan woman questions Jesus, asking whether he is greater than their father Jacob (John 4:12). Jesus implies that he is greater even than he, and she immediately turns to a question of worship. This too is an intentional connection between these two passages. Jacob had come to the well after an encounter with God involving a stairway and angels ascending and descending to God. Jesus declares, "[A]n hour is coming, and is now here, when the true worshipers will worship the Father in Spirit and in truth" (John 4:23). Thus Jesus is telling the woman at the well, who asked if he was greater than Jacob, that the stairway Jacob saw is standing right in front of her.

Jacob had been sent out to find a wife and ensure that the promise would come to pass through his offspring. The Samaritan woman says that when the Messiah comes he will explain all things (John 4:25). And when she turns the conversation back to the promise, Jesus says that it is fulfilled in her presence. Jesus does not look at this woman the way Jacob looked on Rachel, however, with erotic love. Rather, he looks at her with a sacrificial love and says he will give her living water (John 4:10). He will provide for her not only better water but a better place of worship. She and her people will no longer go to a traditional temple; they will instead offer their hearts to God as living sacrifices. Jacob had been willing to do whatever it took to pursue a bride that he first encountered at the well. In a similar way, Jesus is signaling to the Samaritan woman at the well (and to all of us) that he is willing to do whatever it takes to pursue a spiritual bride for himself.

Jacob Is Deceived by Laban (29:20-30)

When the agreed-upon seven years of work for his bride are complete, Jacob goes to Laban and asks that Rachel be given to him as a wife. In response, Laban throws what seems like a wedding feast and Jacob marries (vv. 20-22). But what happens after this suggests there are large quantities of wine at the feast and that the bride wears a heavy veil. Regardless, Jacob is not officially given his bride until evening, when he goes into the tent to consummate the marriage. He is doing so without any light and without seeing the veiled face of his bride. Given these circumstances, it is not surprising that Jacob does not realize whom he has married until the next morning. When Jacob wakes, he realizes that he is not married to the daughter he desires but to her less attractive older sister, Leah. Whereas verse 17 says Rachel "was shapely and beautiful," Leah is described only as having "tender eyes."

Angry that he has been deceived, Jacob demands to know why Laban has done this (v. 25). His new father-in-law responds by hiding behind custom and culture—as if it is news to him that Jacob sought to marry the younger sister while Leah was yet unwed (vv. 26-27). The irony here is that deceptive Jacob, the younger brother who desires the younger sister, has been deceived, receiving the older sister as his wife. In fact, Jacob uses the same Hebrew root word for "deceive" when complaining about Laban as Isaac does earlier when complaining about Jacob's deception (v. 25; cf. 27:35). The deceiver has been deceived.

When Laban suggests that Jacob may have Rachel if he'll agree to working for Laban for an additional seven years, Jacob does not hesitate. He takes the deal. Only a week later, Jacob is a man with two wives. And verse 30 reports that "he loved Rachel more than Leah."

Jacob Fathers the Twelve Tribes
GENESIS 29:31–30:24

Verse 31 says Leah is "neglected" by her husband. Nevertheless, Leah gives Jacob six sons and a daughter over the course of time. So while Leah is unloved by her husband, she is blessed by God with children. The Lord has compassion on Leah and opens her womb. Though Leah steadfastly holds onto hope that her bearing children for Jacob will cause him to love her, that is not the case. Her desperation for approval from her husband, however, is forever acknowledged in the meaning behind the names she gives to her first several sons (vv. 31-35).

Meanwhile, for a long time Rachel remains barren. As result, Rachel becomes filled with envy toward her sister and develops an unhealthy attitude toward Jacob (30:1).

Among Leah's children are Levi and Judah, making her the mother of the priests and kings of Israel. Through Judah, in fact, God will continue the lineage of the Messiah all the way to Joseph of Nazareth. Thus Leah, the despised wife, becomes a spiritual grandmother to all believers. God blesses her by making her a kind of new Eve, though Leah will not see this. Rather, the poor woman lives out her life in bitterness, failing to understand the providence of God. From her perspective, her circumstances appear to be desperate and evil, yet all along God works through them to bring about the lineage of Judah and Jesus, the ultimate offspring of Eve and of Abraham. This is another reminder that God is able to take evil, desperate situations and turn them around to accomplish his good purposes.

This idea should comfort the modern believer. So too should the reality that we know more than Leah, Jacob, and Rachel could. Unlike Jacob, for instance, who receives only the vague promise of a future blessing, the Christian knows the name and birthplace of the Messiah as well as the saving actions of God in the course of history. The Christian knows of the fulfillment of the seed of Abraham in Jesus. And the Christian knows that God uses all things to conform us to the image of Christ (Rom 8:28-30). Therefore, the Christian should not be surprised by the suffering and evil we encounter in our lives, nor should we be surprised to see such things in the life of Leah. Rather, we can choose to respond to such trials with a sense of joy, not mistrust or anger (Jas 1:2-3).

Moses shows the reader that out of Leah's heartbreaking situation arises something she could not imagine: the genesis of the twelve tribes of Israel. While Leah would serve as matriarch to most of them, Jacob's wife Rachel as well as their two slaves, Bilhah and Zilpah, would mother the others. These twelve tribes, birthed of the messy family dynamics created by Jacob, Laban, and Laban's impatient daughters, nevertheless serve as the next building blocks of God's people, and from the tribe of Judah will come Jesus the Messiah.

Also, from this extended family group, Jesus will choose twelve men to help lead his mission. Through those twelve apostles, God establishes his church, which will culminate in what John sees in his Revelation vision of 144,000 people sealed by God (Rev 7:4). In the end these twelve tribes lead to a number no person can count. And all of this comes through a dark and depressing marriage birthed from deception. Even so, God remains faithful. He chooses to bless Leah even if she does not know it.

The significance of Jesus descending from neglected Leah is not just based on the fact that he comes from someone like her but also that he comes for people like her. In a spiritual sense, all outside of Christ are as undesirable as Leah was to Jacob. But Tim Keller powerfully observes that the reason God

> goes after Leah and not Rachel, why he makes the girl who [sic] nobody wanted into the mother of Jesus, the bearer of the Messianic line, the bearer of salvation to the world, is not just that he likes the underdog, but because that is the gospel.

Keller also points out that Jesus doesn't just come as the son of Leah but comes like Leah herself:

> He became the man nobody wanted. He was born in a manger. He had no beauty that we should desire him. He came to his own and his own received him not. And at the end, nobody wanted him. Everybody abandoned him. Even his Father in heaven didn't want him. Jesus cried out on the cross: "My God, my God, why have you forsaken me?" ("The Girl Nobody Wanted," 70)

Whom Jesus comes from reflects how Jesus came for us. Jesus comes from the unlovable, and he comes for the unlovable.

Reflect and Discuss

1. Why is Jacob's securing a wife such an essential point in the story? Why is the blessing of Abraham contingent on it?
2. Esau appears to be blessed. He has wives, lives in the land of promise, and has strength. However, God affirms that the blessing will come through Jacob. What does this reveal about God's use of the weak and unassuming for his purposes?
3. The ladder Jacob sees in his dream is coming down from heaven, not going up. What does the stairway narrative reveal about the relationship between God and humanity?
4. How does the purpose of Jacob's stairway differ from the purpose of the Tower of Babylon? How should that shape the way we pursue a relationship with God?

5. Although Isaac does not know whom he is blessing, God does. How does God's blessing Jacob fulfill his promise? How does it accomplish his plan to glorify his Son?

6. Why do you think some modern people are uncomfortable with the idea of being afraid in the presence of God? What is it about the presence of God that inspires fear?

7. Jacob's desire for Rachel brings to mind the holy desire between a man and woman. What does holy desire look like for the single? For the married?

8. Jacob's continual pursuit of Rachel, even after being deceived by Laban, evidences the strength of his desire for her. In what ways can husbands keep pursuing their wives over the course of a lifetime?

9. Leah is unloved by her husband even though she is destined to be the mother of Israel's line of kings (Judah) and of the line of priests (Levi). How are Christians to understand the providence of God in this situation? How are we to consider the unloved and disregarded within the story of Scripture? Are they truly forgotten?

10. Jesus comes from the line of unloved Leah rather than desired Rachel. Whom he comes from reveals whom he came for. What does this reality show us about the gospel?

Wrestling Jacob

GENESIS 30:25–33:20

Main Idea: Jacob reconciles with his father-in-law and brother, entrusting himself and his future to the sovereignty of God. His struggle with God and his new name, Israel, set the stage for Jacob to become the head of the people of God.

I. **Jacob Tricks and Struggles with Laban (30:25–31:55).**
   A. Jacob prospers and works for Laban (30:25-43).
   B. Jacob angers and reconciles with Laban (31).
II. **Jacob Fears and Struggles with God (32).**
   A. Jacob and the fear of man (32:1-12)
   B. Jacob and the blessing of God (32:13-32)
III. **Jacob Reconciles and Struggles with His Past (33).**

Jacob has spent twenty years working for Laban. After Rachel gives birth to Joseph, Jacob desires to return to the land of promise but is at first delayed (30:25-27). Following a vision from God commanding him to return home, Jacob finally sets out for Canaan.

Before he can enter the land of promise, Jacob must deal with two individuals: Laban and Esau. Jacob knows he is not viewed favorably by his father-in-law or brothers-in-law. Laban is angry because Jacob has left with his daughters and grandchildren, as well as with Jacob's herds— livestock that formerly belonged to Laban. Jacob initially deceives Laban in order to flee Haran. However, in the ensuing confrontation with Laban, Jacob illustrates the integrity of a believer who recognizes the source of his blessings. He testifies to the integrity of his actions and insists that he never defrauded Laban, even as Laban repeatedly did so to him (31:38-42). In his righteous conduct toward Laban, Jacob serves as a model for how believers should interact with unbelievers shrewdly.

Jacob's later interaction with Esau is also an example of shrewd conduct from a believer toward an unbeliever. Jacob does not meet Esau with an air of superiority as the chosen one of God. He knows that Esau is not favored by God, yet he responds to him with humility because he recognizes that he has indeed treated this brother unkindly. Moreover, he knows that the favor he personally enjoys is unmerited. Just as Jacob seeks to live peacefully with his brother, believers should seek every recourse to live at peace with others (Rom 12:18). There is no place for haughtiness or pride in or from the church. Only by the grace of God does the believer know the blessings of God.

The most important event in Jacob's life is his wrestling with God at the Jabbok River. Following this event, God gives Jacob a new name, Israel. As Israel, he is now the head of the nascent nation that consists of his wives and children. He will forever carry the mark of his struggle with God in his body. This pattern of struggling with God in the wilderness, and subsequently receiving the blessings of God, will be repeated in the life of Jesus, the True Israel. In this way, Jacob is the head of a multitude that will find its culmination in one man, Jesus, the head of an innumerable people.

Jacob's transition from deceptive individual to patriarch of the nation of Israel illustrates the move from old to new that occurs in the life of every believer. Jacob's former identity is left on one side of the river, and his new identity goes forward. And from this moment forward, in fact, he is not just a man but an embodiment of the people of God. In the same way the believer also receives a new identity. But instead of struggling with God, the believer shares in the identity of Christ. Through faith in what Jesus accomplished at the cross and tomb, every believer is brought into God's spiritual covenant family and shares in the blessings of God.

Jacob Tricks and Struggles with Laban
GENESIS 30:25–31:55

The tension between Laban and Jacob reaches a breaking point. Jacob departs for Canaan with his family and possessions but is pursued by Laban. They will reconcile after Laban is assured that his children and grandchildren will be treated fairly and that Jacob means Laban no ill will. As Jacob is entering the promised land again, this episode is a fulfillment of the blessing of God. When Jacob entered Paddan-aram, he had only his staff and a desire to find safety and a wife (32:10). He now desires to leave there with multiple wives, his many children, and large herds. God has been faithful in beginning to fulfill the promised blessing he spoke to Jacob at Bethel twenty years prior (28:13-15). Laban, however, will not make it easy for him to go.

Jacob Prospers and Works for Laban (30:25-43)

The growing tension between these two men is apparent after the birth of Joseph, the first child of Rachel. Jacob expresses to Laban his desire to return home to Canaan (vv. 25-26). Though he has become wealthy and prosperous in the land of Haran, Jacob knows the land of Canaan, not Haran, is promised to the descendants of Abraham. Therefore, staying there is inconceivable. He has accomplished what he set out to do when he arrived. Not only has Jacob escaped the wrath of his brother, but he has married a wife (two in fact!) and fathered multiple children. Now that the seed of the promise is firmly secure, there is no reason to remain with his father-in-law who has only continued to deceive him after initially tricking him into marrying Leah.

Nevertheless, Laban convinces Jacob to stay longer by offering him the chance to name his own "wages." After all, Jacob's work has increased Laban's wealth, and the Lord has blessed him as a result of his son-in-law (vv. 28-31). Jacob agrees to stay for a time, asking only for the "spotted" and "speckled" livestock and "dark-colored" lambs (vv. 31-32). Laban agrees to this but orders his own sons to take all the speckled sheep from his herd so far away that it would take Jacob three days to reach them (vv. 35-36).

Jacob's response to this latest trick is a form of selective breeding that is not scientific but supernatural. He knows, after all, that God will give him the animals that are speckled and streaked (31:12). It is unclear how he knows that this method involving "peeled branches" at the watering troughs will cause the livestock to produce speckled animals (30:37-42). Regardless, through it Jacob increases his flock. And in these dealings, he is exercising dominion over the animals just as God called Adam to do. Jacob even judges between the animals and breeds the stronger together in such a way that they produce spotted animals, while the weaker produce offspring that will belong to Laban (v. 42). Jacob is further blessed by God as his animals multiply and his riches increase (30:43).

This whole portion of the Genesis text portrays Laban as an oppressor over Jacob in several ways that parallel the exodus story. For Moses's readers, the previously enslaved Israelites, all this injustice with which their patriarch wrestles would seem familiar. While their oppression had been larger in scale, it was similar in kind. And in both cases, in spite of it, both Jacob's flocks and the people descended from him continue to multiply (Exod 1:7), even as they face "difficult labor" from their oppressors (Exod 1:14). In both cases, God sees the oppression and eventually empowers his people to flee (Exod 3:7-10). Just as the Israelites are led out of Egypt by Moses, God speaks through a leader (Jacob) to his people (Jacob's family) and leads them out of oppression in due time. Yet in both cases their oppressors pursue them (Exod 14:8), though God delivers them (Exod 14:30-31). The point is that when God blesses Jacob in spite of his oppressor and then frees Jacob from the oppression of Laban, his life is pointing ahead to the experiences of his descendants. It also anticipates the coming of the greatest offspring of Jacob, a true Israel, who will defeat the seed of the serpent and forever deliver his people from oppression through another exodus yet to come.

Jacob Angers and Reconciles with Laban (31)

After an undisclosed period of time, Jacob hears that Laban's sons are angry with him because he has grown prosperous while their father's herds have decreased (v. 1). This means they have lost a portion of their own inheritance. By this point Laban no longer favors Jacob either. The time is ripe for God to direct Jacob to return to Canaan (v. 3). Jacob thus summons Rachel and Leah to tell them why they must leave Haran. In his explanation, the actions of God are set against those of Laban. While their father has cheated Jacob and changed his wages repeatedly (v. 7), God has continually blessed Jacob and shown him favor. Moreover, God, he tells his wives, has now spoken to him in a dream and told him to go back to his "native land" (vv. 11-13).

The response of Leah and Rachel is to repudiate the actions of their father. Through his wicked dealings, after all, his disfavor extends past Jacob to them and Laban's own grandchildren. Leah and Rachel affirm that they will support Jacob in journeying back to the land of promise (vv. 14-16).

Just as Laban deceived Jacob, so now does Jacob deceive Laban to flee from him (vv. 17-20).

Next the passage includes mention of one of the first instances of idolatry in the Bible. The topic comes up because when Jacob and his family are preparing to leave Laban, Rachel steals the "household idols" of her father (v. 19). This action could suggest that Rachel shares her father's idolatry and desires to have the household gods with her to worship on the difficult journey. If that is the case, then this text serves as a reminder of the danger when parents establish bad spiritual practices in their homes. However, it is also possible that Rachel is not an idolater at all. It could be she is not driven by a desire for illicit worship but for revenge. If that is the case, her actions represent an act of vengeance toward her father who has cheated her husband and manipulated Jacob's wages multiple times. In either case, Rachel's secret actions put the entire journey (and her own life) at risk (v. 32).

Two things should be noted concerning Laban's abrupt arrival in Jacob's camp and related search for the missing household gods. First, Rachel's actions toward him seem to display her disregard for his idols. She knows that when her father enters her tent she should customarily stand and greet him as a sign of respect, but she tells him that she is menstruating and that she "cannot stand" (v. 35). She has hidden the figures inside the saddlebag on which she is sitting. Laban does not ask her to stand. Perhaps he quickly looks things over and leaves in embarrassment. Rachel's menstruation would be understood by the Israelite readers as rendering Rachel's seat unclean. By sitting on the idols at such a time, she is consciously defiling them, even as she seeks to protect herself from her father's wrath.

The second thing to note is Laban's desperation. In verse 33, he enters tent after tent, pursuing mere idols as items of utmost importance. Why? He believes they are powerful and fears what will happen to him if he does not have them, especially in the absence of Jacob, who has been a conduit of divine blessing over the years (30:27). So, though Laban has been blessed by God through Jacob, he does not personally trust in the God of Jacob. He trusts instead in man-made idols.

Laban reveals a pattern that is common among fallen humanity in this broken world. When we face adversity and life feels out of control, one temptation is to turn to idols of our own—whether it is the household gods as Laban did or the modern-day idols in the form of success, significance, security, or satisfaction. Rather than turning upward in dependence, fallen humanity easily follows the path of Laban and turns inward in idolatry.

In verses 36-42 Jacob responds to Laban's claims by sharing his resumé. He describes his scrupulous and honest care for the flocks and herds of Laban. Jacob reminds him that he did not defraud Laban even when Laban deceived and mistreated him. But Jacob's key defense when it comes to proving his innocence before his father-in-law is not the greatness of his resumé but the greatness of his God. He says, "God has seen my affliction and my hard work, and he issued his verdict" (v. 42). For Jacob, the source of his protection and the source of his deliverance and the source of his wealth is the power and presence of God. Thus Laban relents, and the men make "a covenant" of peace (vv. 44-45).

As Jacob prepares to enter the land of promise, he knows he has already experienced the initial fulfillment of God's covenant with Abraham.

Jacob Fears and Struggles with God
GENESIS 32

After reconciling with Laban, Jacob braces for the inevitable meeting with his brother. First, he attempts to make amends by sending gifts. But Jacob also turns to God to ask for protection based on the covenant of God. Before he sees Esau, Jacob will meet God face-to-face and be given a new name: Israel. Jacob's struggle with God sets the pattern for the future experience of the true Israel. Just as Jacob struggles with God and is blessed, the true Israel succeeds, enduring the judgment of God and securing the blessing of his people.

Jacob and the Fear of Man (32:1-12)

Having made peace with Laban, Jacob still faces a big problem. He will soon encounter his brother. As far as Jacob knows, Esau is still angry with him. In their last interaction, after all, Esau declared that he would kill Jacob after their father's death (27:41). In an effort to test the state of things, Jacob sends a messenger to Esau seeking his "favor" (32:5).

Imagine Jacob's alarm when the messenger returns with news that Esau is coming to meet Jacob with "four hundred men" (v. 6). His first reaction is terror over what he assumes to be an approaching army, as the text describes him as being "greatly afraid and distressed" (v. 7). He fears this is the end of his family. He thus divides the camp in the hopes that at least part of his family and some possessions will be spared Esau's wrath. But Jacob's fear of man leads him to do something else. He calls out to God to seek "rescue" for the promise and his family (vv. 9-12).

Here, then, Jacob finally acts like a patriarch and man of deep faith. He stands before God and reminds God of the covenant by quoting him: "You have said, 'I will cause you to prosper, and I will make your offspring like the sand of the sea, too numerous to be counted'" (v. 12). Jacob also asks God to pass over his sin, acknowledging that he does not deserve the love and blessing of God (32:10). Yet despite Jacob's unworthiness, he asks God to keep the promises made to Abraham, Isaac, and himself. What Jacob evidences in this moment is that he doesn't just care about himself. He cares about the future of his family, the chosen family, and the future of God's covenant.

A pattern of seeking favor from the covenant Lord will appear throughout the rest of Scripture. When the Israelites worship a golden calf at Sinai and God plans to destroy them, Moses will intercede on their behalf. He will use the same form as Jacob does here. He will ask for protection by reminding God of the covenant made with Abraham, Isaac, and Jacob (Exod 32:13). Moses stands in the place of the people and, although he has not committed this particular sin, he will ask God to pass over their collective sin. In the New Testament, the writer of Hebrews tells the reader that Jesus Christ does something similar for believers before the throne of God (Heb 7:24-25). In his intercession for us, perfect Jesus reminds God continually of his promise to redeem a people through the shed blood of Christ. Here Jacob stands before God, believing that God will answer, grant forgiveness, and keep his covenant promises. Jesus, then, is a new and better Jacob who doesn't just plead for the deliverance of his people but who also purchases the deliverance of his people.

Jacob and the Blessing of God (32:13-32)

The next major moment in Jacob's life helps reveal that the blessing of God often comes on the other side of a battle.

"During the night" Jacob sends his family across the river Jabbok, but he remains behind. Then, while he is asleep, he wrestles with a man until "daybreak" (vv. 22-24).

The text parallels this man with Jacob's brother Esau. For many verses now, Jacob has been worried about the threat of his brother; instead, he should have been worried about the threat of this man. Jacob wrestled with Esau even in his mother's womb and came out grasping Esau's heel (25:22,26). Jacob has been wrestling his entire life, first against his brother and then later against Laban. But now, when he expects yet another encounter with Esau, he finds himself wrestling with a stranger in the dark. And at some point Jacob realizes that the one he is battling is not a mere man but the God with whom he has just wrestled in prayer (32:29-31).

Even as Jacob wrestles with God, God reaches over and strikes "Jacob's hip socket." Jacob is wounded in a way that he will carry his entire life. Jacob will now walk with a limp (vv. 25,31). This is significant because up to this point Jacob has been a strong, self-reliant individual. He wrestled vigorously with Esau in the womb. He could single-handedly move a large stone from the mouth of the well to impress a pretty girl. But from here out, Jacob will have an uneven gait. This historical insight was sure to connect with Moses's earliest readers because of its direct impact on their dietary habits. In verse 32 Moses writes that "the Israelites don't eat the thigh muscle that is at the hip socket: because he struck Jacob's hip socket at the thigh muscle" in memory of what happened to this patriarch (v. 32).

In verse 26, Jacob's refusal to release the stranger until he is blessed sounds strange to the modern reader but would be less so to Moses's first audience. After a night of wrestling, Jacob recognizes that this person is a force of importance. And Jacob has a long habit of struggling to secure blessings. He had to deceive Esau for the birthright. He deceived Isaac, who was blind, for the blessing. Now it is Jacob who cannot see, and he is asking for a blessing from this stranger. The stranger asks Jacob's name, just as Isaac did (27:18). However, Jacob does not lie this time. He is then given a new name, Israel, from the stranger "because [he has] struggled with God and with men and [has] prevailed" (v. 28). Thus, Jacob undergoes a radical transformation in this scene. The old man dies here at the river so that the new man, Israel, can cross over in his place.

From this point forward throughout the Bible, the name *Israel* will be used to describe not just Jacob but the entire nation descended from him. It means "one who has wrestled with God and has prevailed." Throughout the Bible, *Israel* is a reference not just to one man but to a nation that started with one man and became a multitude of people—a great nation. God's plan for this nation reaches its fruition in the person of Jesus, who is the true Israel. One thread of the promise made to save people from the curse of sin begins in one man, Jacob, and culminates in another man, Jesus. The meaning of this name, *Israel*, continues throughout the narrative of Scripture: this is the one who has wrestled with God and has prevailed. The battle brings about the blessing.

When God names Jacob, he is declaring his authority over him.
Throughout Genesis, naming is a practice of authority. Adam exercises
dominion over the animals by naming them (2:19). Adam names his
helper Eve (2:23). Later in Scripture, Jesus will give Simon the new
name Peter (John 1:42). Thus, when God renames Jacob, he is declaring his authority over him. And thus, Jacob is no longer the servant of
his father-in-law, nor is he the runaway younger brother. He is the head
of a chosen nation that will become a multitude. His new name demonstrates God's authority over his life to make this promise a reality.

The book of Revelation opens with Jesus's promise that he will give to
those who understand and persevere "a white stone, and on the stone a
new name is inscribed that no one knows except the one who receives it"
(Rev 2:17). This means he will give all believers new names one day, signifying his authority and indicating their adoption into a new family: his own.

The idea of national Israel struggling with God and being blessed
after the battle is picked up in Ezekiel and later by Jesus. The prophet
Ezekiel, in fact, prophesies about Israel's rebellion and the coming judgment of God in ways that parallel the instance when their forefather
Jacob wrestles with God. He writes from the Lord's perspective:

> *I will bring you from the peoples and gather you from the countries*
> *where you were scattered, with a strong hand, an outstretched arm,*
> *and outpoured wrath. I will lead you into the wilderness of the peoples*
> *and enter into judgment with you there face to face.* (Ezek 20:34-35)

A few verses later, Ezekiel adds this: "I will make you pass under the rod
and will bring you into the bond of the covenant" (Ezek 20:37). Just as
God allowed Jacob to be separated from his family to wrestle with him,
he will bring Israel out from the peoples. Just as God struggled with
Jacob, using a strong hand and an outstretched arm, he will do the same
to rebellious Israel in his outpoured wrath. Just as God entered into
judgment with Jacob face-to-face in the wilderness, he will do the same
with Israel. Just as God's struggle with Jacob was part of the way God
brought him into the blessing of the covenant, his judgment of Israel
through the rod is how he will bring them into the bond of the covenant.

God's encounter with the person of Israel in Genesis 32, however,
doesn't just set the stage for God's judgment that falls upon the nation
of Israel in the future. It also anticipates God's judgment that falls upon
the True Israel, Jesus Christ, the ultimate son of Israel, who takes on
God's wrath for the sake of his sinful brothers and sisters. One parallel

is seen in an account related to the birth of Jesus. One of the first people to encounter him is a prophetess whose name is Anna (Luke 2:36). Her father's name, Phanuel, derives from the name "Penuel," which Jacob gives to this place where he wrestled with God (Gen 32:31). Just as Jacob came face-to-face with God at Penuel, the daughter of Phanuel comes face-to-face with God as she looks at the ultimate son of Jacob, Jesus.

But the parallels are even clearer in the death of Jesus. Much like Jacob, Jesus is separated from the people and goes outside the camp into the wilderness in an important struggle. This one will culminate in his enduring the wrath of God on their behalf (Heb 13:12). Much like Jacob, he will come face-to-face with God in judgment as he, the Messiah, personally encounters what Ezekiel calls the strong hand and outpoured wrath of God that the people have earned, but this time it is Jesus who is the one with outstretched arms (Mark 15:24). Also, much like Jacob, he is struck on the side of his body as a Roman spear pierces him and takes not his gait but his life (John 19:34). Much like Jacob, this struggle with God marks Jesus—not with a limp but with scars on his hands and feet (John 20:25-27). Much like Jacob, Jesus is proven to be not just the hope of Israel but the True Israel because he, being perfect though his fallen people are not, "struggled with God and with men" and then ultimately "prevailed" through his resurrection (Gen 32:28; cf. Col 2:15). Thus, just as Jacob received the name Israel, Christ is given a name "that is above every name" (Phil 2:9).

Jesus is the new and better Jacob who becomes the True Israel through his victorious death and resurrection. God gives to Christ all the blessings of the covenant, and those are then given to the people of God. Jesus leaves the grave as a new man, True Israel. Jesus's reenactment of the struggle of Israel establishes a new people, who are not the product of flesh and blood but of the promise and the work of the Spirit. So while True Israel refers to Jesus, the phrase *true Israel* also refers not to the physical descendants of Jacob but to those who share in the covenant blessing because of their union with Christ. He has secured the promise for his people through his own lonely struggle.

Jacob Reconciles and Struggles with His Past
GENESIS 33

Finally it is time for Jacob to confront his brother, Esau. Jacob fled from Canaan after stealing the blessing and birthright from this man

(27:42-45), so to finally meet him with four hundred men clearly on Esau's side must be nerve-racking (33:1).

Esau's response to seeing Jacob, however, is not a cold rejection but a warm reception (v. 4). This foreshadows a coming day when Joseph's brothers will fear encountering Joseph only to be warmly received by him (Gen 45:4-9). But while Esau seems to reconcile with his brother, he never reconciles with the God that both Jacob and later Joseph highly esteem (Mal 1:2-3).

How does Jacob react to their surprisingly pleasant reunion? With humility and grace toward Esau. Jacob has a duty to protect the family, but he does not have a duty to be the aggressor. In fact, in all his late dealings with his brother, he does all that is possible to avoid conflict, just as the apostle Paul says a believer is to do (Rom 12:18). He even refers to Esau as his "lord" (Gen 32:4). And again he offers him extravagant gifts (33:10). Moreover, when asked by Esau who the children and women traveling with him are, Jacob does not refer to the blessing, which would have been accurate. Instead, Jacob intentionally avoids reminding Esau of the matter. He thus refers to his family as the undeserved gift of God (v. 5). Jacob is speaking in terms of humility and grace. He looks back and sees this multitude that is only a hint of the nation and people that are to come.

As Jacob sets up camp in the place of the promise with the first fruits of the people of the promise all around him (vv. 17-18), it gives a glimpse of what God does for us in Christ. Jacob stands before Esau and tells him these are "the children God has graciously given your servant" (v. 5). In a similar way the new Israel will stand before God and triumphantly declare, "Here I am with the children God gave me" (Heb 2:13; cf. Isa 8:18). Both the first group, a small struggling herd, and the second, a people without number, are signs of God's grace and his covenant faithfulness.

Reflect and Discuss

1. Even though Jacob has prospered in Haran, he remains aware that it is not the promised land of Canaan. Why must Christians set their minds on the promises of God even in the midst of prosperity?

2. What does the story of Laban searching for his household gods reveal about Laban? About Rachel? About human tendency?

3. The stones set up by Laban and Jacob are to serve as reminders of their covenant with each other. What moments have you memorialized to remind you of the covenant faithfulness of God toward you?
4. Jacob calls out to God because of his fear of Esau. What does this suggest about the purpose of fears and feelings of desperation?
5. Jacob asks God to be faithful to the promise made to Abraham, even though Jacob is unworthy of it. Why does God keep his promises even when his people fail?
6. Jacob intercedes on behalf of his family, seeking God's protection. Is there a time when you have served as an intercessor or when someone has interceded on your behalf? If so, explain. What does interceding for others in prayer have to do with the life of faith?
7. The story of Jacob wrestling with God results in a new name and identity for Jacob: Israel. What does this story of struggle reveal about the nature of God? About the nature of Jacob?
8. What connections do you see between the first Israel (Jacob) and the ultimate and True Israel (Jesus)?
9. Jacob does not attack his brother; rather, he meets him in a posture of humility. What lessons should Christians take from this?
10. Esau's response to Jacob is one of reconciliation and peace. How are Christians to be peacemakers? How are they to respond to requests of forgiveness?

Righteous Anger and Israel's Tribes

GENESIS 34–36

Main Idea: The eldest sons of Jacob act against the passivity of their father as Levi and Simeon defend their sister against the abuse of Shechem but take their vengeance too far. Reuben even attempts to usurp the authority of Jacob altogether by having an illicit encounter with his concubine, Bilhah. As a result of all this, Jacob will eventually remove the place of preeminence from these sons and bestow it on his next oldest child, Judah, who will become the head of the messianic line.

I. **Jacob's Sons and Righteous Anger (34)**
   A. Shechem's abuse and Dinah's humiliation (34:1-4)
   B. Jacob's cowardice and his sons' bargain (34:5-24)
   C. Levi and Simeon's anger and Jacob's response (34:25-31)
II. **Jacob's Son and Rebellious Lust (35)**
   A. Jacob returns to Bethel (35:1-15).
   B. Rachel bears another son (35:16-20).
   C. Reuben usurps his father (35:21-29).
III. **Esau's Sons and Reigning Chiefs (36)**

The family life of Jacob is anything but simple. He deceived his father and brother, was cheated by his uncle, was forced to marry the sister of his true love, and lived for years without a home or family structure. Life after the birth of his children is no less chaotic. In these chapters two major events occur that contribute to growing tensions among Jacob's immediate family for the rest of the book. (I say "growing" because the fact that Jacob was forced to marry the sister of his true love first and then ended up fathering children by a total of four women paved the way for further problems. See, for instance, Gen 30:14-16.)

The first major future-shaping event in chapter 34 is the abuse of Dinah by Shechem and her full brothers' subsequent revenge. Their actions are contrasted with the cowardice of their father, who proves himself more fearful of the surrounding nations than he is protective of his daughter. Tragically, the brothers' actions go too far, leading to them being described as "vicious" and violent later in the book (49:5-7).

The second event follows the birth of Jacob's twelfth and final son, Benjamin. Reuben, Jacob's firstborn, rebelliously sleeps with his father's concubine. Reuben's actions represent an attempt to usurp the authority of his father and assume the position of authority over the whole family. But in this matter, too, Jacob does nothing. Only at the end of Jacob's life, his blessing of Reuben will note his strength while also removing from Reuben the place of prestige that was his right as firstborn son (49:3-4).

These two episodes set up Judah, the fourth born, to be the one through whom will come the seed of the promise: Jesus. Nevertheless, chapter 35 closes with a recounting of all twelve sons of Israel. Despite their flaws, they will be the heads of the twelve tribes. Genesis 36 provides a genealogy of the descendants of Esau, which anticipates the later moments in redemptive history in which the Edomites figure into the story of Israel.

Jacob's Sons and Righteous Anger
GENESIS 34

Once Jacob reconciles with Esau, he doesn't live happily ever after. Jacob and his family are staying near a place called Shechem when his daughter is seized by the son of the local chieftain, Hamor. This son is also named Shechem. After the resulting rape, the guilty man's father seeks Jacob's consent for their two children to marry. He makes this request in the hearing of the girl's well-informed and angry brothers (vv. 1-4,8-9). When Jacob shirks his responsibility to protect his daughter by failing to react, his sons take the matter into their own hands (v. 13). They come up with a way to deceive the men of the offender's town and execute vengeance on all of them to vindicate the honor of their sister (vv. 14-29). Poor Dinah is thus abused by one man, disregarded by her father, and used by her brothers to justify their crimes. The episode reveals the danger of a culture commodifying and objectifying women.

Shechem's Abuse and Dinah's Humiliation (34:1-4)

The objectification of women by men is no new phenomenon. This passage in Genesis 34 recounts the way the daughter of Jacob is abused by a son of the neighboring tribe. There is some textual ambiguity concerning precisely what happened to Dinah. It could be that Dinah was forced into a sexual act entirely against her will. Or it is possible that she was seduced into it—meaning that she may have seemed to consent to the act of intercourse but was violated nevertheless. Either way, Shechem "defiled" and humiliated her (v. 5). The text does not offer any details regarding whether her will has been violated. The issue is not her will but Dinah herself. Although the current culture may hold up consent as the only inviolable standard—where consent is present all actions are permissible—the Bible does not view sex in these categories. While an assault against the will is horrible and awful, so is an assault against a woman's integrity and dignity. No matter the particulars of this case, Shechem, who is the prince of his tribe, abuses his power when he defiles Jacob's daughter.

Curiously, Shechem becomes "infatuated with" Dinah after he violates her (v. 3). This is the exact opposite of what happens later when a young man named Amnon rapes his half sister Tamar. Amnon starts out infatuated with Tamar but despises her once he's "disgraced her" (2 Sam 13:14-15). Here Shechem defiles her, becomes infatuated, and then wishes to marry her. Shechem goes to his father and tells him to get the girl for him "as a wife" (Gen 34:4). Here too, then, is a parody of the normal progression of a relationship. Jacob and Rachel's relationship, for instance, followed the usual romantic pattern. Jacob saw Rachel; Jacob pursued Rachel; Jacob married Rachel; Jacob slept with Rachel. But for Shechem, all the steps are disordered. He violates Dinah; he then becomes infatuated with her; he asks his father to go pursue her; and finally, he attempts to marry her.

Interesting here too is that Hamor is presented as a slave to his son's appetites. In fact, Hamor's response to the demand of his son is acquiescence (v. 8). He thus becomes culpable in the abuse and humiliation of Dinah because he is doing all he can to help his son continue to objectify and use this woman. To Hamor as well, Dinah is not a person with value but a product to be consumed.

Jacob's Cowardice and His Sons' Bargain (34:5-24)

Jacob's reaction to news of the humiliation of his daughter is an act of cowardice and a rejection of his obligation to protect his household. He neither seems angry about it nor demands restitution or justice. He simply remains "silent," reverting to passivity and evidencing cowardice (v. 5). All this runs counter to Jacob's prior behavior. Formerly, Jacob was impulsive and reactionary. He stole Esau's birthright. He deceived his way to his father's blessing. He secretly fled from Laban with all he owned. But in this matter of injustice against his daughter, Jacob chooses to be a passive participant.

The reason for this switch in expected response is not entirely clear. It is possible that Jacob reacts this way because Dinah is the daughter of Leah, not Rachel. It is possible that age is mellowing him. But the strongest potential explanation is that he is simply afraid of the Shechemites and the other larger nations that surround his own people. Jacob, after all, later expresses fear because his family is outnumbered by the nations and peoples around them (v. 30). But this is merely cowardice. Jacob's fear of the people of Shechem causes him to fail to protect the integrity and dignity of his daughter. The fear of man can drive us toward passivity instead of protection.

Jacob's sons swing the emotional pendulum in the opposite direction. In contrast to the passive reaction of Jacob, his sons are filled with anger and indignation. Why? Moses tells the reader that the sons of Jacob are angry because "Shechem had committed an outrage against Israel by raping Jacob's daughter, and such a thing should not be done" (v. 7). In saying this, Moses is placing himself on the side of the sons. At least to a point. His editorial comment that "such a thing should not be done" makes clear that Jacob's reaction is itself condemnable. Initially, the sons have the proper reaction. Also, whereas Jacob is concerned with himself ("You have brought trouble on me, making me odious"; v. 30), the sons are concerned with Dinah. They are thinking about the integrity of their sister ("Should he treat our sister like a prostitute?"; v. 31).

At this point in the narrative Moses contributes something else of great note. He begins to talk of the sons of Jacob in the collective, as Israel. In fact, Moses's same editorial comment, briefly mentioned above, takes the name God has given to Jacob and applies it to Jacob's sons. He writes, "Shechem had committed an outrage *against Israel* by raping *Jacob's daughter*" (v. 7; emphasis added). The point is that the sons are becoming a people. And moved by their shared righteous anger, the men plot to avenge their sister.

The defilement of Dinah is not just a bad incident. When Shechem violates Dinah, this is a matter of grave consequence. This is the serpent trying to destroy the seed of promise. This is the dragon seeking to destroy the child of the woman (cf. Rev 12:4). Moses will later tell the children of Israel that they are not to intermarry with the people of the land because they would absorb the Israelites (Deut 7:3-4). Shechem's father is not just trying to tempt Jacob and his family but trying to adopt them. In this way, Hamor is imaging his father, the devil (John 8:44). When Satan offers the three wilderness temptations to Jesus (Matt 4:1-11), he is not just trying to deceive the son of Jacob but trying to adopt him. In either case, if the Israel of God is adopted through these temptations, then the promises of God may fail. When Hamor attempts to graft Israel into their people, it is actually an attempt by Satan to stop the promises of God by destroying the line of the Messiah.

Understandably, the sons of Jacob, namely Simeon and Levi, are filled with righteous anger and outrage in the matter of their sister. But in what they do with it, they demonstrate that they are truly the children of Jacob, the deceiver. The sons old enough to do so "agree" to the offer of marriage from Hamor and Shechem on the condition that the men of Shechem be "circumcised" (vv. 15-17). Hamor responds in agreement and promptly goes to his own city gate to share with his people about the monetary and economic benefits ahead if only they will go along with the brothers' demands (vv. 18-24). Thus, even though Shechem did not get consent from Dinah to be his wife before he took her purity, he and his father honor the men of their tribe by currying their support and assent in following through with this step. For Hamor, this circumcision matter is no more than a necessary step in an economic arrangement. It has nothing to do with converting to the faith of Jacob. When Hamor approaches the men of his city to undergo circumcision, all his reasons are pragmatic. He uses the promise of Jacob's "livestock . . . possessions, and . . . animals" as incentives (v. 23). And whereas Shechem was enticed by the beauty of Jacob's daughter, the other men are enticed by the bounty of Jacob's wealth. So they readily agree to do whatever is necessary to make it their own.

The physical circumcision devoid of any spiritual meaning Hamor and the men of Shechem undergo is but a parody of the real thing. How so? Paul describes in Romans 2 how circumcision is not just an outward operation. He writes,

> *Circumcision benefits you if you observe the law, but if you are a lawbreaker, your circumcision has become uncircumcision. . . . For a person is not a Jew who is one outwardly, and true circumcision is not something visible in the flesh. On the contrary, a person is a Jew who is one inwardly, and circumcision is of the heart—by the Spirit, not*

the letter. That person's praise is not from people but from God. (Rom 2:25,28-29)

Though they do not realize the significance of what they are doing, the men of Shechem are trying to become part of the people of God by marking their flesh so that they can receive the benefits of the promise without the responsibilities of faith. This is not unlike the way Shechem desires and therefore takes Dinah without first accepting the attendant responsibilities of honoring her and protecting her reputation and future. The New Testament also repudiates the idea of trying to receive the benefits of the new covenant without any commitment (Matt 16:24-25; John 6:53-60). But, as Paul says in Romans 2:29, the path to that promise does not come by transforming our skin but by letting God transform our hearts. The point is that Shechem and the others in his tribe remain outside the Abrahamic covenant, even after their skins look more like those of the men of Israel.

Levi and Simeon's Anger and Jacob's Response (34:25-31)

Levi and Simeon's actions toward Shechem are not praised or condemned in the text. Therefore, Moses's view of the deception and attack are unknown. For this reason, it is best to say that the text presents Levi and Simeon as having the proper core motivation even if their actions go beyond what is just. After all, they punish the innocent along with the wicked. This understanding is defensible in part because Moses gives the last word to Levi and Simeon. When confronted by their father Jacob, they do not resort to a response of, "He harmed us, so we harmed him." Rather, they make clear their interest is in avenging Dinah and her integrity: "Should he treat our sister like a prostitute?" (v. 31). For this reason, it is sensible to conclude that Moses approves of the rationale behind the attack even if Levi and Simeon may go too far in punishing the innocent along with the wicked. Regardless of their intentions and actions, it seems clear that these brothers are attempting to protect both Dinah and the future promise of the covenant.

The response of Jacob to his son's actions is contrasted with the response of the True Israel, Jesus. When the sons tell their father what they have done, he does not praise their sense of righteous anger or condemn their murder of innocents. Rather, he expresses outrage that they have endangered *him*: "You have brought trouble on me, making me odious to the inhabitants of the land" (v. 30). Jacob is more worried about the nations and fearful of potential reprisals than he is concerned about Dinah or the character of his sons. His numerous references to "me" make clear Jacob is focused only on protecting himself (v. 30).

In contrast, Jesus will respond to his own Dinah figure with compassion and protection. The Samaritan woman at the well, mentioned in John 4, bears similarity to Dinah in that she was engaged in a sexual relationship with a man to whom she was not married. That he was fifth in a series of men in her life may suggest she had a history with predatory males. Moreover, Jesus encounters this woman at "Jacob's well" (John 4:6). Jacob, of course, was the father of Dinah. Jesus's response to this woman of Samaria involved speaking to her as a valuable human being. He speaks to her with care and concern.

The woman's question, "You aren't greater than our father Jacob, are you?" (John 4:12), is important in that it invites us to see that Jesus is far greater than their shared ancestor for many reasons. For one, in this particular case he is greater because he offers relief to a woman humiliated and hurt by the men around her instead of remaining silent while she hurts. Moreover, he does not cower in fear of the Samaritans (who dislike full-blooded Jews like him) the way Jacob cowers before the men of Shechem. Jesus's courage reflects what Paul is describing in Ephesians 5 when he says that a husband does not just pursue his bride, but he protects her and washes her and purifies her (Eph 5:25-27). Though the parallel with Ephesians is not perfect, Jacob is concerned with himself, not Dinah. But Jesus is concerned with the woman at the well, not with himself, the True Israel. In fact, he seeks out the woman for the purpose of showing her the path toward restoration.

Jacob also suffers from a lack of faith. Jacob fears that the people of the land have the power to wipe him out. This is after God has promised to make him a great and mighty nation and has done much in that direction already (28:13-15). In the future the people of Israel will find themselves outnumbered. And they too will repeatedly respond in the same faithless way Jacob does by asking, "How can we survive when they are more numerous or larger or more powerful than we are?" (e.g., Exod 5:21; Num 14:1-4).

Jacob is trying to protect the seed through political negotiation. Instead, he should recognize that the kingdom of God comes through the Spirit of God, not the diplomacy of man. Jacob is reliant on his own power to bring about the promise and forgets that he is the underserving recipient of the promise and blessings only God can provide. We face that same temptation today to rely on ourselves rather than God. The constant refrain from God is that his people are "more than conquerors," but only because of his presence and power (Rom 8:37).

Jacob's Son and Rebellious Lust

GENESIS 35

Sometime after the incident at Shechem, Reuben attempts to usurp from Jacob the position of preeminence in the family by having a sexual encounter with Bilhah, Jacob's concubine. But instead of elevating Reuben, this treachery results in Jacob rejecting him so that the lineage of the promised Messiah eventually comes through Judah (49:8-12).

Jacob Returns to Bethel (35:1-15)

After the actions of Jacob's sons, God calls Jacob to return "to Bethel and settle there" (v. 1). Jacob's resulting command to "his family" to put away the "foreign gods" indicates his awareness that some polytheism is being practiced in his household (v. 2). Perhaps the household idols once hidden in Rebekah's saddlebag had become dear to the hearts of some in the family. In any case, Jacob recognizes that the people under his leadership will not faithfully turn toward God in worship at Bethel while unfaithfully turning away from him in idolatry too. A pattern of God's requiring the renunciation of idols, in fact, will be repeated throughout the Old Testament (Deut 7:25; Josh 24:14; 1 Sam 7:3).

Jacob plans to build an altar to the God who provides protection and who "has been with [Jacob] everywhere [he has] gone" (Gen 35:3). Thus, the same Jacob who was fearful in the previous chapter remembers here that God is with him and for him. Indeed, the protection of God continues as they journey toward Bethel because "a terror from God" comes on the surrounding cities (v. 5). While the text is not specific about the nature of this terror, it is sufficient to prevent anyone from seeking vengeance on the sons of Jacob for the murders of Hamor, Shechem, and all the men of their tribe.

Upon arriving in Bethel, Jacob builds his altar. He names it "El-bethel" or "the God of Bethel" in recognition of God's appearing to him at Bethel years earlier when he fled Esau (v. 7; 28:10-22). Moreover, God *appears* and offers a blessing that affirms the previous blessing given him (35:9; cf. 28:13-15). This places Jacob on the same level with Abraham and Isaac who received similar blessings (cf. 24:1; 25:11).

In a sense, this blessing is much the same blessing given to Abraham in Genesis 17:6 and Adam in Genesis 1:28. But as in the case of his grandfather Abraham, the covenant commitment Jacob receives in 35:11-12 centers on the promise of a *new people* ("Be fruitful and multiply") in a *new place* ("I will give the land to your future descendants") living out a *new purpose* ("kings will descend from you"). The connection between God's kingdom and God's purpose cannot be overlooked—the "kings" who will come from their shared line, leading to the coming of the King of kings who will ultimately accomplish God's covenantal purpose.

Jacob's pouring of "oil" on the "stone marker" he sets up to memorialize his latest encounter with the Lord invites the reader to consider that God chooses to pour out the blessings of the promise on a man who, in many ways, has proven to be a scoundrel (vv. 14-15). Jacob is a thief, a usurper, and a coward. However, throughout Scripture God often uses figures such as this to advance his work. Moses, for instance, has an anger problem. David falls into adultery, murder, and displays of pride. Even the disciples that Jesus chooses are shown to be people who cannot agree, constantly jockeying for positions of prominence (Mark 10:35-45). Apostles Peter and Paul get into a shouting match over the Gentile believers (Gal 2:11). Why does God choose to use such flawed human beings? Because in spite of all those flaws, they have a faith that is not centered on themselves but is ultimately focused on one man—Jesus Christ of Nazareth.

This should give hope to both the believer and the skeptic. God uses imperfect people who simply place their faith in Christ. There is no prerequisite of perfection. The spiritual grandparents of the church were flawed and so are those brought into the church today. God's people, past and present, are made righteous solely because of their union with the one who is perfect.

Rachel Bears Another Son (35:16-20)

After an undisclosed period, the family of Jacob sets "out from Bethel," most likely heading for Mamre (Hebron) where Isaac resides. Along the way, Rachel goes into labor and dies while giving birth (v. 16), a tragic turn that will fill Jacob with sorrow. She names her second son Ben-oni, which can mean "son of my struggle" or "son of my sorrow."

Thus, Rachel gives him a name that describes the dark and dismal circumstances in which he enters the world. But to his credit, Jacob renames him Benjamin, which means "son of the right hand" (v. 18). Jacob therefore gives him a name of promise and strength. This name is one that looks to the future. So Jacob, in spite of his grief, is looking to the future and expecting the promise to come to fulfillment through these twelve sons.

The significance of this birth scene is not just based on what happens but on where it happens. Benjamin is born on the outskirts of a place called "Ephrath," also known as "Bethlehem" (v. 19). By God's providence, then, the birthplace of this last direct son of Jacob is the same location destined to be the birthplace of the coming and greatest son of Jacob, Jesus the Messiah. Long past Jacob's lifetime, in fact, the prophet Micah says this:

> Bethlehem Ephrathah,
> you are small among the clans of Judah;
> one will come from you
> to be ruler over Israel for me. (Mic 5:2)

So, centuries later, just as Benjamin was born in Bethlehem, the True Israel is born in Bethlehem as the prophet foretold. And just as Benjamin's name means "son of the right hand," the True Israel will take his own place in victory at the right hand of the Father (Acts 7:55-56; Heb 1:3; 1 Pet 3:22). Even in Rebekah's death, she anticipates the Messiah through the birth of Benjamin.

Reuben Usurps His Father (35:21-29)

While Reuben's decision to sleep with his father's concubine may have been prompted by unrestrained lust (49:4), its effect is an attempt to wrest control from his father. By sleeping with Bilhah, after all, Reuben puts himself in a position reserved for his father. Later, in fact, during the reign of David, his own son Absalom sleeps with the concubines of David in view of the people after chasing David out of town (2 Sam 16:22). Why? To assert his dominance over his father so that he might be king in David's place.

The rebellion of a son against his father is not just an intra-family dispute. An earthly father's authority is derived from the authority of the heavenly Father. Therefore, when Reuben rebels against his father,

Jacob, he is rebelling against God, too. Paul says that all the families on earth are named from God the Father (Eph 3:15). So, when Reuben turns his heart away from his biological father, he is actually turning his heart away from his ultimate Father as well. When Reuben sleeps with his father's concubine, it is not immoral just because he is sexually out of control; it is a sin against the authority of the father and therefore a sin against God.

Long past Reuben's earthly lifetime, the prophet Malachi will speak of the ministry of a future Elijah (John the Baptist) who will "turn the hearts of fathers to their children and the hearts of children to their fathers" (Mal 4:6). One reason for this is that the same underlying rebellion that causes Reuben to turn away from his father in such a shameful way will show up in generation after generation of this family.

Jacob's immediate response to what Reuben does is not recorded. The text only tells the reader, "Israel heard about it" (Gen 35:22). So again, just as in the case of the sexual abuse of Dinah, it appears Israel does not react in a manner that is appropriate to the situation. Nevertheless, when Jacob gives his final blessings to his sons in Egypt, what he speaks to Reuben references this incident:

> *Reuben, you are my firstborn,*
> *my strength and the firstfruits of my virility,*
> *excelling in prominence, excelling in power.*
> *Turbulent as water, you will not excel,*
> *because you got into your father's bed*
> *and you defiled it.* (49:3-4)

Because of Reuben's actions, he will be denied the preeminence that should be his by birthright. This firstborn son's attempt to wrest authority from his father has resulted in his forfeiture of ever inheriting that authority. In this situation, then, Reuben follows in the way of Esau. Just as Esau squandered his birthright for the fleeting pleasure of food, Reuben squanders his birthright for the fleeting pleasure of sex.

Later in the Old Testament, we learn that Reuben's birthright and his blessing end up being divided between two of his brothers. For instance, the text says, "Although *Judah* became strong among his brothers and a ruler came from him, the birthright was given to *Joseph*" (1 Chr 5:2; emphasis added). While Reuben's birthright goes to Joseph, the blessing of the messianic promise now goes through Judah. When Jesus comes as the ruler from Judah, he recovers the role Reuben abandoned in that he becomes "the firstborn among many brothers and sisters" (Rom 8:29).

Genesis 35 draws toward its close with a recounting of the male children of Jacob: Reuben, Simeon, Levi, Judah, Dan, Naphtali, Gad, Asher, Issachar, Zebulun, Joseph, and Benjamin. God has given Jacob these twelve sons who represent the future of the covenant. With the renaming of Jacob as Israel in 32:28, and the movement of that name from just the father to the collective sons in 34:7, God is telling Jacob that his life and progeny are not about him. Jacob's life is about the promise and the covenant. It is about the coming of the ultimate seed of Abraham, the True Israel, whom the New Testament will identify as Jesus Christ. From this point of Genesis forward, God's promises to this family will march on and continue even as Jacob fades into the background.

Perhaps to underscore this point, Isaac, who has been absent from the narrative since Jacob fled to his uncle's, is now brought back into the picture (vv. 27-29). But only so that his death can be noted. As the death of Isaac occurs, we learn both that his life was "full of days" and that the reconciliation of Esau and Jacob is complete, as seen in the fact that they bury him together (v. 29). The Genesis text has moved from Abraham to the child Abraham received (Isaac), to the child blessed as the promised son (Jacob), and is swiftly passing on to the nation of Israel (represented by Jacob's twelve sons). Yet, as Scripture unfolds, even these will fade into the background as the Bible narrows the story of the promise down into the line of Judah, then to that of David, and eventually to Jesus. The text is making clear that the focal point is not the patriarchs but the child of the promise.

Esau's Sons and Reigning Chiefs
GENESIS 36

Throughout Genesis there has been a pattern of advancing the storyline through the recounting of family records (5:1-32; 10:1-32; 11:10-32). Prior to this point in the book, most lineages have focused on the descendants who are in the messianic line promised in Genesis 3:15. But Genesis 36 recounts a line of the human family that's in league with the serpent. This genealogy of the descendants of Esau (collectively known throughout Scripture as "Edom") is a departure from the norm already established. So, why does Moses include this genealogy in Genesis? There are five reasons (36:1).

First, the genealogy introduces the Edomites because they will reappear throughout the Bible as a foil for the people of God. Here Moses connects these people back to their originator, Esau, the one who rejected the birthright and rejected the covenant blessing of God. This is a helpful insight because the descendants of Esau will mirror their forefather's reckless attitude toward God's plans and will prove to be a thorn in the side of the Israelites, including in the time of their wilderness wanderings and during the settlement of Canaan (Num 20:14-21). It is noteworthy that the lineage of the people of God recounted in 1 Chronicles also includes the lineage of Esau (1 Chr 1:34-54). Both here and there, the biblical narrative helps us see that these two lineages follow divergent directions.

Second, Genesis 36 establishes that the Edomites receive both land and protection from God. Verses 6-9 describe the mountainous land "of Seir" in Canaan as the place where Esau's family settles. When national Israel later enters the promised land officially, in fact, Deuteronomy 2:4-5 details how God protects this area of land given to Esau's descendants. The Israelites are not allowed to conquer the land of Seir because of the command of God. This is exactly why the author of Hebrews says, "By faith Isaac blessed Jacob *and Esau* concerning things to come" (Heb 11:20; emphasis added). Of course, a great blessing was given to Jacob (Gen 27:27-29). But a promise of blessing was also given to Esau (27:39-40). And even though Jacob and his family receive the primary messianic blessing, a blessing is still reserved for Esau and his own descendants that God is committed to protect. In fact, this causes Esau to prosper to the point that he is so abundantly wealthy that he and his brother Jacob must separate (36:7). This echoes the prior separation of Lot and Abraham (13:1-18). Although Esau, like Lot, is separate from the covenant people of God, both men experience the blessings linked to their association with the lineage of Abraham.

Third, the genealogy connects the rebellion of Esau against God to the rebellion of Edom against the people of God. The pattern established by Esau with the rejection of the birthright will continue with his descendants. Like their forefather, the Edomites will be characterized by immorality and rebellion. Earlier in Genesis, Moses noted that the first two wives of Esau "made life bitter for Isaac and Rebekah" (26:35). That his brides were so troublesome may also be a contributing factor in the trajectory of Esau's line. Regardless, in days to come, the rebellion of Edom will contribute to the hardship of Israel in a manner mirroring the situation between Isaac and Rebekah and their Canaanite daughters-in-law. Just as Esau rebelled against God and went his own way, his descendants will rebel against the people of God and go their own way (2 Chr 21:8-10). Moses is noting the pattern established by Esau that his descendants will continue to repeat.

Fourth, the genealogy connects the lineage of Esau to the future destruction of Edom. The prophets of Israel will continually make reference to Edom and other wicked nations as facing a coming judgment for their rebellion against God and his people. There are myriad prophecies that refer to the destruction and judgment of Edom, in fact (Isa 34:5-9; Jer 49:7-22; Ezek 25:12-14; 35:1-15; Obad 1:1-14; Mal 1:4-5). Basic familiarity with the history and actions of the nations surrounding God's people, Israel, proves helpful in grasping the intricacies of the biblical narrative. These nations will face judgment for their rebellion against God and his people.

Finally, the genealogy shows how God has bestowed his covenant love on Jacob as well as his judgment on Esau. Genesis 36 brings clarity to Paul's claim in Romans 9:13 that God loved Jacob and hated Esau. The hatred was a covenant judgment on the rebellion of Esau against the birthright he gave up and the blessing Jacob received in his place. It is also a judgment against the rebellion God foresaw in the descendants of Esau against God and his people. Genesis 36 helps the reader understand the meaning of this phrase: "Even so, I loved Jacob, but I hated Esau" (Mal 1:2-3) This statement is not an arbitrary preference, nor is it an abstract hyperbole. Instead, it is a personalized reality based on the sovereign election of God.

The lineage of Esau recounts that there were "kings who reigned in the land of Edom before any king reigned over the Israelites" (Gen 36:31). This is important because it appears to be an early fulfillment that through Abraham would come kings and nations (17:6). Although this promise is most fully met later in the messianic lineage, Esau's line too evidences the blessings spoken to Abraham and Isaac. The kings of Edom, however, would have been among the rulers of nations the Israelites later envied because of their own lack of a human king (1 Sam 8:5). When Israel longs for a king, the text repeatedly mentions that one of their primary motivations is to be like the nations around them (1 Sam 8:19-20).

Within the lineage of Esau's descendants, one name deserves special attention. One of the descendants of Esau is a man called

"Amalek" (Gen 36:12). The descendants of Amalek are known as the Amalekites. This group would develop into a hostile tribe by the time of the conquest of Canaan by the Israelites. When the Israelites seek a king because of the surrounding nations, God chooses Saul of the tribe of Benjamin. However, because of King Saul's actions toward the Amalekites, God would remove his right to rule and give the kingdom to a new king, David of the tribe of Judah. What exactly does Saul do to earn this punishment? Though tasked with the utter destruction of the Amalekites for their actions against the Israelites at the time of the exodus (1 Sam 15:2-3; cf. Exod 17:8-15; Num 24:20; Deut 25:17-19), Saul chooses to spare the best of their herds and possessions—as well as their king. For his disobedience to God's commands, the prophet Samuel pronounces judgment against Saul. The rebellion of the Amalekites and the related disobedience of Saul thus ultimately prepare the way for David to become king of Israel and carry forward the lineage of the promise that will be fulfilled through the ultimate son of King David.

When Genesis 36 is considered in light of the larger story of Scripture, its messianic significance begins to emerge. One of the most extensive prophecies of judgment against the Edomites is found in the book of Obadiah (Obad 1:1-14). But, curiously, at the end of Obadiah's prophecy of coming judgment is a promise of messianic strength. Verse 21 mentions "the hill country of Esau" and notes "the kingdom will be the LORD's." This is the promise that the descendants of Israel will rule over the descendants of Edom. The lineage of the promised seed will rule over the lineage of the serpent. The kingdom that will come from that rule will belong to the Lord. The concept of a kingdom of God coming through the messianic lordship of Christ grows more clear in the New Testament. Indeed, that kingdom ultimately expands over all nations under the messianic rulership of King Jesus (cf. Luke 1:33; 1 Cor 15:24-27; Rev 11:15). The recounting of Esau's lineage in the people of Edom is one of the unexpected ways that Genesis shows that God keeps his promise to restore the kingdom of earth to its rightful ownership through the work of the messianic Savior.

Reflect and Discuss

1. The actions of Shechem toward Dinah suggest cultural disrespect for women. How can Christians help protect women and help hold abusers accountable?

2. Even though Jacob does not abuse his daughter the way Shechem does, he does not stop her objectification either. Do you think his silence and cowardice increase Dinah's trauma? Why or why not?

3. What, if anything, does the Shechem story reveal about the justice of God for the abused? Do you agree with the actions of Levi and Simeon in the Dinah matter? Explain your answer.

4. In the Old Testament, the people of God are repeatedly instructed to put away false gods. What does this instruction have to do with modern Christians?

5. Why does God continue to affirm the promise made to Abraham throughout the lifetimes of his son and grandsons? Why do you think Moses records it for the people of God at multiple points?

6. Reuben's actions with Bilhah are an attack not just on the authority of his father but on the authority of God. Give an example of how a modern individual's actions toward a parent help reveal something about his or her relationship to God.

7. Reuben's actions result in his loss of the preeminent position among the brothers. What does this have to do with Judah?

8. The movement of the text from the patriarchs to the twelve tribes is important to redemption history. Explain why.

9. God causes Esau to become father to a great people. How does the genealogy of Esau reflect the blessing and promise made to Abraham?

10. Though great, the Edomites are not the chosen people of God. How does the genealogy reflect the reality of God's judgment on Esau?

Joseph the Favored One

GENESIS 37–39

Main Idea: God is working through the wicked actions of Joseph's brothers to prepare both protection and a place for the Israelite people in the future. Meanwhile, God preserves the promised line despite the sinful actions of Judah and his family. And God shows innocent Joseph favor in spite of his years spent in prison. God can use the evil of others to accomplish his promises and advance his purposes in the lives of his people.

I. **Joseph's Pride and His Brothers' Anger (37)**
    A. Joseph brags about his dreams (37:1-11).
    B. Judah barters for Joseph's life (37:12-36).
II. **Judah's Hypocrisy and His Daughter-in-Law's Deception (38)**
III. **Potiphar's Wife and His Servant's Integrity (39)**
    A. Joseph and the favor in Potiphar's house (39:1-6)
    B. Joseph and the deception of Potiphar's wife (39:7-20)
    C. Joseph and the favor in Pharaoh's prison (39:21-23)

Genesis is full of prominent figures. Yet none of them are featured more extensively than Joseph. Why? Joseph serves as a bridge between the books of Genesis and Exodus. Moreover, his life conveys a key theme for Genesis: the people of God advance the purposes of God as the plan of God assures the promises of God. Furthermore, the birthright (that is, the greater inheritance portion of the firstborn) that Reuben forfeited through his sin is destined to fall to Joseph (1 Chr 5:1-2). It is therefore not surprising that his story appears so prominently in Genesis.

In chapter 27 the main account involving Joseph begins on a note of familiarity. Joseph, like his father, grandfather, and great-grandfather, is not a figure who immediately garners sympathy. By age seventeen, he is a prideful and arrogant son who repeatedly draws the ire of his brothers. The brothers decide that they will deal with this arrogant little brother by getting rid of him. They intend to kill him but settle with selling him into slavery. However, this is part of God's plan to ensure the protection of his people. And here God works through the wicked actions of the brothers to further his own plans. The key to understanding the story of Joseph, in fact, is found at its conclusion:

> But Joseph said to [his brothers], "Don't be afraid. . . . You planned evil against me; God planned it for good to bring about the present result—the survival of many people." (50:19-20)

At the beginning of this story, it is difficult to imagine how Joseph's slavery and imprisonment could be used as part of God's plan. But God is continually working through the actions of people. By the end of his life, Joseph can see that even the hardest turns of his personal history became the very tools used by God to protect the people of Israel.

A similar reality rises to the surface with regard to the troubling story of Judah and his daughter-in-law Tamar. At first, its inclusion seems like an unnecessary disruption in the flow of the story of Joseph. But ultimately God uses the sin and brokenness in this narrative, too, to bring about his divine purpose. Through the illicit union of the pair, the line leading to the Messiah who would one day deliver his people from sin and brokenness continues.

Christians reading these particular stories involving Joseph and his half brother Judah should take comfort in this shared theme: God is at work in every season and can redeem every situation. As Paul reminds the church at Rome, for "those who love God," all circumstances are being worked together for their "good" by God (Rom 8:28). Moreover, Joseph emerges as someone who grasps this at the end of his life, even if he is not an admirable figure at the beginning. Again we see Moses making clear that the promises and provision of God are not about the worthiness of God's people but about his grace and determination to accomplish his will.

Joseph's Pride and His Brothers' Anger
GENESIS 37

The final segment of the book of Genesis is the story of Joseph. He is introduced as a proud young man whom his brothers come to resent. Their resentment culminates in the decision to sell him into slavery. However, what they intended for evil, God is using to further his plans. In all circumstances, God is ensuring the survival of the family of Jacob and the lineage of the promised seed.

Joseph Brags about His Dreams (37:1-11)

For the final time in Genesis, we see the familiar *toledot* structure appear in the text in verse 2 as it declares, "These are the family records of Jacob." However, the last part of Genesis is not primarily about Jacob but his son Joseph.

The text introduces Joseph to the reader by describing his vocation and age. Joseph is a young man who tends his father's sheep alongside his many brothers. This inclusion proves important in that the image of a despised shepherd is one repeated throughout the Scriptures. Abel, for instance, was a shepherd hated by his own brother Cain (4:8). David, though destined to be Israel's king, will be despised by his brothers and considered of little worth as he tends the sheep in his earliest years (1 Sam 16:1-13). Ultimately, however, Jesus will portray himself as a shepherd hated by his Jewish brothers and delivered up to death (John 10:1-18). Each of these types and images that precede the coming of Jesus foreshadows his arrival as the fulfillment of the promise. Thus, the life of Joseph anticipates that of the coming Messiah. Just like Joseph, in fact, Jesus is also a favored son who becomes a righteous sufferer. And he too provides both deliverance for his people and reconciliation with those who are alienated from him. But unlike Joseph's situation, in which he is thought dead at one point only to later show up alive and in charge, Jesus experiences an actual death and literal resurrection. The image is fulfilled in the reality.

Joseph's relationship with his brothers is fraught with trouble and tension. He is favored by his father because he "was a son born to [Jacob] in his old age" (v. 3-4). And although Jacob has another son, Benjamin, born even later and also by his favorite wife, Rachel, Joseph is her firstborn. Joseph is also the recipient of special gifts from his father. The most striking of these is a "long-sleeved robe" (v. 3). The phrase translated in the CSB as "long-sleeved robe," however, could be translated "robe of many colors" (v. 3). Either way, the robe visually sets Joseph apart as favored and special every day he wears it.

Unfortunately, Joseph's response to his father's favoritism is not gracious humility but pride. He brings "a bad report" about his brothers to Jacob while they are tending the sheep (v. 2). Further, he will tell his brothers about dreams he has that underscore the idea that he is more special than they. Such action suggests that young Joseph is a man who has been blessed but does not recognize that he is undeserving of the blessing. Jacob's favoritism feeds Joseph's immaturity, which only leads to worse and worse relationships with his brothers. Joseph minds the sheep. But a problem emerges because he can't help but mind his brothers as well. Eventually, his brothers hate "him and [can]not bring themselves to speak peaceably to him" (v. 4).

The two dreams Joseph relays to his family, which exacerbate already hostile relationships, are similar in theme. The first, outlined in verses 6-7, involves him and his brothers gathering grain. After they've bound the grain, his brothers' sheaves bow down to his. In the second dream, summarized in verse 9, eleven stars bow to Joseph. And the sun and moon do too. These two dreams anticipate the future actions of the brothers and family toward Joseph that will be explained in Genesis 42. But upon hearing about them, the brothers react only with more anger toward Joseph (37:8). Even Jacob finds the second one worthy of a rebuke (v. 10).

Joseph's brothers receive his words as insults. But the text soon reveals a different reality: these words are not insults from a prideful brother but insights into the future from the same promise-keeping God whose interest in their family had been long apparent. The dreams are actually visions from God. Joseph tells his family that they will at some point in the future give him honor, something that would invert the normal family order (v. 10). But in fact, not only would the boy's elder brothers bow before him and accord him the honor of the firstborn, but also his mother (here most likely a reference to Leah because Rachel has already died) and father would bow down as well. Despite their skeptical reaction, this vision is eventually fulfilled because of the wicked actions of Joseph's brothers. In the moment, his brothers reject him, and his father rebukes him (v. 10). Yet even though his brothers are filled with jealousy, Jacob is filled with curiosity, as the text tells us "his father kept the matter in mind" (v. 11).

Judah Barters for Joseph's Life (37:12-36)

Joseph doesn't yet know that he is about to risk losing his life, and he also doesn't yet know that he will one day save the life of his brothers. Sometime after the dream incidents, Jacob sends Joseph to his brothers, who are tending the flocks "at Shechem" (vv. 12-14). At this point, Joseph is yet to realize that his life is in danger. Previously, Shechem was the site where the brothers exacted bloody revenge against a man named Shechem for his actions toward their sister Dinah. Thus, Moses may mention the place-name three times here to remind the reader that these brothers are capable of extreme acts of violence (34:24-29). Indeed, by the time Joseph is within their sight, they have already determined to kill him (37:18). That their decision to do so is related to their disgust over his dreams is made clear in their sarcastic statement about Joseph being the "dream expert" (v. 19). It also shows up in what they say in verse 20: "Let's . . . throw him into one of the pits. We can say that a vicious animal ate him. Then we'll see what becomes of his dreams!"

Joseph's eldest brother, Reuben, however, mercifully intervenes. He pleads with them, urging that they not "shed" his "blood" (v. 22). It is unclear why Reuben wishes to save Joseph's life. It is possible that he truly wishes not to murder his brother because he recognizes that murdering would be wrong and doesn't want it on his conscience. However, the text points out he wants to "rescue him from them and return him to [their] father," which could indicate that his real concern is regaining favor from Jacob following the Bilhah incident (v. 22). Reuben might even be attempting to regain his position as the blessed firstborn (35:22). Regardless of his motivations, Reuben is able to persuade the brothers not to kill Joseph immediately but instead to place him in a pit until they decide what to do (37:22).

Ultimately, however, it is not Reuben who saves Joseph's life but Judah (vv. 26-28). After all, at some point Reuben leaves Joseph without any protection he might offer and only later comes back to the pit to discover that he has been sold (v. 29). Reuben's plan to save Joseph, it seems, did not account for the greed of his brothers. Nor did he consider that a group of slave traders might happen by. When Judah saves the life of his brother, in fact, he only does so because he and the other brothers see in it a chance for monetary gain, for personal profit (37:26-27). So, far from showing mercy or compassion to Joseph, Judah intends to help himself as he harms his brother!

How much do Joseph's brothers sell him for? "Twenty pieces of silver" (v. 28). This amount is not unlike the thirty pieces of silver Judas receives for betraying Jesus (Matt 26:15-16). The same motivation that drives the brothers to sell off Joseph, in fact, is what drives the disciple to sell out the Lord.

Amazingly, this awful day in Joseph's life is the beginning of the chain of events that will culminate in his declaration that what others planned for evil, "God planned . . . for good" (50:20). Even as the brothers hand Joseph off to the traders, God is at work behind the scenes to ensure the survival of the people of Israel in the future. It is no coincidence, for instance, that the slave traders are headed to prosperous and powerful "Egypt" (v. 28). In fact, through the brothers' actions, the plans of God are being brought to fruition. Joseph being sold becomes key to the brothers and the rest of his family receiving grain and therefore surviving a coming famine. While they plot and scheme to advance their own desires, they are completely unaware of how their actions dovetail with the purposes of God. They are not thinking about their father's lineage or protecting the promise made to him and earlier forefathers, but God is.

The brothers decide to sell Joseph into slavery and then use an animal to deceive their father. As there was an animal substituted for Isaac, in a different way an animal is substituted for Joseph (37:31). After the brothers present Joseph's torn, bloodied, and familiar cloak to Jacob, Jacob responds by tearing his clothes and wearing "sackcloth"—traditional actions of mourning in this period (v. 34). Though Jacob had experienced much hardship and loss by this point, the loss of his favorite son leads Jacob to believe that he will continue mourning all the way to his own descent into "Sheol" (v. 35). The word "Sheol" refers to the realm where the souls of the dead were believed to reside, but in Jacob's day there was not an extensive knowledge of the afterlife.

The chapter ends by noting that Joseph was sold "to Potiphar," the captain of Pharaoh's guard (v. 36). Then the Joseph narrative gets interrupted by insight into the life of Judah and his children.

Judah's Hypocrisy and His Daughter-in-Law's Deception
GENESIS 38

Why does Moses interrupt the Joseph narrative to recount a series of episodes involving Judah's branch of the family? Moses is connecting the story of Joseph to the broader theme of Genesis by showing how God preserves the messianic line, which will run not through Joseph but through Judah.

This chapter centers on the abuse and abandonment of a woman named Tamar, and most of the troubles recounted in it befall her at the hands of those expected to protect her. Sometime after the brothers sell Joseph, Judah takes a Canaanite wife who gives birth to three sons: Er, Onan, and Shelah (vv. 1-5). When the oldest of these is ready to be married, his father gets a wife for him: Tamar (v. 6). Er, however, is an "evil" individual, so much so that he is struck down by God (v. 7). The text does not indicate what actions preceded his death. But this is the first time Scripture documents God putting an individual to death.

In line with an ancient custom, it falls to Er's younger brother, Onan, to take Tamar as a wife in order to provide a son who will be considered Er's firstborn (v. 8). This practice of levirate marriage is detailed in Deuteronomy 25:5-10. The widow is to be taken in by her brother-in-law (her *levir* in Latin, hence the phrase "levirate marriage"), with the understanding that he will both give her a child and care for her. This system would ensure a family line's continuation. Childlessness, after all, was not just a problem for a woman experiencing it but also for the community. The cessation of Judah's family line was a threat to the promise from God regarding a future seed.

The practice of levirate marriage features prominently in the later story of Ruth and Boaz (Ruth 4:1-13). But importantly, the practice is not one Christians need to follow. In Christ the promise of the seed has been fulfilled, so widows may marry "in the Lord" whomever they wish (1 Cor 7:39).

Tamar soon finds that her new marriage to Onan is marked by sexual abuse. Though Judah tells Onan to perform his duty to the family and community by impregnating Tamar, Onan decides to shirk that responsibility because the child of such a union will not be counted as his own. Yes, he sleeps with Tamar to satisfy his passions, but he does so in such a way that he is just using her. Each time he is intimate with Tamar, Onan practices a form of birth control in which he withdraws and spills his seed on the ground. This did not happen just once. Instead, it occurred "whenever he slept" with Tamar, which was no doubt humiliating to his wife (v. 9). To do such a thing, in fact, is also dishonoring to the memory of his own brother and defies his father. "What he [does is] evil in the LORD's sight," so God kills him as well (v. 10).

Christ's family tree confirms that Judah's was the line destined to give rise to his coming. And Jesus, as this commentary is establishing, is the ultimate seed referred to not just in God's promises to Abraham but is also the hero-seed promised to Adam and Eve in Genesis 3:15. Therefore, the actions of Onan are wicked in part because they jeopardize these wonderful plans. They work against the necessity of continuing the line of Judah past his sons' generation. But in killing Onan, God is showing that he doesn't need Onan any more than he needed Er. He can raise up a Messiah without them.

After this point in the narrative, Tamar faces a new problem. She finds herself back in her "father's house" but abandoned by her husbands' family. Why? Because following the death of not just one son but two who'd been married to Tamar, Judah also decides to shirk responsibility and prevents her from being given to his third son, Shelah (38:11). Judah uses the excuse that this son is too young, but "after a long time" Tamar sees that this is merely a delaying tactic and decides to take matters into her own hands (v. 12). When Judah sends her back to be a widow in her father's house, he creates the appearance of care for her though he is only caring for himself and his third son. Why? He is worried that his last son, Shelah, might die too if she marries him (v. 11). Judah sees her as a problem to manage rather than as a victim to dignify or as a daughter in need of ongoing compassion and protection. Tamar thus experiences what the survivor community today calls "the second abuse," which is what happens when those who are meant to care for survivors of abuse instead compound their pain. The secondary abuse she experiences is entirely Judah's fault.

Tamar's desperation and Judah's despair result in an illicit sexual encounter that ends up in her pregnancy. Judah does not intend to give his son to her, so Tamar takes matters into her own hands (v. 14). After Judah's wife dies and his time of mourning ends, he journeys to "Timnah to his sheepshearers" (v. 12). Tamar, receiving news of his travels, decides it is time to do something drastic about the fact she still has not "been given to [Shelah] as a wife" (v. 14). Her scheme involves pretending to be a prostitute—later the text will refer to her disguise as one befitting a "cult prostitute" (vv. 21-22)—and luring Judah into sleeping with her. Essential to her plan is the obtainment of his personal items, including his "signet ring," as security against payment. And just as she hopes, Tamar becomes "pregnant by" Judah (v. 18). Thus he inadvertently fulfills the point of levirate marriage himself.

After the encounter, Judah attempts to pay his obligation to the mystery woman and recover his personal effects (v. 20). In doing so, he shows more commitment to fulfilling his promises to what appears to be a prostitute than to his own daughter-in-law. Even so, when Judah's friend can't find her, Judah's fear of becoming "a laughingstock" reveals that he is more concerned with his safety and reputation than righteousness in even this matter (v. 23).

Months pass and Judah receives word that his daughter-in-law has disgraced herself and his family by being with child, though without husband. But when Judah decides to confront the sins of Tamar, even demanding she "be burned to death," he is instead confronted by evidence of his own sin (v. 24-25). Tamar, being forced to defend herself, produces the items she obtained from the man who mistook her for a prostitute (v. 5). Her coming infant, it turns out, is his own.

Can you imagine the shock when Judah realizes that the items the woman presents are undeniably his? In this scene he comes face-to-face with his own sexual sin in a manner just as humbling as when his later descendant, King David, is confronted by the prophet Nathan over his own sexual misdeeds (2 Sam 12:7).

One of the most important things about us is how we respond when we come face-to-face with our sin. Do we overlook our sin or own it? Judah faces that same decision. Tamar had called for him to examine the items, but now he is forced to examine himself. So, what does he do with such stark evidence of his own sinfulness and hypocrisy? His reaction in Genesis 38:26 appears to bear the marks of true repentance. He does not sweep the matter under the rug or brush it off. Rather, he responds by admitting that Tamar "is more in the right than [he], since [he] did not give her to [his] son Shelah" (v. 26). Having been ready to burn her to death, then, he is now burned with a sense of conviction. He recognizes not only his culpability in the sexual immorality but also his failure to uphold his commitment to honor and protect his daughter-in-law. He is well aware that his own failure to give her to Shelah in marriage heavily contributed to their shared sin. In verbally recognizing this in such a way, Judah repents before Tamar. And he bears fruit in keeping with repentance as "he [does] not know her intimately again" (v. 26; cf. Matt 3:8).

The interruption to the surrounding Joseph story culminates in the birth of Tamar's twins. But just as in the case of Esau and Jacob, there is an intense struggle within her womb related to their delivery (vv. 27-30; cf. 25:22). First, Zerah extends his hand (and the midwife wraps a scarlet thread around it to designate him the official firstborn). But Zerah withdraws it back inside his mother before his brother Perez is born. This inclusion is important because again, as in the account of Jacob and Esau, Moses aims to highlight the most important line in the Israelite family. The featured lineage is not that of Zerah the firstborn, but of Perez, the younger son. That the scarlet thread is mistakenly placed on the hand of Zerah helps emphasize that, in God's providence, the scarlet thread of redemption will move instead through Perez and on down toward the Messiah. Perez's descendant Boaz, after all, will marry another Canaanite through Levirate marriage and become the great-grandfather of King David. And the surprising blessing given to Boaz when he marries Ruth is that his house will be "like the house of Perez, the son Tamar bore to Judah" (Ruth 4:12). Thus, this messy episode of deceit, dishonor, and sexual immorality in Genesis 38 nevertheless leads to blessing. And ultimately, this story is an essential inclusion in Scripture because in it God works even through the cowardice and corruption of Judah to prepare the way for the coming of the lion of the tribe of Judah: Jesus.

Tamar figures not only in the lineage of Boaz but also in the lineage of Jesus. Matthew 1 lists Tamar as one of the five women mentioned in his genealogy. The others are Rahab, Ruth, Bathsheba, and Mary. Tamar's name goes from being rebuked in Genesis 38 to being revered in the genealogy of Jesus in Matthew 1:3. While Tamar was defiled by the son of Judah and rejected and used by Judah himself, a greater son of Judah has come since. And he was defiled and rejected for us so that none of us should have to carry the shame born by Tamar. Tamar and Judah are not thinking about the future and the coming Messiah when they commit these acts of deception and sexual immorality. God, however, is using this to further the promise and bring about his purposes. This vulnerable woman made a way for Jesus. Now, Jesus makes a way for the vulnerable, like Tamar, to find hope and healing and become valued members of the family of God.

Potiphar's Wife and His Servant's Integrity
GENESIS 39

In this section, Joseph finds favor and position in the household of Potiphar. Until Joseph's refusal to sleep with Potiphar's lustful wife leads to an unjust accusation of rape and Joseph's imprisonment. Nevertheless, Joseph is continually blessed by God and finds favor with those around him. God continues to be faithful to Joseph and works even this latest evil toward his ultimate plan to preserve the promised family line of Abraham, Isaac, and Jacob.

Joseph and the Favor in Potiphar's House (39:1-6)

This chapter opens with Joseph in "Egypt," separated from the other people of the promise and the place of the promise (v. 1). However, God will work through these developments that seem to endanger the promise to preserve his people and to keep his promises.

Joseph finds himself as the property of an Egyptian man named Potiphar, "the captain of" Pharaoh's "guards" (v. 1; cf. 37:36). Potiphar is in a position of prominence and prestige in Pharaoh's court. But though Potiphar initially brings Joseph on as he would any new slave, it isn't long before he comes to trust Joseph with all that he has (39:4). Because all Joseph does flourishes, he finds favor with his master. However, the text makes clear that Joseph is successful in his work because "[t]he LORD [is] with Joseph" and makes him so (v. 2-3). The presence of God, in fact, will be connected to the person of Joseph multiple times throughout the final chapters of Genesis (45:5,7-8; 48:21; 50:24-25). Further, this fact will be mentioned by Stephen the martyr in Acts 7:9 when he gives his history of the Jewish patriarchs. Stephen says, "The patriarchs became jealous of Joseph and sold him into Egypt, *but God was with him*" (emphasis added). This idea of God's presence in Joseph's life is the key to understanding how God is working to fulfill the Abrahamic promise in spite of what Joseph can and cannot see.

That God's presence causes Joseph to prosper hints at something that is true of Christians. This is not, however, a guarantee of material prosperity (as will be evident later when Joseph is placed in prison) but rather of spiritual prosperity. The blessing for Christians comes spiritually through Christ so that we receive the spiritual riches of the covenant through the Spirit's presence with us (Eph 1:3). The Spirit's presence precedes covenantal prosperity for the people of God who find themselves in Christ. God causes Joseph to excel in all he does. The psalmist declares that the one who trusts in God . . .

> *is like a tree planted beside flowing streams*
> *that bears its fruit in its season,*
> *and its leaf does not wither.*
> *Whatever he does prospers.* (Ps 1:3)

God's presence leads to God's favor in Joseph's life. The theme of "favor" resting on Joseph, introduced in Genesis 39:4, initiates a pattern of God's favor resting on his chosen people (cf. 18:3; 19:19; 33:10). The favor of God not only benefits his chosen people but also those around them. Because of Joseph, for example, God blesses Potiphar's house. And just as Laban was blessed by God because of Jacob's presence (30:27), Potiphar is now blessed by God because of Joseph's (39:5-6). Joseph is the conduit through which the blessings of God extend into this Egyptian household.

The opening of the chapter documents what seems like a complete reversal of what we might expect to happen in Joseph's story. Whereas before he was a hated brother, he is now a favored servant in a position of prominence. Joseph has moved from the auction block to having full authority in Potiphar's household. Potiphar trusts Joseph so much that he delegates authority over all things to him. The only thing Potiphar thinks about is what he himself will eat (v. 6). By this point in the story, Joseph seems to have found a way to enjoy the remainder of his life in spite of what his brothers did to him.

Joseph and the Deception of Potiphar's Wife (39:7-20)

Tragically, the false accusations of Potiphar's wife upend the favor Joseph has enjoyed. But before that, the text describes the dangerous dynamics within Potiphar's household. Potiphar's wife "looked longingly at Joseph," the young Hebrew slave who was "well-built and handsome" (vv. 6-7). The verse 7 phrase "looked longingly" brings to mind the words of Genesis 3:6 when Eve looked at the tree and noted that it was "delightful to look at." In a similar way, Potiphar's wife looks overlong at the forbidden fruit in her home and decides to reach for him. This situation points back to the sin cycle described previously as well.

In time, Potiphar's wife grows determined to lure Joseph into her bed. The firm way Joseph resists her sinful advances is instructive. It shows us how to better fight against temptation in our own lives. First, Joseph remembers *what God has called him to do.* He is in a position of leadership and responsibility, and he thus reminds Potiphar's wife that her husband has "put all that he owns under [Joseph's] authority" (v. 8). Joseph is a man of integrity who does not forget the significance of his leadership role. To give in to this particular temptation would be to reject the opportunities and responsibilities God has given him. Saying yes to Satan's ploys always means saying no to God's design for our lives.

Second, Joseph remembers *who God has called him to be.* He grounds his refusal in the uniqueness of his personal identity. In addition to reminding Potiphar's wife of his responsibility, he reminds her of who he is: "No one in this house is greater than I am" (v. 9). Indeed, why would he do anything to tarnish his reputation as a trustworthy leader? For the Christian, a proper understanding of who we are in light of who God has called us to be will empower us to have a stronger resistance to the pull of deception in our lives. Joseph recognizes that he has gone from being a slave under everyone's authority to a leader with authority and respect. In the same way, the Christian has moved from enslavement to sin (Rom 6:15-18) to being a coheir and conqueror with Christ (Rom 8:31-39).

Third, Joseph remembers *how God has provided for him.* He tells Potiphar's wife that her husband has "withheld nothing from [him] except [her], because [she is] his wife" (v. 9). No doubt aware his position in Potiphar's household is the result of God's favor, Joseph recognizes that everything he has is linked to God's abundant provision. And he dare not reach for another man's wife, for she is off limits in both Potiphar's eyes and God's. As Joseph combats the temptation to take what he lacks, he carefully considers all that he has been given. Unlike Adam and Eve, who were swayed by their desire for more than they had received, Joseph stands firm and is content with what God has provided to him.

Finally, Joseph remembers *how God sees sin.* He understands the depths of the evil of humanity's sin. In his rhetorical question to the temptress, he recognizes that sin toward his master is also sin against God: "So how could I do this immense evil, and how could I sin against God?" (v. 9). In saying this, Joseph displays his "fear" of God (cf. 42:18). As the writer of Proverbs declares, "[T]he fear of the LORD is the beginning of wisdom" (Prov 9:10). It is also the beginning of the Christian's ability to resist temptation. As sure as Joseph knows that to commit adultery would infuriate Potiphar, he knows that it would be a sin against the Lord (cf. 2 Sam 12:13; Ps 51:4). Sin, even sexual sin, is never just a private matter involving only the individuals engaging in it. Rather, it is always an affront to the holiness and honor of God. Joseph recognizes that what Potiphar's wife wants would not just be improper but a transgression against the holiness of God.

After Joseph rejects her advance, it becomes obvious that this is not just a single request (v. 10). She relentlessly pursues him and tempts him toward sin. However, Joseph repeatedly rejects her advances. To his credit, Joseph refuses to be persuaded by the ongoing enticements of his boss's wife (Prov 1:10). So she decides to force the issue one day when

Joseph enters the house when no one else is around. Potiphar's wife seizes her moment by taking hold of Joseph's garment and demanding that he sleep with her (Gen 39:11-12). Here too Joseph's actions are instructive on the topic of refusing to cave in to temptation. Joseph *flees*, leaving his garment behind (v. 12). Similarly, Paul later urges the Corinthian believers, "Flee sexual immorality!" (1 Cor 6:18). And he says,

> *No temptation has come upon you except what is common to*
> *humanity. But God is faithful; he will not allow you to be tempted*
> *beyond what you are able, but with the temptation he will also provide*
> *a way out so that you may be able to bear it.* (1 Cor 10:13)

God has provided Joseph a way of escape from the temptation. He leaves behind the garment and runs from the house.

The circumstances behind this instance in Potiphar's home provide a caution when it comes to temptation. The risk of giving in to it rises in cases of isolation. Because there were no servants in the house, Joseph could have more easily given in to Potiphar's wife with less fear of being found out. The same is true of the Christian life. Isolation makes temptation even stronger.

In some ways, that Joseph resists these advances is a reversal of events connected to the fall. For instance, though Eve listens to the voice of the serpent, Joseph refuses to listen to the voice of Potiphar's wife—even though she entices him "day after day" (v. 10; cf. 3:1-5). Though Eve succumbs to the serpent's seduction when she is essentially isolated, Joseph resists the temptation of Potiphar's wife—even though "none of the household servants [are] there" (v. 11; cf. 3:1). Though Eve covers over the shame of her nakedness with fig leaves after her sin, Joseph is willing to have the shame of his nakedness uncovered as he flees from seduction (v. 12; cf. 3:7).

Once Potiphar's wife realizes she has been rejected in spite of her best efforts, she uses Joseph's garment, which he's left in her grasping hand in his hurry to get away, to make a vengeful attempt to ruin Joseph for spurning her. She brings in the other servants and provides them with a different narrative from what really happened. She even goes so far as to place the blame on her husband in verse 14, making a judgment on his intent, which is meant to escalate the situation. Everything she says in this section is deceptive (39:13-18). In this way, she reflects the way of the serpent, who uses those twin powers of deception and accusation habitually (Rev 12:9-10). Christians should realize that Satan often works using these same patterns, enticing us toward sin and then turning to accuse us for that sin.

Things grow worse when the woman speaks directly to her husband beginning in Genesis 39:17, reminding Potiphar that Joseph is nothing more than a "Hebrew slave," denigrating Joseph's standing within the household. "These are the things your slave did to me," she cries (v. 19). In all she says, Potiphar's wife is clearly out to ruin, and most likely end, Joseph's life with these accusations.

Potiphar's response is understandably one of fury. He is outraged by the account that his wife provides. He has Joseph thrown into the prison reserved for "the king's prisoners" (vv. 19-20). This punishment is in reality a lighter sentence than Joseph could have received. Potiphar would have been within his rights to have Joseph executed, but his choice proves that God is providing for Joseph. And while there is little hope of deliverance from the king's prison, the Lord is working in even these events to ensure the protection of the people of Israel and the future fulfillment of his promises to Abraham.

Joseph and the Favor in Pharaoh's Prison (39:21-23)

Even in prison, Joseph prospers. Just as God was with Joseph in the pit and with Joseph in Potiphar's house, he is "with Joseph" in prison. Moreover, God grants Joseph "favor" in the eyes of the prison warden (v. 21), resulting in Joseph's being elevated to a position of authority and responsibility there too. Repeatedly throughout the Bible, the people of God are granted favor with those around them, both individually as in the case of Joseph (v. 3; Acts 7:10) and nationally as in the case of Israel with the Egyptians before the exodus (Exod 3:21; 11:3; 12:36). Even though God's people are sometimes terribly mistreated, he is able to bless them even in the most unlikely circumstances.

The life of Joseph mirrors and foreshadows the coming life of Jesus. Like Jesus, Joseph is portrayed as a favored son but also a righteous sufferer. In the same way, Jesus takes on flesh as God's beloved Son in whom he is "well-pleased" (Matt 3:17). He is a righteous sufferer (1 Pet 3:18). Like Joseph, Jesus spends much of his short earthly life as a servant. As Paul reminds us in Philippians, Jesus chose to become "a servant . . . obedient to the point of death—even to death on a cross" (Phil 2:7-8). And like Joseph, Jesus was destined to rise from that humble role to a position of authority. Indeed, he is over all things "in heaven and on earth" (Phil 2:9-11). Just as with Joseph, this rise to kingship and rule comes through persecution and false accusation. In the death and resurrection of Jesus, God showed kindness to him in the same way he showed kindness to Joseph in prison. The Lord sustains Jesus through his presence just as he sustained Joseph in prison. Joseph is not just a model in terms of how to find deliverance from temptation, then. At many points, he is also a model of the Deliverer himself.

Reflect and Discuss

1. The favoritism Jacob evidences creates strife within his family. What might parents do to ensure that they are valuing each child and creating an atmosphere in the home that does not contribute to strife?
2. Joseph is introduced as an arrogant son. Repeatedly God uses characters who fail to generate sympathy (at least at first) to advance his storyline (Abraham, Jacob, Judah). What does this reveal about God's character? About Scripture?
3. Judah's actions near the pit result in Joseph's life being spared. How does this anticipate the salvation that will come from a descendant of Judah for believers?
4. Give an example of how God works through the evil motivations of others to further his plan.
5. How does the story of Judah and Tamar contribute to the larger storyline of Scripture and point to God's plan for Israel's family as well as for humanity?
6. Tamar's story is used as a blessing in a later passage of Scripture (Ruth 4:12). In what ways has God turned a painful situation in your past into a point of reference evidencing the blessing of God?
7. The blessings of God flow to Potiphar through Joseph. What does this have to do with Christians?
8. Joseph sees the sin of adultery with Potiphar's wife as not only against Potiphar but also against God. Why is sin always primarily against God, even as it is against others?
9. What does Joseph's resistance to the advances of Potiphar's wife teach us about resisting sin?
10. What parallels do you see between the lives of Joseph and Christ?

Joseph the Interpreter of Dreams

GENESIS 40–41

Main Idea: Joseph is elevated from his position as imprisoned slave to ruler of Egypt because of God's favor and providential working. In this action, God further prepares the way for both the survival of Jacob's family and ultimately for the exodus, when God will officially bring the people of Israel into the land he promised to Abraham.

I. **Joseph the Servant of Prisoners (40)**
   A. Joseph is the servant of servants (40:1-8).
   B. Joseph interprets for the cupbearer (40:9-15).
   C. Joseph interprets for the baker (40:16-23).
II. **Joseph the Interpreter of Dreams (41:1-36)**
   A. Pharaoh's dreams and lack of interpretation (41:1-8)
   B. The cupbearer's memory and praise of Joseph (41:9-14)
   C. Joseph's interpretation and plan for salvation (41:15-36)
III. **Joseph the Savior of Nations (41:37-57)**
   A. Joseph is elevated in Egypt (41:37-45).
   B. Joseph flourishes in Egypt (41:46-57).

The previous chapter closes with Joseph unjustly imprisoned by the lies of Potiphar's wife. Despite that inauspicious turn in his biography, Joseph is the second most powerful individual in Egypt by the end of Genesis 41. He has a wife and two sons as well as servants. Joseph's circumstances have changed because God is preparing a way to save Jacob's family from a coming famine. In fact, Joseph is the means for the salvation of not just the fledgling nation of Israel but also part of God's plan to save the rest of the world. Through Joseph's life, God is working to ensure that his promise of the seed will come to pass.

The passages depicting Joseph as interpreter of dreams bear resemblance to the other major section of Scripture featuring a descendant of Jacob working in a foreign court: Daniel. In both accounts, God uses a Hebrew captive to interpret dreams for the ruler (Gen 41:1-36; Dan 2:1-45). These dreams were beyond the ability of the court's wise men and magicians (Gen 41:8; Dan 2:2-11). And their interpretation led to the elevation of the Hebrew in the ruler's court (Gen 41:37-45; Dan 2:46-49). These similarities indicate the way God uses his people even amid circumstances of captivity and suffering to bring about the salvation of his people. Joseph's interpretation provides physical salvation from starvation. Daniel's interpretation anticipates a coming Messiah for the people of God (Dan 2:44-45). In both instances, then, God is at work to show himself faithful to his people and his promises.

Joseph the Servant of Prisoners
GENESIS 40

While unjustly imprisoned, Joseph attends to two of Pharaoh's court officials. He interprets their dreams of what will come to pass. Although he is forgotten by the one who most benefits from his gifts, God remembers Joseph, and he is soon brought forth from prison.

Joseph Is the Servant of Servants (40:1-8)

While imprisoned, Joseph is soon joined by two officials from the court of Pharaoh. The Pharaoh's "cupbearer and baker" have offended "their master" in some way (v. 1). The text sheds no light on the nature of their transgressions.

The previous chapter noted that Joseph was given authority within the prison because of his success and the favor of the warden (39:23), so here that authority and responsibility extend to serving these two imprisoned officials (40:4). Joseph has gone from being a favored son to the servant of imprisoned servants. Surely, this point in his life, Joseph feels he cannot sink much lower.

Nevertheless, as Joseph is attending the two men, he astutely notices that they are "distraught" (v. 6). It is not unusual for prisoners to be distressed, so the fact Joseph even notices their sadness indicates these men must have been in an unusual state of anguish. Joseph then learns their distress is the result of dreams: "Both had a dream on the same night, and each dream had its own meaning" (v. 5).

By highlighting the fact that the dreams have distinct interpretations, Moses subtly indicates that the two men will face different outcomes. Unlike the two upcoming dreams of Pharaoh in Genesis 41 that mean the same thing, these two dreams are unique to each man. Ultimately, the two are distressed not by the dreams but by their inability to know what the dreams mean: "[T]here is no one to interpret them" (40:8). The pair feel confused and anxious.

Joseph's response to his fellow prisoners marks the trajectory of his life going forward: he invites them to tell him their dreams. But before doing so, he reminds the two men, "[I]nterpretations belong to God" (v. 8). Thus, Joseph makes clear that any interpretation he might offer is not his own; it comes from the Lord. Joseph will make a similar claim later, when he interprets Pharaoh's dreams (41:16; cf. Dan 2:28). And in a similar way, at the end of his life, he will credit all that happened to him not to his own ability but to the will of God (50:19-20). Joseph recognizes that every blessing he has received is not due to his skill or excellence but to the kindness of God (cf. Dan 2:19-30).

Joseph Interprets for the Cupbearer (40:9-15)

At Joseph's request, the cupbearer tells his dream. Both his and the baker's dreams, it soon becomes apparent, are connected to their official roles in the court of Pharaoh. The cupbearer dreamed of a flowering grapevine with three branches. As the grapes ripened, the cupbearer took the grapes, crushed them into the cup of Pharaoh, and delivered the cup for the king to drink (vv. 9-11). This kind of access to the king would likely give the cupbearer access to the wise men and magicians of Egypt were he not imprisoned. But he is reduced to waiting on this foreign slave to reveal this dream's meaning.

Joseph reveals to the cupbearer the meaning and then makes a request of him. Based on its details and the Lord's revelation, Joseph prophesies that the cupbearer will be restored to his position of influence in the court of Pharaoh in "three days." Joseph then asks that the cupbearer remember him by "mentioning him to Pharoah" when he is restored to his position (vv. 12-14). With this comes a declaration of the injustices committed against him. And interestingly, when Joseph describes his current situation in verse 15, he uses the same Hebrew word for the "dungeon" they sit in that Moses uses to describe the "pit" into which his brothers previously threw him (37:24). Joseph therefore sees his current situation as a reprise of his past unjust suffering. At this particular moment, his future prospects, he feels, are wholly reliant on the favor of a man who will be restored to power.

By this point, Joseph feels forgotten by everyone in his former life. Surely even his father, if still living, has given up on him by now. Indeed, humanly speaking, he is truly alone with no one to care if he spends the rest of his life in the dungeon, Nevertheless, Joseph petitions the cupbearer to show him "kindness," as Joseph has shown kindness to him (v. 14). The term translated *kindness* that Joseph uses here is translated elsewhere as "faithful love" (Hb. *chesed*). It refers to a commitment to help based on a promise that has been made. Throughout the Old Testament, this term will be used to describe the relationship between God and his people (Ps 89:1; Isa 63:7). Indeed, faithful love defines a central aspect of God's relationship to Israel (Lam 3:22-23). But though God never fails to show his people his faithful love, we soon learn that the cupbearer forgets to show that brand of kindness to Joseph (Gen 40:23).

Joseph issues these requests to the cupbearer for two reasons. Joseph has been unjustly taken and unjustly imprisoned (v. 15). He appeals to his status as a victim of crime and injustice. His mistreatment included being kidnapped and sold as a slave. He was also jailed for a crime he did not commit. Joseph implores the cupbearer to help him for reasons beyond a sort of *quid pro quo* arrangement by appealing to this servant's sense of justice. This has significant implications for the Christian: Christians should be people who seek justice. Later, Joseph's request to be remembered becomes a command for the believer. Hebrews 13:3 says, "Remember those in prison, as though you were in prison with them, and the mistreated, as though you yourselves were suffering bodily" (Heb 13:3). The Christian is to respond to those in prison with remembrance and grace.

Joseph Interprets for the Baker (40:16-23)

After listening to the prophecy of restoration, the chief baker shares his dream. In it he walked with "three baskets" of bread on his head for the table of Pharaoh, but the bread was being eaten by birds. The baker probably hopes that in three days he will also be restored to his position of honor (vv. 16-17). However, as the text made clear in verse 5, "[E]ach dream had its own meaning." And the interpretation of this dream is not favorable for the baker.

Joseph tells him that his head will be lifted (like the promise made to the cupbearer in v. 12). But in this case the baker's head will be lifted away from his body. So whereas the cupbearer is lifted up for restoration, the baker is lifted up for judgment. In three days, in fact, the baker's body will be hung from a tree, and the birds will feast on his flesh (v. 19). An awful end is ahead for the baker.

Beginning in verse 20 the text records the fulfillment of the interpretations given by Joseph. Indeed, three days later, the cupbearer and baker are both lifted up out of the dungeon and "elevated" back "among [the] servants." The former is restored to his position. The latter is executed.

The fates of these two men point toward the two eternal futures faced by every human. Just as both men failed Pharaoh, all people have failed their true King (Rom 3:23). As a result, all of us will die and then face judgment (Heb 9:27). Each of us deserves punishment like the baker because of our sins (Rom 6:23). Yet like the cupbearer, some will be restored to eternally serve before our King. How? Through faith in the death and resurrection of Jesus true restoration comes. Jesus is the bread of life. In trusting in him, we don't have to face judgment like the baker (John 6:35). Jesus offers us living water so we can experience restoration like the cupbearer (John 4:10).

It is easy to imagine Joseph hoping for quick reprieve from his prison sentence even as Pharoah's party gets underway somewhere nearby. *If the cupbearer would only bring my plea to Pharaoh,* he surely thinks, *the king might put an end to this injustice.* However, as the chapter ends, the text emphatically notes that the cupbearer "forgot" Joseph (Gen 40:23). Thus, once again he gets fresh reason to feel mistreated and abandoned. Even this, however, is setting Joseph up for a great reversal. While all others may have forgotten Joseph, God remembers him, as he has done for many others throughout Genesis (8:1; 19:29; 30:22).

Joseph the Interpreter of Dreams
GENESIS 41:1-36

In time, Joseph is called on to interpret Pharaoh's dreams. The encounter between these men sets the stage for the arrival of the people of Israel in the land of Egypt that comes at the end of the book. Joseph's position in Egypt ensures the survival of his family in the coming famine. In each recorded turn of Joseph's life, God continues to show his faithfulness to Joseph and ultimately to the line of Israel through which the promised seed will come.

Pharaoh's Dreams and Lack of Interpretation (41:1-8)

"Two years" after the events of the previous chapter, Pharaoh has dreams that disturb him. This pair of dreams involve the Nile River, cows, and grain. All of these are related to the livelihood of the people of Egypt. The dreams are marked by abundance (well-fed cows and plump heads of grain) followed by scarcity (sickly cows and thin heads of grain). This repeated theme causes Pharaoh to be concerned about their import. Indeed, they are important. Moses recounts the dreams three times: as Pharaoh experiences them (vv. 1-7), when he tells Joseph about them (vv. 15-24), and when Joseph interprets them (vv. 25-27).

In verse 7, the text hints that Pharaoh experiences a sense of relief when he awakes and realizes he has been dreaming (v. 7). But this relief will turn to consternation when he finds no one in his court can tell him their meaning. Pharaoh relays his dreams to all the court magicians and wise men, "but no one [can] interpret them for him" (v. 8). Just as a later king in Babylon will seek answers of his wise men and find them lacking (Dan 2:12-13), Pharaoh finds his servants unable to provide him with any insight into his nocturnal visions. Ultimately this is because, as Joseph previously stated, the interpretation of dreams belongs to God and not individuals (Gen 40:8). The confusion concerning the dreams is problematic for Pharaoh but provides an opportunity for Joseph, a man of God, to be freed from prison.

The Cupbearer's Memory and Praise of Joseph (41:9-14)

When the magicians are unable to interpret Pharaoh's dreams, the cupbearer remembers his promise to Joseph. Moreover, Pharaoh's servant acknowledges his own "faults" as are evidenced in his breaking his promise to Joseph (v. 9). The cupbearer then recounts the past to Pharaoh and explains the events surrounding his own perplexing dream. As he describes Joseph's ability to give interpretation, he tells Pharaoh that things "turned out just the way [Joseph] interpreted them." He "was restored to [his] position, and the other man was hanged" (v. 13). In saying this, the cupbearer is making clear to Pharaoh that Joseph has a proven record of credible interpretation. Given the recent failure of his magicians and wise men, Pharaoh is likely excited to hear that there may be another path toward clarity.

He sends for Joseph, and the prisoner is quickly brought "from the dungeon" (v. 14). Last time he was lifted out of a pit in exchange for twenty pieces of silver (37:28). This time, Joseph is lifted out of one in exchange for something far more valuable—at least temporary freedom and a potential chance to plead his case.

Imagine Joseph's excitement over this sudden reversal of fortune as he shaves and dons new garments before entering Pharaoh's presence—as was customary. Over a decade since being sold to Egypt as a slave, Joseph stands before Egypt's ruler with the possibility of freedom (Ps 105:20; cf. Dan 2:25).

Joseph's Interpretation and Plan for Salvation (41:15-36)

When Joseph stands before Pharaoh, he is aware that he is in a situation with incredibly high stakes. Nevertheless, his audience with the king of Egypt begins in a surprising, if not shocking, manner. To Pharaoh's comment, "I have heard it said . . . that you can hear a dream and interpret it," Joseph replies, "I am not able to" (vv. 15-16). Then, almost in the same breath, Joseph tells Pharaoh that interpretation is given by God. Just as in Genesis 40:8, then, Joseph has deflected credit away from himself and instead gives the glory to the Lord (cf. Dan 2:28-30).

What Joseph says here illustrates his faith in a point that Jesus will later make to his disciples in Matthew 19:26: "With man this is impossible, but with God all things are possible." Joseph knows that the interpretation of Pharaoh's dream is, like the chance to stand before Pharaoh at all, only possible because their Creator is with him. So instead of taking credit for himself and seeking to strengthen his chances of being released from prison or even restored to his homeland, Joseph starts this encounter by giving credit to God.

Importantly, Joseph's claim that it is God who will give an interpretation directly challenges Pharaoh's belief structure. The pharaohs of Egypt, after all, believed themselves to be children of the gods. Moreover, the religious leaders representing the many gods of Egypt have already failed to offer any explanation for the man's dreams. Joseph's claim is therefore a bold statement that the gods of Egypt do not hold the power and ability of the God of Joseph.

Pharaoh is not put off by this and tells his dreams to Joseph. He immediately sets himself apart from other would-be interpreters by starting his reply with the confident words, "God has revealed to Pharaoh what he is about to do" (Gen 41:25). At this point in the narrative, Joseph begins speaking as a prophet of God.

Throughout the Old Testament, prophets play a central role in the storyline of the people of Israel. Moses, who later leads the people out of Egypt, is described as a prophet (Deut 18:15-19). The prophet Nathan confronts David after his inappropriate actions with Bathsheba (2 Sam 12:1-15). The prophets Isaiah, Jeremiah, and Ezekiel speak to the divided kingdoms of Israel both before and during their exiles. And John the Baptist comes in the spirit of another prophet, Elijah, to prepare the way of the coming Messiah (Mal 4:5-6; Mark 1:1-8). The role of prophet will finally culminate in the person of Jesus, who is a prophet after the manner of Moses (Deut 18:15). When Jesus comes as the long-awaited Messiah, he does not come like the prophets of the Old Testament, however, simply *declaring* the words of God. Rather, he himself also *is* the Word of God (John 1:1-18).

Before Joseph gets into an explanation of the dreams, he speaks prophetically about the nature of God first. In 41:25, he draws attention to God's ability to providentially direct the course of history. Such abilities are among the many things that set God apart from humanity and reveal his character and essence (cf. Num 23:19; Isa 46:10-11). Joseph gives Pharaoh several assurances that God will do what the dreams say he will (41:25,28,32).

Modern readers may wish that, like Pharaoh, they could know the future to plan for what lies ahead. In one sense God does show us our future, revealing insights about the heavenly realties ahead for those in Christ. Still, walking by faith and not by sight requires clinging to what God has revealed to us while trusting him with what he hasn't (2 Cor 5:7). So, while we may long for the future to be revealed in dreams, providing clarity about the direction we should move or about how to navigate particular circumstances, God is often most interested in working through our uncertainty to lead us toward deeper dependence on him.

In Genesis 41:26-32, God's Spirit works through Joseph to tell Pharaoh what will happen to the nation. In verse 38, Pharoah remarks on it. The Spirit at work in Joseph is the same Spirit at work in us today, even if how he works may look different. While we are not promised that God will reveal the specifics of our future to us, Jesus does tell us that the "Spirit of truth" will "declare to you what is to come" (John 16:13).

After giving Pharaoh the bad news about the coming famine, Joseph offers a plan for ensuring the survival of Egypt. The key to meeting the challenge ahead, he points out, will require "Pharaoh [to] look for a discerning and wise man and set him over the land of Egypt" (v. 33). The newly appointed leader should appoint overseers to help him ensure that 20 percent of the seven good harvests to come are reserved for use during the years of famine. Securing these reserves will sustain the nation during the famine (vv. 34-36). The plan, of course, is a sound one. Indeed, without Pharoah's dreams and God's graciously working through Joseph to interpret them, Egypt would be as devastated by the famine ahead as any other nation feeling its impact.

The solution offered by Joseph is not just the means through which God is saving the people of Egypt, however. This plan of intervention is also intended to aid the family of Jacob, as the text will soon reveal. The psalmist's later recounting of this period in the life of the nation of Israel details one key way God has proven himself faithful to his chosen people throughout redemptive history. He writes,

> *He [God] called down famine against the land*
> *and destroyed the entire food supply.*
> *He had sent a man ahead of them—*
> *Joseph, who was sold as a slave.*
> *They hurt his feet with shackles;*
> *his neck was put in an iron collar.*
> *Until the time his prediction came true,*
> *the word of the LORD tested him.*
> *The king sent for him and released him;*
> *the ruler of peoples set him free.*
> *He made him master of his household,*
> *ruler over all his possessions—*
> *binding his officials at will*
> *and instructing his elders.* (Ps 105:16-22)

In the psalmist's summary of the famine narrative, four things demonstrate God's faithfulness to Israel and to Joseph. First, Psalm 105:16 speaks of the way God "called down famine against the land." The Lord, then, was actively engaged in causing the circumstances he ultimately used to advance his redemptive purposes. Second, God provided for Israel's needs even before the need was known. God "sent a man ahead of them" (Ps 105:17). Therefore, God was actively involved in preparing Joseph for this moment, allowing circumstances to unfold in such a way as to get him in the right place at the right time. As is true of other situations in Scripture, God prepared a deliverer for his people before their trials even occurred. Third, God tested his deliverer to refine him for the future task. The text speaks of the way "the word of the LORD tested" Joseph (Ps 105:19). This means God himself was refining Joseph's character throughout his experiences so that he could use him to save many from the physical famine they would experience. Fourth, Psalm 105 speaks of the way God delivers slaves and turns them into masters. In verse 21 the psalmist writes that Pharaoh made Joseph "master of his household." God took one who was a slave to prisoners, set him free, and increased his standing to a shocking degree. The parallels with God's work in the gospel of Jesus Christ are unmistakable. God's work in the life of Joseph also illustrates the meticulous care God exercises over the life of every believer as he or she walks the path of redemption.

Joseph the Savior of Nations

GENESIS 41:37-57

Joseph's prophecy quickly becomes reality. His plan proves effective in ensuring the survival not only of Egypt but of the surrounding nations as well. The birth of Joseph's sons marks the arrival of the heads of the last tribes of Israel: Ephraim and Manasseh. Through these sons Joseph will effectually receive a double share of inheritance in the land of Canaan. Amid great suffering, God has shown himself faithful both to Joseph and to the family of Abraham by providing for their survival.

Joseph Is Elevated in Egypt (41:37-45)

God provides Joseph with both the wisdom to instruct Pharaoh and the favor for that wisdom to be received well. After Joseph reveals both the dreams' interpretation and a suitable plan for preventing disaster, Pharaoh asks where such a leader can be found to implement this plan (v. 38). Pharaoh knows no one in Egypt capable of doing this. Since his wise men did not understand the dream, Pharaoh does not trust them to aid in its solution. God leads Pharaoh to see that Joseph is just the instrument of salvation he needs. Later, the martyr Stephen notes that God intentionally granted to Joseph wisdom and favor with Pharaoh

(Acts 7:10). Egypt's king doesn't miss that Joseph is "a man who has God's spirit in him" and notes aloud that "there is no one as discerning and wise as" he (vv. 38-39; cf. Dan 5:14). What he says about Joseph shares parallels with the way Matthew 3:16 describes Jesus as having "the Spirit of God" on him. Indeed, as with Joseph, the Spirit dwells in Jesus and is central to his future exaltation (Rom 1:4).

Pharaoh places Joseph in charge of his household and declares, "All my people will obey your commands" (v. 40; Ps 105:21-22). He confirms his words by giving Joseph gifts: Pharoah's own "signet ring," "linen garments," and "a gold chain" (v. 42). These gifts, especially the signet ring, mark the conferral of power and authority on Joseph by Pharaoh (cf. Esth 3:10; 8:2). They also serve as signs of restoration and celebration in the life of Joseph. Just as the prodigal son is greeted with gifts by his father in Jesus's later parable (Luke 15:22), Joseph is given gifts as recognition of his newfound standing.

Joseph's new position is marked by his receiving of new clothing. His initial troubles, after all, began with his brothers stripping him of his many-colored cloak (Gen 37:23). He was further humiliated and disgraced when Potiphar's wife snatched his clothes from him, leading to his imprisonment (39:12). The loss of clothing has been linked to a loss of standing in the life of Joseph. But here, Joseph is clothed with "fine linen garments" by one who is for him (41:42). This gift parallels the "fine linen" Christ's bride receives once her earthly trials are behind her (Rev 19:7-9). Joseph's new clothes reflect his new status.

Joseph Flourishes in Egypt (41:46-57)

In this section the text further develops the parallels between Joseph and Jesus. Joseph begins his ministry in Egypt at the age of "thirty," roughly the same age at which Jesus began his public ministry (v. 46; cf. Luke 3:23). Joseph has gone from servant of prisoners to being the second most powerful individual in Egypt. He is now accompanied by those who call out before him, "Make way," which in the original language means "kneel" (v. 43). Therefore, though Joseph was formerly a slave, now all in the land must bow and submit before his authority. In this way, too, Joseph anticipates the coming Messiah, Jesus of Nazareth. Paul speaks in Philippians 2:7-11 of the way Jesus assumed the form of a slave and was humiliated to the point of death. Yet every knee on earth will one day bow before him because of his great authority.

Prophecy becomes reality in the remainder of this chapter. During the initial seven years, the harvest in Egypt is so abundant that the grain is "like the sand of the sea" (v. 49). That phrase brings to mind God's promise to make Abraham's descendants "as numerous" as "sand on the seashore" (22:17). This connection is important because just as God would later provide for his people in abundance as they travel through the wilderness (Ps 78:24-27), he provides an abundance in Egypt that will similarly help them. This is not just a common-grace blessing on Egypt, after all. God is working in Egypt to provide grain so that Abraham's descendants can survive.

During the years of "outstanding harvests," Joseph marries and has two sons, Manasseh and Ephraim (Gen 41:47,50-52). Their names are significant for several reasons. To begin with, the boys are given Hebrew names rather than Egyptian ones, which connects them to the heritage of God's people. More importantly, their names reflect Joseph's awareness of God's provision in his life. The firstborn, Manasseh, whose name sounds like the Hebrew verb for "forget," is so called because God has caused Joseph to forget his hardship. Every time Joseph sees him, he gets a reminder of the goodness that can come even through suffering (cf. 50:20). The name of his second son, Ephraim, whose name sounds like the Hebrew word meaning "fruitful," signifies Joseph's awareness of the way God has allowed him to prosper in the land. The name foreshadows the blessing given by Jacob to Joseph at the end of Jacob's life: "Joseph is a fruitful vine, a fruitful vine beside a spring; its branches climb over the wall" (49:22).

When the seven years of abundance come "to an end," the famine abruptly begins. People cry "out to Pharaoh" in their suffering (41:55). Stephen's recounting of this moment in the life of Israel also notes the "great suffering" that falls on Canaan, where Joseph's birth family lives, at this time (Acts 7:11). According to plan, Pharoah directs the people to listen to the wisdom of Joseph. The king wisely recognizes that he cannot prevent or change anything. He can only trust the man who forewarned him of these events, the man whose powerful God saw them coming.

Joseph's plan has prepared Egypt for this moment, and he opens "the storehouses" to sell grain "to the Egyptians" (Gen 41:56). The other nations also come to buy from the Egyptians because they too are suffering from famine (v. 57). Here, then, we witness a partial fulfillment of the Genesis 12:3 promise made to Abraham that God will bless all nations through his descendants. In a way, Joseph is presented as the savior of a multitude of nations because he provides the grain to make the bread to sustain their lives. Later, another descendant of Abraham will not only *give* bread to the masses but will *be* the bread of life (Matt 15:32-39; John 6:35).

As all the nations stream to Egypt for bread in Genesis 41:57, the Old Testament hints of something greater that will happen in the last days. A time is coming when the "nations will stream" in not just to secure the provision of God but to experience the presence of God (Isa 2:2-4; Ps 86:9; Rev 15:4).

Throughout Genesis 40 and 41, Joseph exhibits perseverance through suffering (cf. 2 Cor 4:16-18). This pattern established by Joseph is found later in the life of Jesus (Heb 12:1-3). Likewise, Christians are commanded to persevere through trials and suffering (Jas 1:2-4). Chapters 40 and 41 of Genesis also link Joseph the prophet, who revealed the mysteries of God, to Jesus the prophetic Son of God, who is himself the ultimate revelation of God (Heb 1:1-2). Just as Joseph is bound in judgment for crimes he did not commit, Jesus is sent to the cross as a criminal unjustly charged (Matt 27:28-30). Joseph moves from servant to exalted ruler, just as Jesus will move from servant to exalted ruler (Phil 2:9-11). In many aspects of the life of Joseph, then, God is intentionally foreshadowing the greater Joseph who is to come. The story of Joseph anticipates not only the power of God in the exodus but also the salvation of God in the cross.

Reflect and Discuss

1. Joseph chooses to be a *faithful* servant at even the lowest point of his life. How can Christians remain faithful even in the midst of low circumstances?

2. Joseph's dream interpretations are grounded in a perspective guided by God. How can Christians cultivate godly perspective in their own lives?

3. The theme of "faithful love" (Hb. *chesed*) recurs throughout this passage and the whole Old Testament. How does this concept guide the relationship of God with his people?

4. Joseph pleads with the cupbearer to remember him by appealing to the man's sense of justice. What is justice in this situation? What might Christians do to serve as a force for justice in their communities?

5. Even when the cupbearer forgets Joseph, God does not. What are the ramifications for those unjustly imprisoned? Do believers bear any responsibility for remembering those in prison? Explain why or why not.

6. Joseph's humility before Pharaoh contrasts with his hubris before his brothers (37:9; 41:16). How have Joseph's circumstances shaped him into a more humble person?

7. God grants Joseph favor before Pharaoh, which leads to Joseph's elevation. What might this suggest about how God works today? Does every promotion signal God's favor?

8. When Joseph names his sons, he acknowledges the provision of God in his life. How have you seen God provide for you?

9. How does Joseph's work in Egypt contribute to the fulfillment of the promise God made to Abraham?

10. What can Christians learn from the way Joseph endured hardship and suffering?

A Party, a Cup, and a Substitute

GENESIS 42–44

Main Idea: The work of God in Joseph's life has led to Joseph's ability to provide food for his family to deliver them from the famine, leading to their eventual migration to Egypt. This section concludes with the first instance in the Bible of a person offering himself as a substitute for another. Judah's actions set a pattern that will culminate in the substitutionary death of Jesus.

I. Joseph Meets His Brothers' Need (42).
  A. Joseph's brothers and Jacob's plan (42:1-4)
  B. Joseph's brothers and Joseph's accusation (42:5-26)
  C. Joseph's brothers and Jacob's despair (42:27-38)
II. Joseph Shows His Brothers Kindness (43).
  A. The brothers return to Egypt (43:1-15).
  B. The brothers enjoy Joseph's favor (43:16-34).
III. Joseph Tests His Brothers' Love (44).
  A. Joseph tests his brothers (44:1-13).
  B. Judah pleads for his brother (44:14-34).

At this point the Genesis narrative introduces a more personal twist in that as Joseph deals with the public challenges of the famine, he suddenly encounters a private challenge involving his extended family. His brothers unwittingly seek help from the one they previously harmed. Whereas the brothers' disgust sent Joseph to Egypt in the first place, desperation reunites them with him there. And almost as soon as he sees them, Joseph begins testing his brothers, uncovering much about their character and maturity.

More importantly, this story gives Christians a means for better grasping the breadth of God's goodness, the depth of our sinfulness, and our need for reconciliation. It also spotlights one of the most important concepts in God's covenantal plans—redemption through substitution.

Joseph Meets His Brothers' Need

GENESIS 42

As the prophesied famine clamps down on Canaan too, Jacob learns of the grain in Egypt and sends sons to buy some. Upon setting out, the brothers have no idea they will soon find themselves face-to-face with Joseph, who will test them to learn if they have changed since they were last together.

Joseph's Brothers and Jacob's Plan (42:1-4)

As this chapter opens, Jacob and his sons have most likely been trying to find sources of food for some time. Upon hearing rumors that Egypt has grain, Jacob looks at his adult sons and asks why they "keep looking at each other" instead of acting on the news (v. 1). Jacob, after all, realizes how desperate the situation is getting even if his sons do not. That's why he says, "Go down there and buy some for us so that we will live and not die" (v. 2). Moses includes this particular insight to underscore for the reader that the promised family is facing a life-or-death situation. Later, the martyr Stephen will refer to this story by saying how Jacob sent his sons to Egypt because "there was grain" (Acts 7:12). In the ancient world, grain meant hope and life.

However, Jacob does not send all the brothers. His youngest, Benjamin, stays with Jacob because he fears "[s]omething might happen" to "Joseph's brother" (Gen 42:4). This suggests Jacob is still scarred from Joseph's seeming demise all those years before. He was willing to risk the safety of the other brothers, but he wanted to keep Benjamin safe.

Joseph's Brothers and Joseph's Accusation (42:5-26)

As the brothers arrive in Egypt, they are among countless people streaming into the country seeking relief. Little do they know Joseph is the man in charge of overseeing the distribution of aid (vv. 5-6). All around them is evidence that the promises of Pharaoh regarding Joseph's leadership have become reality (41:40).

Despite the crowd, the sons of Jacob do not go unnoticed. A sense of anticipation builds within the narrative when mention is made of the brothers bowing down "before [Joseph] with their faces to the ground"

(42:6). This is a fulfillment of his early dream involving the bowing sheaves of wheat.

This idea of the oppressors of God's faith-filled people bowing before those chosen by God does not end with the Joseph narrative. The prophet Isaiah highlights this pattern as well. He writes,

> *The sons of your oppressors will come and bow down to you; all who reviled you will fall facedown at your feet. They will call you the City of the LORD, Zion of the Holy One of Israel.* (Isa 60:14)

Indeed, just as Joseph's brothers bow before him in the current Genesis scene, those that afflicted Israel throughout her history will one day bow down to God's chosen people. These indicators in the Old Testament foreshadow the reality that would come with the Messiah. Those who oppressed, reviled, and rejected him will one day bow down at his feet, as Paul highlights in Philippians 2:9-11. Joseph recognizes his siblings but treats them as strangers. This is the first time he has seen them in almost twenty years. From our carnal perspective, it is completely understandable that he speaks "harshly to them" in this encounter (Gen 42:7). However, it is possible that in spite of his tone, Joseph immediately begins to realize that one reason God has brought him to the position he now holds is for them.

It is unclear why the brothers do not recognize Joseph. Many years have passed, and he undoubtedly looks different. He was probably groomed and clothed like an Egyptian. Also, this is not a context in which they would have anticipated to see their brother. They would never expect the ruler of this country to have any connection to the young brother whom they sold into slavery years before. However, Joseph recognizes them and remembers the dream he had when he was just a boy (v. 9). Joseph's brothers bowed down before him (v. 6). This is the first of several instances in this section of the Joseph narrative where we see the literal fulfillment of the dream Joseph had all those years ago of his brothers bowing down before him (37:7-10). Just as the Egyptians bow before Joseph (41:43), now his brothers do the same.

Joseph accuses the visitors before him of being "spies." These words no doubt cause the brothers to fear that rather than dying of starvation in Canaan they will instead face execution in Egypt. Joseph, however, knows his accusation is untrue and is not interested in killing them. What he wants is to set the stage for what happens in chapters 43–45.

The terrified brothers hurriedly assert their innocence. Ironically, they appeal to their honesty (42:11). The last time they interacted with Joseph, they were selling him into slavery behind their father's back and would have had to lie about it to get away with it (37:12-36).

In attempting to acquit themselves, the brothers reveal to Joseph that Benjamin is with their father Jacob, who is still living in Canaan (42:13). These insights likely brought relief to Joseph, as he may have feared that the brothers had disposed of Benjamin just as they had disposed of him.

Nevertheless, to discern whether they are telling the truth, Joseph proposes a test. He announces that all the brothers before him will remain in Egypt except for one who is to go and bring Benjamin to Joseph. The one sent for Benjamin will not be allowed to return without him (vv. 14-16). As if to show the power he holds over them while also giving them a taste of what they subjected him to, Joseph allows the group to sit in prison "for three days" (v. 17).

The brothers know that accomplishing what the hostile Egyptian ruler demands will prove almost impossible. Benjamin, after all, hadn't been allowed to come to Egypt the first time in spite of the fact that there was no real danger in doing so. But now the young man must not only travel to Egypt but face the angry foreign ruler. Jacob, they realize, will assuredly reject this proposal.

The time comes when they again must stand before Joseph-in-disguise. Here there is a parallel with the situation of the cupbearer, who was released from prison after three days. The brothers' first surprise comes when Joseph declares to them, "I fear God" (v. 18). What was implicit in Genesis 39:9, then, is now made explicit: the fear of the Lord is indeed a guiding principle in Joseph's life.

This concept does not just end with Joseph. Throughout the Old Testament this theme of fearing God and acting on that continues. Israel, for example, is instructed to allow "fear" of God to impact the way they "rule" (Lev 25:43). Nehemiah is commended for his fear of God, which shapes everything he does in the book that bears his name (Neh 5:15). The writer of Proverbs states, "The fear of the LORD is the beginning of wisdom, and the knowledge of the Holy One is understanding" (Prov 9:10). The theme culminates in the life, death, and resurrection of Jesus. Rather than fearing man or even fearing the schemes of Satan, Jesus resists the temptation to fear those around him. Instead, he set his face like flint toward the cross (cf. Isa 50:7; Luke 9:51). He knows that honoring God is the only path to righteousness set before him.

The second surprise Joseph gives his brothers is the assurance that none of them need to feel doomed. In fact, he puts an easier path to success with him in front of his brothers. He tells them, "Do this and you will live" (Gen 42:18). He presents them with an alternative solution for their desperate situation. Rather than making almost all of them stay behind for the mission to present Benjamin, he says he will send all of them home, except one. The brothers recognize that they have little choice and consent to this plan (v. 20).

This is not the last time the people of Israel are confronted with a command like, "Do this and you will live" (cf. Lev 18:5; Deut 4:1; Ezek 20:13,21). When an expert in the law asks Jesus how to have eternal life, in fact, Jesus affirms the greatest commandment and tells him, "Do this and you will live" (Luke 10:25-28). The problem all of Israel faces throughout the Old Testament, however, is that they can never fulfill the requirements necessary to find life. Thus, as Paul later declares, "The commandment that was meant for life resulted in death for me" (Rom 7:10). Only One successfully rescues his brothers and brings them back from a far country. Only One keeps the law perfectly. Jesus comes as the new and greater Joseph who finally fulfills the command to "do this and you will live."

In verse 20, the distraught brothers turn toward one another and start voicing their certainty that they "are being punished" for their actions toward Joseph so many years before (v. 21). They see their current situation through the lens of judgment for past disobedience. They have lingering guilt and shame after all these years. Even so, their personal suffering in this moment causes them to think a little differently about how they disregarded the "deep distress" of Joseph "when he pleaded with" them (v. 21). They were like the priest and the Levite in the parable of the good Samaritan, as they passed by on the other side, refusing to help their brother (Luke 10:30-37). Perhaps Jesus has a moment like this in mind in Luke 10 when he tells the expert in the law, "Do this and you will live," immediately before telling the story of the good Samaritan (Luke 10:28). Joseph's brothers see their current situation through the lens of judgment for past disobedience. At the same time, they are still pointing fingers and shifting blame.

At this point in the story, Reuben brings up the fact he told the group "not to harm" Joseph. Then he adds, "Now we must account for his blood!" (v. 22). Which suggests he suspects Joseph died long ago thanks to what was done to him. It is possible Reuben's stated conclusion has something to do with either God's words to Cain following Abel's murder or God's promise to Noah, recorded in Genesis 9:5-6. There the Lord says,

> I will require a penalty for your lifeblood; I will require it from any animal and from any human; if someone murders a fellow human, I will require that person's life. Whoever sheds human blood, by humans his blood will be shed, for God made humans in his image.

Reuben recognizes this reality. Joseph, presented as a prophet in Genesis, will be avenged by God (Luke 11:49-51).

The brothers' first trip to Egypt ends with Simeon being bound and jailed while the others are sent away. The last time a brother was bound, it was Joseph.

Before the men depart, Joseph has them loaded with grain and provisions and their money returned to their sacks (42:25). So despite all his obvious displays of hostility toward them, he begins their journey with a blessing.

Joseph's Brothers and Jacob's Despair (42:27-38)

When the brothers stop for the night, one of them discovers the silver in his sack. Almost immediately the brothers' confusion gives way to concern: "Their hearts [sink]" and they are "trembling" (v. 28). Though they may silently wonder, *Should we go back, or should we go home and get Benjamin before returning?*, only one question is given voice in the text: "What has God done to us?" (v. 28). This is the first time they have acknowledged him with regard to their situation. Until this moment, they have looked at their challenges from a human perspective. But now they consider this one from God's perspective. They consider whether his hand, his providence, might be at work behind things. This is a critical step for God's people when they face adversity. Indeed, when presented with difficulty or hardship, we should consider whether God might be at work behind the situations we encounter (Rom 5:2-5). The brothers attempt to do this now.

The brothers decide to return home to Jacob. They are probably greeted with joy, until he notices that Simeon is absent. Regardless, the brothers tell their father of all that happened in Egypt, saving their troubling request for the final moment of their tale. They want to impress on Jacob how desperate the situation they all face is before asking for permission to take Benjamin to Egypt. But no sooner has mention of his name been made than the brothers discover that each of them has been implicated in the theft of the silver because all their "silver," intended to pay for the grain, has been returned. Previously, they had sought God's perspective when they first discovered the silver in one of their sacks. However, "they were afraid" once they discovered the silver in all of their sacks because they had lost sight of God's providence (Gen 42:35).

How does Jacob respond to this troubling discovery? With raw emotion: "It's me that you make childless" (v. 36). Few things can cause despair like losing a son. Jacob lost Joseph years before. By this point, he knows Simeon is imprisoned. Now, facing the possible loss of Benjamin, Jacob is distraught. His anguish is evident when he cries, "Everything happens to me!" (v. 36).

Reuben, the eldest, attempts to confront and comfort his father. He promises that he will protect Benjamin and return him to Jacob, but Jacob will not be persuaded. Worse, mirroring his response to the loss of Joseph (37:35), Jacob insists that losing Benjamin will cause him to be brought "down to Sheol in sorrow" (42:38).

The chapter ends with the family at an impasse. Joseph is in Egypt, refusing to allow Simeon to go to Canaan, while Jacob is in Canaan refusing to allow Benjamin to go to Egypt. But unless Benjamin is sent, Simeon will remain captive, and the family will run out of food.

Joseph Shows His Brothers Kindness
GENESIS 43

Ultimately, Jacob decides his sons must return to Egypt to buy grain. But on their return there, the brothers are not met by the hostile ruler they expect. Instead, they are reunited with Simeon and treated to all the favor and extravagance Joseph can extend.

The Brothers Return to Egypt (43:1-15)

After the grain brought back from the first trip runs out, Jacob decides his sons must return to Egypt for more. But as Judah reminds his father, they cannot return without Benjamin. He is necessary both for receiving more grain and getting Simeon out of prison (vv. 1-5). Jacob, feeling himself in an impossible situation—he must choose his son or his family—lashes out (v. 6). But Judah persists, turning his father's own words on him. The brothers must take Benjamin so that the family of Abraham, Isaac, and Jacob "may live and not die" (v. 8; cf. 42:2). Indeed, Judah's insistence in this matter is important because he is essentially pleading with his father to empower him to rescue their family from death by starvation. This foreshadows what Judah's ultimate offspring, Jesus Christ, the bread of life, does for all those found in him (John 6:35; Heb 2:14-15).

Judah strengthens his case by taking responsibility for protecting Benjamin as well as the rest of the family. Judah tells Jacob to hold him "personally accountable" for his safe return (Gen 43:9). The time for action and salvation is now (Gen 43:10). Jacob only has one way to save his family.

Jacob relents and admits that what Judah is insisting on is the only course of action. He encourages his remaining sons to take "the best" produce and gifts of Canaan to curry favor with the lord of Egypt. He also insists they take plenty of "silver" (vv. 11-12). Jacob expects the brothers will need to buy the ruling Egyptian's favor. Nevertheless, he expresses some optimism that the silver left in their bags "was a mistake" (v. 12). And he not only allows them to "take" Benjamin but offers a blessing over their trip: "May God Almighty cause the man to be merciful to you" (v. 14). Thus, Jacob recognizes that the only hope the brothers have of receiving mercy is not the gifts he's sending but God's favor. With his final words, Jacob acknowledges that he may lose more sons, but he has no choice (v. 14).

The Brothers Enjoy Joseph's Favor (43:16-34)

When the brothers return to Egypt, they find themselves before Joseph. Every one of the brothers is likely wondering what is going to happen in this moment. However, though they fear a confrontation, no sooner does Joseph see Benjamin than he calls for a celebration. Though the brothers cannot understand what he says, he tells "his steward" to prepare food for them because the men will join him for his noonday meal (v. 16). Then they are ushered toward his home.

At play in this moment are parallels with the parable Jesus would tell about the prodigal son (Luke 15). But rather than the runaway son

knowingly coming home from a far country to his father to pursue reconciliation, here the wayward brothers leave their home unknowingly to
enter a far-off country to reconcile with the son who was lost. Fittingly,
it is Joseph—the one who was mistreated and suffered harm—who initiates reconciliation.

The brothers are unaware of the preparations made by the steward
and enter the ruler's residence with trepidation. Yet again, they respond
to the providence of God not with faith but fear, saying among themselves, "They intend to overpower us, seize us, make us slaves, and take
our donkeys" (v. 18; cf. 42:35). Eager to avoid such a fate, the brothers immediately confess to their apparent wrongdoing with the silver
before they can be confronted. They stretch the truth, however, by saying they all found the silver the night they left (43:21), when in reality
only one did (42:27). As they try to avoid punishment, they declare their
righteous intentions and point out that they have brought the money
back. This is a drastically different approach to money than the group
evidenced in Genesis 37:28 when they sold Joseph for twenty pieces of
silver. Before, they were eager to profit by thrusting Joseph into slavery.
Here, they are eager to give money to Joseph in hopes of keeping themselves out of slavery.

The steward brings comfort to the brothers when he tells them,
"Don't be afraid" (43:23). Rather than pressing them on the details of
their confession, he reassures them and gives credit to their God for this
turn of events: "Your God and the God of your father must have put treasure in your bags. I received your silver" (v. 23). This Egyptian servant
thus shows more faith in the providence of God than these sons of Israel.

At this point, Simeon is brought out to them, and they are ushered
into the reception area of their brother-in-disguise, where the steward
provides water to wash their feet. As seen previously in Genesis (18:4;
19:2; 24:32), visitors receiving an invitation to wash their feet signals they
are welcome and indicates warmth from the one receiving the guests.

When Joseph arrives, the brothers present their gifts and bow down
(43:26). This is another example of the fulfillment of Joseph's dreams
that his brothers would bow down to him (37:5-11). The kind words of
the steward may have eased their concerns a bit, but the brothers know
their fate is in the hands of this man.

Genesis 43:27 says that Joseph responds to the bowing by asking
them if they are "well." In the original language in which this text was
penned, the term used here is *shalom*. In fact, it's used three times in this

passage (vv. 23,27,28). The use of this term means Joseph wants to know whether their family is experiencing peace. This is a valid concern in light of not just the events that brought them to Egypt but also because of Genesis 37:4: "When [Joseph's] brothers saw that their father loved him more than [they], they hated him and could not bring themselves to speak peaceably to him." Just as the sin of Adam and Eve shattered *shalom* in Eden, the sin of Joseph's brothers shattered *shalom* in their family. If the brothers were honest, they would have admitted that they had perhaps never felt less peace than they do at this moment. How the brothers respond to this question is not shared. But they do assure him Jacob is "well" (43:28). At least he will be if their audience with this ruler goes smoothly.

Joseph shows concern for his brothers even when they have only been concerned about themselves. When Joseph sees that Benjamin is with them, he is "overcome with emotion" (vv. 29-30). Or more literally, "his compassion [grows] warm." Benjamin is Joseph's only younger brother and the only other son of their mother Rachel (35:24). Joseph is so relieved to see that the half brothers have not treated him as badly as they treated him that he declares, "May God be gracious to you, my son." He is so touched that he must leave the room to collect himself (vv. 30-31).

Imagine the brothers' surprise when the man they have long feared re-encountering returns from his abrupt leave and invites them to a meal there in his home. Though they expected punishment and condemnation, they receive provision and celebration.

There are five things to note about this meal. First, the Egyptians and Hebrews eat separately. Why? The Egyptians find eating with Hebrews "detestable" (v. 32). This hints at the tension that exists between the Egyptians and the surrounding nations, especially the Hebrews, at even this early point in history (cf. 46:34; Exod 8:26).

Second, the seating chart of the dinner is important. The brothers are arranged according to their birth order. The brothers look "at each other in astonishment" over this because they can't imagine how their host knows their ages (v. 33).

Third, the portions of the dinner are extravagant. For people who were overcome by famine, they were likely grateful for any food they received. A feast would have seemed an incredible treat. Even so, the guests could not help but notice and wonder why Benjamin's portion was "five times larger" than everyone else's (v. 34).

Fourth, the dinner includes free-flowing wine. Its presence eases the brothers' tension to the point that they become intoxicated and enjoy themselves (v. 34). All of their worry has turned to joy. Here too is a parallel with the parable of the prodigal son. He leaves to visit his father, expecting punishment. Yet when the father sees him, he is received instead with restoration and celebration (Luke 15:22-24).

Finally, the dinner is a glimpse of the gospel. Think about what happens in this moment: a favored son who endured hardship as a righteous sufferer prepares a table before him in the presence of his enemies (cf. Ps 23:5). The brothers, of course, do not deserve to be at a feast because they are enemies of this royal figure at whose table they sit. Nevertheless, in his grace and kindness, Joseph welcomes undeserving sinners to dine alongside him and gives them a generous portion as an act of reconciliation and restoration. Isn't that what God does for us in Christ? In Jesus, because of his grace, we underserving sinners are given a generous portion of his Spirit as an act of reconciliation and restoration. And Jesus compares what is ahead for his followers to attending a "wedding banquet" (Matt 22:1-14). The book of Revelation, too, anticipates this final victory feast as "the marriage feast of the Lamb" (Rev 19:6-9). In the gospel Jesus mirrors the grace of Joseph by welcoming undeserving sinners to the table to receive a generous portion of his Spirit as an act of reconciliation and restoration. In Christ we are invited to his table so that we might taste and see that the Lord is good (Ps 34:8; 1 Pet 2:3).

Joseph Tests His Brothers' Love

GENESIS 44

Joseph has one final test for the brothers. It will reveal whether they have changed in the intervening years since mistreating him. It will also help introduce the idea of a substitute coming from the line of Judah to atone for the sins of another (cf. 42:37). This pattern will culminate in Judah's descendant, Jesus, becoming the ultimate substitutional sacrifice atoning for the sins of the world.

Joseph Tests His Brothers (44:1-13)

As the brothers prepare to depart, Joseph gives his steward instructions that will test the brothers again (cf. 42:15). Just as before, the steward places their money in their bags. But this time, he also puts Joseph's silver cup in "the youngest one's bag" (v. 2). Why the brothers do not check their bags before setting out, particularly considering what happened when they left Egypt previously, is unclear. Perhaps the lingering effects of their drinking have something to do with it. Regardless, they make haste to return home from their successful journey on the day after the feast, having not only secured additional grain but also Simeon's liberation and Benjamin's safe return.

Only a short while after their departure, they are halted by Joseph's steward. As instructed, he says, "Why have you repaid evil for good? Isn't this the cup that my master drinks from and uses for divination? What you have done is wrong!" (vv. 4-5). This encounter surely provokes great fear among the brothers. In an instant, their freedom and good fortune are in jeopardy again. The steward's description of the cup is of interest because later God will forbid divination among his people (Lev 19:26; Deut 18:10). It is possible that Joseph was given the position of "diviner" in Pharaoh's court because of his ability to interpret dreams.

In response to the steward's accusations, the brothers protest their innocence. They are so certain they are not at fault that they propose a severe punishment if any of them is found guilty: If the cup "is found with one of us, . . . he must die, and the rest of us will become my lord's slaves" (v. 9). The steward consents to their offer but limits the potential punishment to the guilty party rather than the whole group. Interestingly, the brothers sound much like their father Jacob, who once declared his innocence to Laban when accused of stealing the household "gods" (31:32). But while Laban did not discover that Rachel had the idols, the steward does discover the cup he'd placed in Benjamin's bag.

Proceeding from oldest to youngest, the steward searches the bags. As each bag is opened, the brothers are probably relieved, and their confidence increases. But when the cup is found in Benjamin's bag, the last to be searched, the brothers are so distraught that they rip their clothing in grief (v. 13).

Judah Pleads for His Brother (44:14-34)

When the brothers once again find themselves before Egypt's second-in-command, they fall down before him in yet another fulfillment of his dream (37:5-11). After only a question or two from him, they collectively declare their guilt. Thus, they do not accept the steward's decision to punish only Benjamin. Rather, together they declare themselves to be Joseph's "slaves" (44:16). Joseph, however, insists he will only punish the supposedly guilty party, Rachel's only remaining son, and send the rest of them back to their "father" (v. 17). Before, Joseph was thrust into slavery because of the actions of these brothers; now, Benjamin will become a slave if the brothers choose to abandon him. Joseph's telling the brothers that they can go in "peace" (*shalom*) is ironic in that there will be no peace in the tents of Jacob's family if Benjamin is left behind (v. 17). In Matthew 4 Jesus goes into the wilderness after his baptism and is tempted by Satan three times. The third temptation has the same offer as that made to Joseph's brothers (Matt 4:8): Jesus could have peace (all the kingdoms of the world) through slavery (bowing down to worship Satan). However, both Judah and Jesus reject the offer.

To his credit, Judah speaks up on behalf of his family throughout this scene. Woven into his response are threads of a pattern of confession and repentance consistent with what God calls Christians to do when we are wrestling with sin in our lives. First, Judah owns their most glaring sin by saying that Benjamin's only full-blooded brother "is dead" (v. 20). Though he doesn't elaborate on this, he acknowledges the one he has sinned against, having no idea that he is speaking to that very person. Moreover, his words in verse 16 admit they have no justification for their sin: "What can we say to my lord? . . . How can we justify ourselves?" (v. 16). Though innocent in the matter of the cup, they are guilty of other crimes and have no credible defense before Joseph. Owning our sin is the first step in repentance. "How can we justify ourselves?" is a question every sinner must confront in his or her own heart. Repentant Christians recognize that there is no place for defending or justifying themselves amid sin.

Second, Judah acknowledges God's role in revealing secret sin. He says, "God has exposed your servants' iniquity" (v. 16; cf. Num 32:23). Similarly, Christians must recognize the Holy Spirit's role in exposing and convicting us of sin as we seek forgiveness (John 16:8). The kindness of the Lord brings us to repentance by exposing our iniquity (Rom 2:4).

Third, Judah surrenders to the authority of the master when he declares he and his brothers are now Joseph's "slaves" (Gen 44:16).

Christians must recognize that everyone who seeks repentance must come to the same point of surrender. Though they have turned away from their heavenly Father by seeking the forbidden fruit of sin, their only hope of forgiveness is to surrender to his mercy. Just as Judah declares they are now slaves of Joseph, the believer must declare through action that he or she is no longer a slave of sin but a slave of righteousness (Rom 6:17-18).

Judah makes a final appeal, in what is one of the longest speeches in Genesis (vv. 18-34). After pleading with Joseph not to be angry (v. 18), Judah tells Joseph all that has transpired since they left Egypt the first time. Judah recounts that "the boy's brother is dead" to him, not realizing that Joseph is in fact alive and listening to him (v. 20). The story focuses on Jacob's reluctance to allow Benjamin to come and his eventual acquiescence to Judah's pleas. Judah knows that if he returns without Benjamin, Jacob will be devastated and will die because "his life is wrapped up with the boy's life" (v. 30).

After telling Joseph what Benjamin's enslavement will mean for Jacob, Judah attempts to personally take responsibility for Benjamin's apparent stealing of the cup. Judah states that he is "accountable to [his] father for the boy," which of course is true (cf. 43:9). He also humbly acknowledges the shame that his sin will carry if he returns without Benjamin: "I will always bear the guilt for sinning against [Jacob]" (44:32). Judah sees his personal responsibility for sin in the same way we all should. Each of us bears the guilt for our sin. Our sin is not an abstract issue but a personal affront to our heavenly Father. Judah's solution to the mess is to ask Joseph if he can take Benjamin's place (v. 33). He offers himself as a substitute to suffer for Benjamin's sin. Joseph responds to Judah's pleading with the determination to punish only the guilty rather than the entire group.

This is the first instance in the Bible of a human serving as a substitute. Readers must not miss the typological significance of this event. Judah offering himself as a substitute for Benjamin points ahead to the coming Messiah from the line of Judah. Only Jesus doesn't just offer up his freedom but actually offers his own life. Nevertheless, both men trade freedom for the sake of restoring brothers for the sake of pleasing a father. Jesus becomes our substitute both to set us free from slavery to sin and to reconcile us to our heavenly Father (cf. John 15:13; 2 Cor 5:21).

Reflect and Discuss

1. What do you think Joseph first felt when seeing his brothers after so many years and trials? How would you react if you were in his sandals?

2. The fear of God is a guiding principle in Joseph's life. That general theme continues throughout the Scriptures. What does it mean to be guided by the fear of the Lord?

3. Early in the story, the brothers conclude that they are being punished for their previous actions toward Joseph. Initially, they are not fully repentant; they continue to shift the blame. Why is acknowledging guilt a necessary step toward true repentance? How does that set the stage for the future reconciliation in the family?

4. Initially, the brothers respond to the silver's surprising presence in one of their sacks by considering what God might have to do with it. How often do you consider whether God might be moving and acting behind the scenes in your life?

5. Judah is shown to be preeminent in the family when he asks to be held accountable for the actions of Benjamin. How does this foreshadow the coming one who will be exalted because of his obedience to the will of the Father?

6. Jacob recognizes that the only hope his sons have of returning with Benjamin in tow is if God grants them favor with the demanding ruler in Egypt. Yet he also attempts to give the best impression possible by sending the man gifts and luxuries from the land of Canaan. What is the relationship between the favor of God and the actions of people?

7. The brothers are told repeatedly not to be afraid. Why would holding on to the promises of God toward their family give them assurance of protection? What promises does God make to believers that can help us fight fear?

8. Judah does not try to justify himself or his brothers before Joseph. He has finally acknowledged the severity of their sin. Why do you think he does so at this point in the narrative but not before?

9. Does Judah understand his sin as a real or an abstract thing? How does that inform the way he seeks forgiveness?

10. Judah offers himself as a substitute for Benjamin. What parallels do you see between what he does here and what Jesus does for us?

A Pilgrim's Promise

GENESIS 45–47

Main Idea: As the Joseph narrative nears its conclusion, Joseph is reunited with his brothers and father. Joseph provides for his family and fulfills God's plan to preserve for himself a remnant. In this way, Joseph anticipates the coming Messiah, who would go before his people to provide them a way of salvation in the midst of spiritual famine.

I. **Joseph Revealed to His Brothers (45)**
   A. Joseph's response to his brothers (45:1-8)
   B. Joseph's instructions for his brothers (45:9-15)
   C. Joseph's summons for his father (45:16-24)
   D. Jacob's journey to his son (45:25-28)
II. **Jacob Reunited with His Son (46)**
   A. The departure of Jacob's family (46:1-7)
   B. The genealogy of Jacob's family (46:8-27)
   C. The arrival of Jacob's family (46:28-34)
III. **Israel Received by Pharaoh (47)**
   A. A gift of land (47:1-12)
   B. A payment of land (47:13-26)
   C. A promise of land (47:27-31)

Genesis 45 opens at a critical moment in the Joseph narrative. The brothers have returned to the presence of Egypt's ruler in fear, and Judah has made his case to him about serving as a substitute for the perceived sins of their brother, Benjamin. So, will Judah's offer be rejected or received? What we find in Genesis 45–47 is that Joseph's response provides a path to reconciliation and forgiveness and, ultimately, a future for Jacob's family. Through the mercy he extends, God is faithful to preserve a remnant to sustain his promises.

Joseph Revealed to His Brothers

GENESIS 45

At last, Joseph reveals himself to his brothers. And almost as soon as he does, he begins to explain his plans to provide for them. Ultimately, these plans will be the fulfillment of God's work to save Israel, his fledgling people, from starvation. Joseph shows his brothers that what they intended for evil was actually part of God's plan to fulfill his promises.

Joseph's Response to His Brothers (45:1-8)

Judah's plea to be a substitute for Benjamin overwhelms Joseph to the point of tears. Though he had previously left the room to regain his composure (43:30), he now sends his servants out and speaks to his brothers alone (45:1). When he declares to them, "I am Joseph!" and asks, "Is my father still living?" they are understandably stunned. In fact, they are "terrified in his presence" (v. 3). They do not know if this is good or bad news. The one they once cruelly sold as a slave is now ruler of the country and in control of their fate. Any uncertainty they have about his identity vanishes when they do not answer and Joseph becomes more specific: "I am Joseph, your brother, . . . the one you sold into Egypt" (v. 4; cf. 37:18-36).

Joseph's tearful response to this group that has wronged him so terribly reveals how God had reoriented his perspective on suffering in a way that is instructive to believers even today. First, *Joseph embraces the right heart.* If anyone in this situation has the right to be "angry," it is Joseph. Yet he not only chooses to let go of any anger he once carried but tells them not to be "angry with" themselves (v. 5). They have spent the last several years in fear of famine and starvation. But nothing could have fully prepared them for this moment. In drawing them near and reassuring them, Joseph models the right attitude to take in the midst of suffering.

Second, *Joseph recognizes the greater good that God is doing through his life's twists and turns.* Joseph explains to the brothers, "God sent me ahead of you to preserve life" (v. 5). So Joseph isn't fixated on himself in this scene. He isn't even focused on his family. Instead, he is consumed with knowledge of the broader way God has been at work in the midst of his suffering for the common good. God's role in Joseph's life to sustain him in suffering would help preserve the lives of countless others from many nations in the midst of the famine. He is certain that work will continue to bless his own family. Big-picture awareness, it seems, enables Joseph to endure hardship more faithfully. The same can help the modern sufferer.

Third, *Joseph also understands the challenges still ahead.* He informs his brothers that there are "five more years" of famine still to come (v. 6).

So, while Joseph recognizes that God has brought about this moment of reconciliation and peace with his family, he does not assume the external source of their suffering is also over. Nevertheless, perhaps this healing in their family will better equip them to continue to endure hardship until the land's productivity is restored. Knowing that hardships of some sort will remain a part of life until Jesus's return similarly helps us.

Fourth, *Joseph identifies God's redemptive purposes.* Joseph notes that he was sent before his brothers "to establish [them] as a remnant within the land and to keep [them] alive by a great deliverance" (v. 7; cf. Ps 105:15-17). This theme of a remnant delivered by God recurs throughout the Bible. Indeed, throughout the book of Genesis, God is refining a remnant for himself to and through whom the covenant promises come. This begins with Adam and Eve, is brought into focus with the family of Noah being protected in the ark, and eventually culminates in the person of Abraham and his descendants. All of this is groundwork for the arrival of the Messiah—God's ultimate chosen servant—who will fulfill the covenant promises to the people of God, purchased by his blood, in full. The New Testament presents the church as the remnant of God's faithful people who are delivered by God's saving grace (Rom 11:5).

Finally, *Joseph appreciates God's sovereign providence.* He remarks that God will keep them "alive by a great deliverance" (v. 7). This deliverance through the famine sets the stage for the central deliverance of the Old Testament, the exodus, in a way that anticipates the ultimate deliverance experienced in Christ. Joseph tells his brothers, "It was not you who sent me here, but God" (v. 8; cf. 50:20). Joseph realizes his earthly experiences are intimately connected with heavenly intentions. Even though the brothers meant to harm him, Joseph recognizes that God was working all things for good in spite of them (Rom 8:28-29).

God's sovereign hand at work in Joseph's life is unmistakable. When Christians today face trials of many kinds, they can endure them more faithfully if they embrace the patterns displayed by Joseph in his hardship.

Joseph's Instructions for His Brothers (45:9-15)

Even before the brothers respond to Joseph, he gives them instructions to bring their father to Egypt. Notice that nothing about what he says here is haphazard. Joseph has designed the situation involving the cup with a particular goal in mind.

Joseph knows that Jacob may feel reluctant to leave the land promised to Abraham and Isaac behind, so he offers several reasons to explain why Jacob should come to Egypt. The first is the power Joseph wields. He explains to his brothers that he is the "lord of all Egypt" (v. 9). Therefore, Jacob should come to Egypt as instructed with the knowledge that he has an advocate with authority there who can properly care for him. Second, Joseph describes the place where they will dwell. He will settle his extended family "in the land of Goshen" so that they are "near" to him (v. 10). Israel will thrive in this fertile section of the nation and will later find protection there from the devastating plagues God brings against Egypt (Exod 8:22). Third, Joseph gives a promise to his father, which includes insight into the longevity of the famine. At this point, there are still five years of famine remaining (v. 11). So, if Jacob intends to endure the situation in Canaan, Joseph is assuring him that things will get much worse. The family, however, will be sustained by settling in Egypt. For Jacob, who has worried about feeding his family for the past two years, this would come as a welcome relief. Finally, Joseph makes another attempt to get his brothers to respond to what he's saying. He says, "Look! Your eyes and the eyes of my brother Benjamin can see that I'm the one speaking to you" (v. 12). This is important because the eyewitness testimony of his brothers will serve as further evidence to convince Jacob to come to Egypt.

Although the brothers are still stunned, Joseph embraces them as a sign of forgiveness and reconciliation. Though Joseph's brothers had cast him out, he now embraces all of them, instead of only Benjamin, who was not involved in their scheming (v. 15). What a picture of grace, then, as the favored son shows undeserved favor to his wayward siblings!

Joseph is able to forgive because he has reoriented his perspective in light of God's purposes (v. 5). Understanding more about God's plans frees him to forgive those who have wronged him.

As this dramatic scene concludes, the brothers talk "with" Joseph (v. 15). Before, they were unable to speak because they were terrified (v. 3), but now they are able to converse openly together (v. 15). Joseph's forgiveness paves the way.

When reading this passage, it is tempting to see oneself as Joseph. But while we certainly should consider our need to forgive others, the more relevant comparison here is between us and Joseph's brothers.

Like them, we cannot avoid the reality of our sin and its consequences. Therefore, we must meditate on our need for forgiveness and reconciliation. Indeed we cannot escape the fact that we are sinners just as they were (Eph 2:1-3). And just as bitterness and jealousy provoked them to sell Joseph, we too are provoked by bitterness and jealousy to sin against our neighbors (Heb 12:15). The glory of the gospel is that Jesus comes as a new and better Joseph who forgives us for our sins, welcomes us, and offers us a future far brighter than any we deserve.

When confronted by the reality of our sin, we can easily react with fear. That, after all, is what happens with Joseph's brothers. But instead we must recognize our faults and seek forgiveness. Often, it takes as much humility to be forgiven by others as it does to forgive. Moreover, like Joseph, when we have been wronged, we must resist the urge to withhold forgiveness from others. We can do this because of Jesus, who not only freely forgives us of our sins but models for us the way we are to extend forgiveness and love (Luke 7:47; Col 3:13).

Joseph's Summons for His Father (45:16-24)

When Pharaoh and his servants hear the report about the arrival of Joseph's brothers, they are "pleased" (v. 16). Though Joseph had at one time been in Pharaoh's prison, and though his family worked as shepherds (a job detestable to Egyptians; 46:34), Pharaoh and the Egyptians are excited for Joseph about his family reconciliation. Pharaoh demonstrates his favor toward Joseph by offering "the best of the land of Egypt" to his family (v. 18; cf. Deut 32:9-14). Moreover, Pharaoh offers them possessions and encourages them not to worry about their "belongings" (Gen 45:20). Such generosity would have been shocking in the midst of the famine, but to Joseph's family it signals the prosperity that awaits them.

Previously, Joseph's brothers returned to Jacob with dread, but they now return with joy. The brothers follow the instructions of Joseph as they journey toward Canaan. This demonstrates that reconciliation includes submission. Joseph also provides gifts as a sign of his forgiveness: silver, clothes, donkeys, and provisions. These gifts serve as a tangible expression of the restoration that has occurred for this broken family (vv. 22-23).

Jacob's Journey to His Son (45:25-28)

When the brothers reach their father and tell him the news, Jacob is "stunned" (v. 26). More literally, the original phrase used means "his heart [is] numb." After worrying the entire time his sons were away, Jacob receives news he never expected: "Joseph is alive, and he is ruler over all of Egypt!" (v. 26), and his initial reaction is disbelief. Nevertheless, as his sons tell him all that has happened and show him the gifts, Jacob realizes that they are telling the truth. He rejoices that "Joseph is still alive" (v. 28). Until now, Jacob had likely thought only of Simeon's slavery and Benjamin's departure. But at this point, his focus shifts to the first son he thought he had lost. This reaction is quite the contrast with the sadness Jacob experienced at Joseph's "death" in 37:35, for he is so excited that his spirit revives and he announces that he will make the long journey to him before he dies (45:27-28). Here Jacob is receiving a foretaste of what Jesus promises in the Beatitudes in Luke 6:20-21. There he says,

> *Blessed are you who are poor,*
> *because the kingdom of God is yours.*
> *Blessed are you who are now hungry,*
> *because you will be filled.*
> *Blessed are you who weep now,*
> *because you will laugh.*

Jacob and his family had been on the path to ruin for many months. Sorrow and weeping have filled his days. But in this moment God shows unmistakable favor and kindness to the house of Jacob. For Jacob, in fact, it is as if Joseph has experienced a resurrection.

This resurrection turns his despair into delight. How much more so should this be true for those of us who have come to know not just the apparent resurrection of Joseph but the actual resurrection of Jesus? His resurrection reshapes our hearts with rejoicing.

Jacob Reunited with His Son
GENESIS 46

Jacob sets out for Egypt, joyful that Joseph is alive. On the journey, God promises Jacob that, although his family is going "down . . . to Egypt," God will eventually bring them "back" to Canaan (v. 4). God is going with them to preserve them and bless them even as they live away from the land of promise. Soon Jacob will see the face of Joseph again.

The Departure of Jacob's Family (46:1-7)

Jacob sets out for Egypt "with all that he [has]." Though Pharaoh has promised them belongings, Jacob is not taking any chances.

When he arrives in Beer-sheba, he offers "sacrifices to" God in the same place as "his father Isaac" (v. 1; 26:23). In this moment we see how awareness of the provision of God leads Jacob to worship God. And after he celebrates God's goodness, he receives a "vision" (v. 2; cf. 28:13). Just as God had earlier done with Abraham, he now appears to his grandson Jacob and transforms his perspective.

Several things stand out in God's address to Jacob. First, God displays his special relationship to Jacob by calling him by name (v. 2). This indicates that the God of the universe knows him intimately. Moreover, it is a reminder to Moses's earliest readers that Israel is not a forgotten group but God's chosen people to fulfill his covenant promises. Second, God establishes an identity for Jacob. The Lord highlights the continuity between Jacob and Isaac, which is a reference to God's promises of blessing for this family (v. 3). Jacob is therefore urged to view himself as God sees him. Third, God offers direction to Jacob. God tells him not to fear as he relocates to Egypt (v. 3). This command is no doubt comforting to the patriarch, especially in light of the fact that each family member who has gone to Egypt has faced difficulty. Joseph was a slave and imprisoned there, and the brothers were accused as spies and imprisoned, too. Nevertheless, God instructs Jacob to walk in faith and not fear. Jacob can move forward confidently, assured by God's promise that Joseph will be with him at the time of his death (v. 4; cf. 50:1). For an ailing father who has experienced severe trauma, this would have been significant encouragement. Fourth, God provides Jacob with a purpose. He promises to make Jacob "into a great nation" (v. 3). In this statement God is revealing how he will advance his covenant promises even in Egypt, through the multiplication of Jacob's line (cf. 12:2; 15:13-14). This promise is realized in the exodus account (Exod 1:7; Deut 26:5). It is the fulfillment of what God told Abraham in Genesis 15:13-14. Israel's time in Egypt was not God's plan B, as if God were making the most of an unexpected famine, then. The famine was part of God's plan to place Israel in Egypt, fulfilling the prophecy in Genesis 15. Finally, God promises to "go . . . with" Jacob. He promises to be with Jacob in Egypt and to have a hand in bringing him back to Canaan (v. 4; cf. 28:15; Exod 3:8).

The promise of the presence of God is a recurring theme in Joseph's narrative (48:21; 50:24)—one that continues to show up throughout the Old Testament (Exod 3:12; Deut 31:6; Josh 1:15; Isa 43:2). In fact, one of the most significant prophecies regarding the coming Messiah describes him as "Immanuel" or "God is with us" (Isa 7:14; cf. Matt 1:23). When Jesus the Messiah gives the Great Commission right before his return to the Father, however, he promises his presence with the apostles and disciples will not depart with his body (Matt 28:20).

So, how does this presence manifest itself in Christians today? God's presence with his people in the new covenant era is experienced through the indwelling of the Holy Spirit (Ezek 36:26-27; Joel 2:28; Eph 1:13-14). This indwelling points toward the conclusion of God's redemptive story when his people will be present with him for all eternity: "Look, God's dwelling is with humanity, and he will live with them" (Rev 21:3). God's presence with Jacob as he journeys to Egypt is the same presence we experience through the Spirit. In both cases, the idea of God's presence being with his people anticipates eternity.

The Genealogy of Jacob's Family (46:8-27)

In this section Moses lists those who arrive in Egypt alongside Jacob, as per Joseph's invitation (Acts 7:14). Throughout Genesis, genealogies and lists often function as hinges connecting one generation to another or marking an important moment in the life of God's covenant community. In Christ this is our family tree. As the list begins, the text states, "These are the names of the sons of Israel who came to Egypt—Jacob and his sons" (v. 8; cf. Josh 24:4; Ps 105:23). The martyr Stephen will describe this as Joseph's invitation to Jacob to come to Egypt (Acts 7:14). These names will be repeated near the beginning of the book of Exodus, which demonstrates continuity between the first two books of Moses (Exod 1:1-5). This genealogy is one of two markers that bookend collective Israel's time in Egypt, those years when "Jacob lived as an alien in the land of Ham" (Ps 105:23). It occurs here as the family of Jacob journeys down to Egypt, and it is repeated when the descendants of Jacob are about to be delivered from the place. The genealogy brackets their time in Egypt and points to the promise that Israel will return to the land of Canaan (Gen 46:4).

The genealogy is also important in that it highlights some initial fulfillment of the promise made to Abraham that his descendants would be as "numerous" as the "stars" of the sky (Gen 15:4-5). What was once a single child given to a couple in their old age has now become a group of "seventy persons" (46:27). The number seventy represents completeness and parallels the Genesis 10 genealogy documenting the seventy who make up the Table of Nations. This particular group of seventy, Moses's earliest readers would know, will become a great multitude by the time of the exodus. In fact, Moses later says to them, "Your ancestors went down to Egypt, seventy people in all, and now the LORD your God has made you numerous, like the stars of the sky" (Deut 10:22). On the edge of the family's return to the promised land, Moses reminds the Israelites of one way God has proven faithful to keep his promises.

Just like the other genealogies of Genesis, this one is not packed with the names of faithful, morally perfect people. Jacob's family faltered, doubted, strayed, and disobeyed. But in spite of all that, God remains faithful to his promise.

This lineage really began with Adam and then Seth. Then it went through Noah and his son Shem. Then things got really exciting with the call and resulting obedience of Abraham. But as we've seen, the Bible will continue to report on this line until its greatest descendant, the Messiah, comes. Jesus Christ is the promised seed. He is the ultimate son of Abraham. He is the greater Isaac and the True Israel. And as sure as his forefathers journeyed to Egypt to escape the famine of Joseph's day, this Messiah would also journey to Egypt to escape a murderous king (cf. Matt 2:13-15). One day he will lead his people, both believing biological and figurative children of Abraham, in a second and greater exodus to bring about the new creation kingdom of the new covenant (Matt 2:13-15).

The Arrival of Jacob's Family (46:28-34)

Judah is "sent . . . ahead" of the family to meet with Joseph prior to their arrival (v. 28). This is yet another confirmation of the primacy of Judah among Israel's offspring. In this scene, Judah acts as a forerunner for the people of Israel; he goes ahead in order to prepare a home for them. This role foreshadows the role of the Messiah, the promised seed from the line of Judah, who goes before his people to "prepare a place for" them in a land of promise (John 14:1-3).

That Joseph, second in command over Egypt, personally hitches "the horses to his chariot and [goes] up to Goshen to meet his father

Israel" adds to the sense of intense happiness and joy accompanying their reunion (Gen 46:28). Neither man ever expected to see the other alive. After a lot of hugging and happy weeping, Jacob declares to his long-lost son, "I'm ready to die now because I have seen your face and you are still alive!" (v. 30). These words foreshadow Simeon's declaration in the temple when he holds the infant Jesus, the greater Joseph: "Now, Master, you can dismiss your servant in peace, as you promised. For my eyes have seen your salvation" (Luke 2:29-30). For both men, at last the promise and hope have come, and they are ready to die because they have seen the fulfillment of the promise of God.

Joseph tells his family that he will go before them to Pharaoh. To prepare them for their audience with the ruler of Egypt, Joseph gives them strict instructions about what to say. Because Jacob's sons work as shepherds, after all, the Egyptians would ordinarily view them with contempt (cf. 43:32; Exod 8:26). However, God has given Joseph such favor with Pharaoh that the king responds in a gracious way toward Joseph's extended family. This audience with Pharaoh results in the family's settling in "the land of Goshen" (Gen 46:34).

Israel Received by Pharaoh
GENESIS 47

In this section, after a lifetime of pilgrimage, Jacob finds rest in Egypt even as he trusts in God's promise to return him and his family to Canaan. This sets the stage for the final chapters of Genesis and the future story of the exodus.

A Gift of Land (47:1-12)

Genesis 47 begins with a major moment in the life of national Israel. Jacob presents "five of his brothers" before Pharaoh, to whom they explain the severity of the famine back in Canaan (vv. 2-4). Easily missed is that this is the beginning of the fulfillment of Genesis 15:13, where God said to their great-grandfather Abraham, "Your offspring will be resident aliens for four hundred years in a land that does not belong to them."

That Pharaoh immediately grants the men's request to "settle" in the Nile Delta and then goes even further by allowing them to take charge of his "livestock" (47:4-6; cf. Prov 22:39) indicates that Joseph's favor with Pharaoh means favor for his family. What they are granted brings to mind the words of Psalm 16:6: "The boundary lines have fallen for me in pleasant places; indeed, I have a beautiful inheritance."

After meeting with Joseph's brothers, the king meets his father Jacob. In a shocking turn of events, Jacob blesses Pharaoh (Gen 47:7,10). This is an important detail because it was customary in that time period for the greater person to bless the lesser. Yet here a lowly Hebrew, who has labored hard as a despised shepherd, offers a blessing to the exalted Pharaoh in his royal garb. This scene is reminiscent of the moment when Melchizedek unexpectedly blesses Abraham (14:18-20). It suggests Jacob is the greater man in the eyes of God. Moreover, it is a reminder that even though Pharaoh is the king of Egypt, Israel is destined to be the father of *many* nations (35:11).

Pharaoh asks Jacob's age, and Jacob responds by describing his life as a "pilgrimage" having already lasted "130 years" (47:9). His answer includes an acknowledgment of the temporary and complex nature of his existence on the fallen earth. His statement encapsulates the pain he has experienced, from the "death" of Joseph, to the famine, to the imprisonment of Simeon, and to his fear of losing Benjamin. Jacob is not alone in thinking of life in this manner. The author of Hebrews applies the idea of a believer's life being a journey toward better things to figures throughout the Old Testament. He says,

> These all died in faith, although they had not received the things that were promised. But they saw them from a distance, greeted them, and confessed that they were foreigners and temporary residents on the earth. Now those who say such things make it clear that they are seeking a homeland. If they were thinking about where they came from, they would have had an opportunity to return. But they now desire a better place—a heavenly one. Therefore, God is not ashamed to be called their God, for he has prepared a city for them. (Heb 11:13-16)

The author of Hebrews thus captures the spirit of Jacob's answer. Jacob is living as a foreigner in the land, longing for a better home. Though he appreciates his temporary home in Goshen, Jacob yearns for the reward of a heavenly one.

Jacob speaks of his life as a pilgrimage. His years have been "few and hard" (v. 9; cf. Job 14:1). While Jacob's cynicism in this scene is understandable, it is important to notice the difference between his statement here and the blessings he gives to his children in Genesis 48–49. As he bestows them, Jacob appears to be fulfilled and satisfied with his life in spite of its hardships. The wearied tone of his statement here stands in stark contrast to Joseph's framing of those same years—the very ones God used for good (45:4-8).

In response to Jacob's answer Pharaoh again promises protection and the best of the land to Jacob's family. Even so, this choice land will eventually become the central location for the oppression of the Hebrews (Exod 1:11).

A Payment of Land (47:13-26)

As Genesis 47 nears conclusion, Moses tells the reader how the power of Pharaoh increased under Joseph's leadership. Over time, the land itself is "exhausted by the famine" (v. 13), and the people become desperate as they hunger. To sustain themselves, the people first give all of their "silver" to Joseph in order to keep purchasing grain from the government's stores (v. 14). The next year, having depleted their silver and valuables, the people trade their "livestock" and then their "land" for grain. Finally, they give themselves into slavery, viewing it as the only way to survive: "'You have saved our lives,' they [say]. 'We have found favor with our lord and will be Pharaoh's slaves'" (vv. 16-19,25). This sets the stage for the opening of the Exodus narrative. Slavery may appear to be the only hope of survival, but it quickly becomes their greatest challenge.

The people of Israel are settled in the land of Goshen. Jacob's family prospers there, and Egypt begins to function as a backdrop for this segment of the story of redemption in the Old Testament. Sadly, the place that saves Israel now enslaves them later. But in the exodus God will deliver the Hebrews from Egypt and from slavery.

A Promise of Land (47:27-31)

As Israel settles in Egypt, there are glimpses of God's promises coming to fruition. The descendants of Abraham, for instance, have a new place in Goshen, even if it is not the land of promise. In it they continue to grow as a new people as they become "fruitful and very numerous" (v. 27).

We have seen references throughout Genesis to the concept to be fruitful and multiply. So far, those have come in the form of promises and directives. Now, however, we see the firstfruits of this command actually becoming a reality. After living in Egypt for "17 years," Jacob knows that his death is approaching (v. 28). Accepting this, he exacts a promise from Joseph to be buried in the family burial plot belonging to Abraham (v. 30; cf. 23:17-20; 25:9-10; 50:5,13). Jacob longs to be returned to the land promised to his fathers. Thus, the author of Hebrews alludes to this moment to note that, even in death, Jacob was walking by faith (Heb 11:21). In this, Jacob is anticipating the next movement in God's redemptive story. His desire is to be buried in the land, even if his family does not yet possess it, because Jacob is trusting that God will fulfill the promise to his descendants. Jacob's pilgrimage has taught him that God is capable of keeping his covenant. Moreover, in urging this promise he exacts from Joseph specifically, Jacob looks forward to the fulfillment of all of the promises God made to Abraham. Jacob anticipates the one greater than Joseph, the one who will bring his pilgrimage to an end and lead him to a better place than a tomb. Jesus welcomes his faith-filled people to a heavenly one, a city prepared for them by God (Heb 11:16).

Throughout Genesis 45–47, in fact, Joseph serves as an anticipation of the Messiah, who would emerge from Israel's lineage. God sends Joseph ahead of Israel to preserve a remnant and bring deliverance (45:5-7). Just as Joseph went before his family, Jesus promises to do the same for his people (John 14:1-3). Just as Joseph provides food for his hungry brothers, Jesus's death and resurrection provide spiritual salvation and nourishment for the spiritually impoverished. Joseph is presented as the beloved son of his father. Though he is rejected by his brothers and sold into slavery, he is eventually exalted to the right hand of Pharaoh. In a similar way, Jesus is God's beloved Son who is rejected by the sons of Israel who conspire to kill him. Jesus becomes as lowly as a slave before being exalted to the right hand of God (Phil 2:6-11). Just as God worked things out for good through the suffering of Joseph, God worked through the suffering endured by Christ on the cross to prepare a way of deliverance for us (Acts 2:23-24).

Reflect and Discuss

1. How does Joseph's ability to identify the redemptive purposes of God reorient his perspective on his life and direct his actions toward his brothers?

2. Throughout Scripture, God is continuously refining and preserving a remnant for himself. The work culminates in the person of Jesus

and his bride, the church. What does this reveal about the faithfulness of God?

3. Why is God's sovereignty over the life of Joseph a comfort for the believer?

4. Joseph's forgiveness of his brothers is one of the strongest examples of reconciliation in the Old Testament. What lessons can you draw from it regarding how to reconcile with those who have harmed you?

5. Joseph's forgiveness of his brothers is total and complete. He not only embraces them but gives them gifts. What is the effect of this total forgiveness on them? How would you respond to such radical forgiveness?

6. Jacob, like the other patriarchs, worships in response to God's faithfulness and promises. What promises of God cause you to break out in joyful worship?

7. God's presence is a continual theme in Genesis. He walks in the garden of Eden and comes down at Babylon. He closes Noah's family in the ark and visits with Abraham. In the events described in this section, he goes down to Egypt with Jacob. The prophets speak of how he will eventually put on flesh and be born in the town of Bethlehem. How does God's presence provide comfort? Why should awareness of it provide strength?

8. The family of Jacob is filled with murderers, adulterers, and deceivers. However, God's grace covers them because of his promise to Abraham. How does the promise made through Jesus cover believers even in the midst of their sin? How can God use sinful people?

9. Judah is sent ahead of the family to meet with Joseph and prepare for their family's arrival. In what ways have you seen Jesus, the ultimate descendant of Judah, preparing the way for you?

10. What steps can you take to help ensure you keep walking by faith the way Jacob did, all the way up to your own death? In what ways does your longing for a homeland and better country guide your pilgrimage here on earth?

Blessings, Deaths, and a Coffin

GENESIS 48–50

Main Idea: The promises of God guide the final earthly days of Jacob and Joseph. When Jacob blesses his sons, it sets the stage for the next segment of the storyline of Scripture. Although Genesis ends without the covenant fully realized, it concludes with the hope that God remains faithful to accomplish his promises.

I. **Israel Blesses His Descendants (48:1–49:28).**
   A. Jacob blesses Joseph's sons (48:1-22).
   B. Jacob blesses his sons (49:1-28).
II. **Israel and Joseph Plan for Death (49:29–50:26).**
   A. Jacob's instructions and death (49:29–50:14)
   B. Joseph's kindness and mercy (50:15-21)
   C. Joseph's instructions and death (50:22-26)

The final chapters of Genesis draw the book to an end with the promises of God remaining unfulfilled. These chapters continue, instead, the theme of longing and hopeful expectation. True, at the conclusion of Genesis, the children of Israel are still in the land of Egypt, and the patriarchs are all dead. Nevertheless, the promise remains as strong as ever: God will bring his people to the promised land (46:4; 50:25) and fulfill his covenant with Abraham. Jacob and Joseph know that God is faithful to keep his promises, even if they are unable to see them. Thus, this part of Genesis helps show that faith consists of hopeful expectation even when God's promises are long in coming to fulfillment.

In these final chapters, the preeminence of Judah is once again highlighted. It is seen specifically in the blessing Jacob bestows on his sons before his death. Reuben forfeited the birthright of the firstborn because of his sin, and the "birthright was given to the sons of Joseph" (1 Chr 5:1). That is why Jacob blesses Joseph's sons before he blesses his own. Nevertheless, neither Reuben nor Joseph's sons receive the place of preeminence and authority in the blessing. That blessing goes to Judah who "became strong among his brothers" (1 Chr 5:2). Judah's line, in fact, will culminate in the coming of the Lion from the tribe of Judah, Jesus, who will wield the royal scepter of the kingdom of God forever (Gen 49:9-10). The blessing Jacob bestows to Judah may not be fully understood, either by Judah or by the other brothers. It becomes clear later, however, in the person of Jesus. Jacob speaks prophetically of the way God is advancing the story of redemption. The promise to Abraham has come down to the twelve sons of Jacob. Now that promise will focus on the line of Judah, from whom rulers will come. It will give rise to the line of David before arriving in Jesus, who is the ultimate son of each of these four men (Matt 1:1).

The final chapters of Genesis are the springboard into the next major phase of redemptive history: the exodus. But the conclusion of this narrative is not merely a bridge. These chapters are intended to teach us that the Christian life is meant to be lived in light of the promises of God. Jacob and Joseph, after all, make plans based on the promises of God all the way up to their deaths. They cling to them even as they die. The Christian should do the same. God promises to conform believers into the image of Christ and give us eternal life (Rom 8:29). Just as each of the patriarchs were part of a larger story, the life of every Christian is a part of the larger story of redemption, too.

Israel Blesses His Descendants
GENESIS 48:1–49:28

As the first book penned by Moses nears its close, Jacob (also called Israel) blesses Joseph's sons and then his own. As he does so, Jacob indicates that the line of Judah will be the line through which the promised seed will come. This prophecy of the coming descendant will find its fulfillment in the person of Jesus Christ as the ultimate seed of promise.

Jacob Blesses Joseph's Sons (48:1-22)

In passing on blessings to his children, Jacob performs his final act as head of the family. He follows the pattern of his father, Isaac, who at the end of his life blessed his sons (27:27-29,39-40).

When Joseph comes to see Jacob with his own sons Manasseh and Ephraim in tow, Joseph seems not to expect the blessing that Jacob will give to his boys. But after Jacob recounts the promise made to him at

Bethel by God (28:13-15)—the promise of a *new people* arising from him and living out a *new purpose* in a *new place*—he announces that he is adopting Joseph's sons as his own (48:5). In the same verse, Jacob says, "Ephraim and Manasseh belong to me just as Reuben and Simeon do." The latter are Jacob's eldest sons, and what is said in this passage confirms that the firstborn's "birthright was given to the *sons* of Joseph" (1 Chr 5:1; emphasis added). This means Joseph's first two offspring are promised an inheritance with the rest of Jacob's sons (that is, with their uncles). This is significant because each of Jacob's sons, biological and adopted, will receive a portion of the promised land and be counted as leader of a distinct tribe in the later history of the Israelite nation (Josh 14:1-5). Though Joseph is ruler of Egypt, the promises of God are to come through Israel. Jacob makes it so that Ephraim and Manasseh (and their descendants) will not be regarded as Egyptians but as Israelites having full status.

As Jacob extends his hands to bless Ephraim and Manasseh, he continues a trend found throughout Genesis of subverting the tradition of preeminence according to birth order. Rather than bless Manasseh, the firstborn, and then Ephraim, Jacob moves to do the opposite. At first, Joseph believes this is a mistake caused by his poor eyesight (49:10). But when he attempts to correct his father, Jacob makes clear that he has made no mistake. Jacob acknowledges that Manasseh too will become "great" and the head of a "tribe," but the second son will receive the greater blessing (v. 19). This move underscores the validity of Judah, the fourth-born son of Jacob, being the one chosen by God to carry forward the messianic line. It is a reminder that the grace of God, not the timing of one's birth, is the conduit through which blessing comes.

The chapter ends with Jacob's anticipation of the return to the land of promise (v. 21). Old as he is, he fondly remembers and honors the promise God gave to him at Bethel so many years prior. The faithfulness of God gives Jacob hope as he enters the final days of his life. His expressed longing for Canaan establishes the theme of the last few chapters of the book. Repeatedly, the major figures will look toward the return of the people of Israel to that place (49:29; 50:24). While the family's return will not be fulfilled by the book's end, this builds anticipation for the next major moment in redemptive history: the exodus of the people from Egypt and their journey toward the land of promise.

Jacob Blesses His Sons (49:1-28)

Finally, Jacob gathers all of his biological sons together so that he may bless them as well. These are more than simple well-wishes. Here Jacob speaks under the inspiration of the Spirit as he prophesies of "what will happen . . . in the days to come" (v. 1). Jacob blesses "each one with a suitable blessing" specific to him (v. 28). In doing so, Jacob links the past actions of each of the sons to the futures of their descendants. He also speaks of an obvious preeminence for Joseph (through his own sons) and for Judah. Combined, their blessings make up nearly half of Jacob's speech. Ultimately, each blessing he speaks has to do with the later history of Israel as Israel's tribes reflect their namesakes.

As the "firstborn," Reuben might go into this meeting expecting to receive the greatest blessing, following traditions of the time (v. 3). But while Jacob agrees that Reuben is powerful and prominent by birth, he is disqualified from receiving the birthright because he "defiled his father's bed" (1 Chr 5:1). Jacob's final words to this son show he never forgot Reuben's actions with Bilhah, in which he rebelled against the authority of his father (Gen 35:21-22). Because Reuben attempted to usurp Jacob's authority, the position of preeminence is removed from him (49:3-4).

Levi and Simeon are the next to receive a prophetic blessing. The two are treated as a pair perhaps because of their actions together in Shechem (34:25-28). Jacob describes them as violent and wrathful. Because of these tendencies, they will be dispersed throughout the tribes (49:7). This promise will come to fruition when the tribes settle in the land of Canaan. The tribe of Levi will receive no specific area of land and will instead be dispersed throughout the tribes as priests (Num 18:20; Deut 18:1-8). The tribe of Simeon will receive land within the territory of Judah (Josh 19:1-9).

The blessings involving several of the brothers are less extensive. In Genesis 49:13 Zebulun is told that his descendants will dwell by the sea, and there is evidence that the coastal trading routes passed through his land even though it did not extend physically to the sea (Josh 19:10-16). Alternatively, Jacob may have prophetically referred to the tribal division mentioned in Ezekiel 48:26. In Genesis 49:14-15 Issachar (and by extension, his descendants) is described as "strong." Nevertheless, his tribe will be forced to work for others in some capacity. Dan's prophecy, in verses 16 and 17, is a play on the sound of his name. In Hebrew

"Dan" is similar to the word for "judge" (cf. Gen 30:6). At the same time, Dan's descendants will be like "a viper beside the path" in terms of their often wicked actions (Judg 18). In Genesis 49:19 Gad's name, which sounds like the Hebrew word for "raiders," references his descendants' need for strength in battle because they will live on the east side of the Jordan River, leaving them susceptible to raiders since they are separate from the other tribes. In line with verse 20, Asher's descendants will occupy a fertile coastal plain and participate in prosperous trade routes contributing to their "royal delicacies." Like the doe Jacob mentions in verse 21, Naphtali's offspring will grow and flourish on the rich natural resources of upper Galilee. That the youngest brother, Benjamin, is described as a wolf that "tears his prey" in verse 27 indicates that aggressive warriors will come from the tribe (1 Chr 8:40; 12:2). Each of these blessings is meaningful, but none give preeminence or special status to a particular son.

The major sections of Jacob's blessing occur in Genesis 49:8-12 (with regard to Judah) and 49:22-26 (regarding Joseph). These two men, and by extension the tribes descending from them, receive special distinction. Through Joseph come the tribes of Manasseh and Ephraim who, in later sections of Scripture, will be the preeminent tribe in the northern kingdom of Israel. Conversely, from the tribe of Judah will come the Davidic dynasty and the rulers of the southern kingdom. Jacob's blessings for both Judah and Joseph indicate their respective lines will hold special significance in the future.

Even within these distinctions, however, Judah is set apart as the most esteemed among Jacob's offspring because he will carry forward the line of the Messiah. Judah is the fourth son born to Jacob. There is no reason, then, that he should receive any mark of distinction. He was not born first—Reuben was. Nor was Judah his father's favorite son—Joseph was. Nor was Judah the one to receive the birthright of the firstborn—Joseph's sons were (1 Chr 5:1). But the Spirit leads Jacob to imply that Judah is the one through whom the seed promised to Abraham will come.

Four images used by Jacob in the blessing he gives to Judah recur throughout Scripture. The first image is that of the *warrior*, found in the description of Judah as "a young lion" (v. 9). A lion cub appears to be weak and powerless. Yet the cub soon grows and becomes a fierce and powerful predator. In the same way, Jacob is saying the descendants of Judah will appear weak and powerless, though in the fullness of time they will give rise to a fierce and powerful figure. The apostle John will use a similar image in speaking of that same figure, but he starts with the image of "a lamb" to describe the one worthy to open the scroll in his vision (Rev 5:6-10). This slain lamb, which is even more powerless than a lion cub, is nevertheless also "the Lion from the tribe of Judah" (Rev 5:5). Jacob's promise to Judah is a promise that his descendant will tear apart his enemies. Long past Judah's lifetime, the renegade prophet Balaam confirms the messianic nature of Jacob's blessing. When Balaam prophesies about the coming Messiah, he describes this coming royal figure by combining this description of the lion in Genesis 49:9 with the calling of Abraham in Genesis 12:3 (Num 24:9).

Judah's blessing will come through battle. This is proven in part in the life of another famous offspring of Judah, David. Led by the Spirit of God, he slays "his tens of thousands" (1 Sam 18:7). David as the warrior king, in fact, is a picture of the ultimate mighty warrior who will come from the tribe of Judah and destroy the enemies of God: the returning Jesus Christ.

The second image to note in Genesis 49:8-12 is that of *ruler*. This idea will be of great importance to Judah's tribe. Verse 10 describes how the "scepter will not depart from Judah . . . until he whose right it is comes and the obedience of the peoples [belong] to him." The ultimate ruler to come from Judah will have authority to rule all nations. Isaiah speaks prophetically of the messianic servant in this way: "I have put my Spirit on him; he will bring justice to the nations" (Isa 42:1). This widespread rulership is previewed not long after the birth of the infant Jesus when the child is greeted by wise men with gifts of "gold, frankincense, and myrrh" (Matt 2:11). These gifts signify his death, but they also signify his rule and authority. They are a foretaste of the "tribute" that is due him (Gen 49:10 ESV) since this descendant of Judah has unmatched authority. Paul confirms that Jesus comes as this messianic ruler to usher in the kingdom of God (1 Cor 15:24-27).

The third image of note in Genesis 49:9-12 is seen in the *prosperity* that comes through this key descendant of Judah's line. Jacob says that the descendant ties "the colt of his donkey to the choice vine" (v. 11). This phrase points toward the abundance that comes from this individual. For the individual who is so wealthy that he has many vines, there is no problem if the donkey consumes the grapes from the "choice vine." This offspring of Judah, then, will have possessions in abundance. Nevertheless, Jesus will come into the world as the poor son of a carpenter. He thus experiences no abundance or prosperity from a worldly standpoint. Indeed, he has no "majesty that we should look at him" (Isa 53:2). So, how is this part of the prophecy true?

To begin with, even when Jesus takes on the humble form of humanity, he is still the Son of the living God who possesses "the cattle on a thousand hills" (Ps 50:10). The incarnation does not rob him of this abundance so much as it puts the experience of it on hold and adds to it something even better. How? The new abundance in view is spiritual in nature and is secured through his death and resurrection. While in his earthly lifetime, Jesus owns no vineyard, he becomes the true "vine" (John 15:5). Though he possesses no colt, he nevertheless rides into Jerusalem on one humbly loaned to him in the triumphal entry (Matt 21:1-11; cf. Zech 9:9). Now, he is seated at the right hand of the Father in the place of abundance (Acts 2:33). And like a victor who disburses the plunder of the conquest to his people, Christ the warrior King pours out the victory gift of the Spirit upon the church (Eph 4:7-12).

The final important image in Genesis 49:8-12 involves the *wine-soaked garments* of the descendant: "He washes his clothes in wine and his robes in the blood of grapes" (v. 11). While Judah can merely guess at the true meaning of Jacob's words here, Judah's ultimate descendant—the One of whom Jacob speaks—will both know and fulfill this prophecy. Later, the prophets anticipate the "crimson-stained garments" of the coming conqueror who accomplishes victory through his wrath-filled judgment that is even now yet to come (Isa 63:1-6). In the first miracle of Jesus, however, he turns water into "wine" (John 2:1-12). During the Last Supper, Jesus explains that the wine represents the new "covenant" in his "blood" (Matt 26:28). In the garden of Gethsemane, his sweat is "like drops of blood" (Luke 22:44). Before his death, Jesus is offered wine to drink (Mark 15:23,36). On the cross, his side is pierced and his garments are soaked in his blood, like the "blood of grapes" (cf. John 19:34). The rule exercised by Judah's offspring is a rule that comes through blood. In spite of all this, as alluded to above, the prophetic picture for Judah also becomes a reality through the return of Jesus and events linked to it. At his return, for instance, Jesus will subdue his enemies while wearing a "robe dipped in blood" (Rev 19:13). Jesus will be the promised warrior King who comes to "trample the winepress of the fierce anger of God" (Rev 19:15). Christ the warrior King will both strike down the enemies of God and extend forgiveness to his people through his own shed blood. In his death and in his return, blood is closely connected to the victory of the Messiah that fulfills the blessing of Judah.

Because of Jacob's blessing, the nation of Israel will be looking for the descendant of Judah who will exercise this rule until the promise is fulfilled. And when that one comes who is destined to fulfill the promise, Judah's ultimate offspring will be preeminent over all of creation. As Paul says of that seed, he is the "image of the invisible God, the firstborn over all creation" and "the firstborn from the dead, so that he might come to have first place in everything" (Col 1:15,18). The firstborn of creation—the preeminent one in the whole universe—is Jesus, the second and better Adam. Jesus is the one through whom all the promises find their "Yes" (2 Cor 1:20). The Messiah will come as the True Israel and the Lion of the tribe of Judah, too.

The other major blessing from Jacob goes to Joseph. Before assessing the blessing that goes directly to him, it is noteworthy to observe the nexus between Joseph and the blessing of Judah. At the start of Judah's blessing, Jacob uses familiar language from the Joseph narrative: "[Y]our father's sons will bow down to you" (v. 8). Remember, after Joseph dreams of his family bowing down to him (37:5-11), the text notes them fulfilling it as they bow before Joseph in Egypt (42:4; 43:26,28). When the blessing of Judah declares that people will bow down, it is saying that the coming Messiah from the line of Judah will one day be exalted like Joseph.

The blessing to Joseph mirrors the life of Joseph. In both abundance (49:22) and in danger (v. 23), God will preserve Joseph's offspring just as he sustained Joseph himself.

Jacob's descriptions of the Lord in verse 24 recur throughout the Old Testament and echo forward to the coming Messiah. When Jacob describes God as the "Mighty One of Jacob" (cf. Ps 132:2,5; Isa 1:4; 49:26), it points forward to Mary's praise of her pregnancy as she celebrates God as the "Mighty One" (Luke 1:49). When Jacob describes God as the "Shepherd" (cf. Gen 48:15; Ps 23:1), it points forward to the way Jesus depicts himself as "the good shepherd [who] lays down his life for the sheep" (John 10:11). When Jacob describes God as "the Rock of Israel" (cf. Ps 118:22; Isa 28:16), it points ahead to Jesus—"the stone that the builders rejected" who becomes the "cornerstone" (1 Pet 2:6-8). The blessings that come from Jacob to his sons anticipate the blessings that will come through the True Israel.

Israel and Joseph Plan for Death

GENESIS 49:29–50:26

After blessing his sons, Jacob prepares them for his departure. Joseph will do the same in the last section of Genesis. Both of these men, though dying, are looking toward the future. Their actions are the result of their faith that God will bring about what he has promised.

Jacob's Instructions and Death (49:29–50:14)

The book of Genesis will close with the people of Israel still living in Egypt, not the land of promise. However, though they are absent from the land, Jacob and Joseph clearly anticipate Israel's return to Canaan. After blessing his sons, Jacob insists that he be buried in the cave in "the field Abraham purchased from Ephron the Hethite as burial property" (49:30). Jacob emphasizes that his family owns this cave, which is within the land of promise. He does not want to be buried in Egypt but within the boundaries of what God promised to his grandfather, Abraham, and father, Isaac. As Jacob draws his last breath (v. 33), then, he dies in faith, actively awaiting the fulfillment of the promise.

In chapter 50, the sons of Jacob do as their father commanded them. Joseph has Jacob's body "embalmed," and the family takes it back to Canaan (v. 2). Mention of the preparation process used is significant because the Egyptians believed that embalming was a way to conquer death. Their techniques were precise and required great skill. They were so sure of its power that their tombs were filled with all the deceased person would need to live. The Hebrews, though, are not trusting in the science of the Egyptians to conquer death. Jacob and his family are looking to the life that comes from the promise. Jacob lived in Egypt, but he was not an Egyptian. Jacob was a Hebrew, a son of Abraham. Though they embalm Israel, they cannot embalm the promises made to Israel—those outlast him until they are fulfilled in Christ.

Just as Jesus's death and burial are not the end of the story of salvation, Jacob's end is not the end for him or his family at all (cp. Matt 8:11). It simply leads to the next movement in the greater story of redemption. Imagine the sight of the sons traveling toward Canaan to bury their father in a grand procession (Gen 50:7-11). While this is not the triumphant entry into the land of Canaan that awaits the people group descended from Jacob, it does foreshadow national Israel's exit out of Egypt. While here they are in mourning, a time is coming when they will leave celebrating.

At the death of Jacob, the Egyptians "lamented and wept loudly" (50:10). Their reaction stands in contrast to the actions of the Egyptians in the next book. Moses, the former prince of Egypt and the human author of this book, knows that the Egyptians' care and protection of the Hebrews will ultimately give way to the domination and enslavement of the Hebrew people by a later Pharaoh. Thus, when God does send Israel out of Egypt in the exodus, reversals of this scene will be apparent. Pharaoh will not send them but attempt to stop them. The leaders of Egypt will not follow them to support them but to enslave them all over again (Exod 14:5-9). The horses and chariots of Egypt won't go out in an impressive procession but will race out and disappear under the surface of the Red Sea (Exod 14:28). But another reversal is yet to come when Jesus is called out of Egypt to lead a new exodus (Matt 2:15).

Joseph's Kindness and Mercy (50:15-21)

Perhaps because they fear Joseph's kindness to them thus far has really been about honoring their father Jacob, the death of Jacob causes Joseph's brothers to worry that they will now suffer punishment for the abuse they once heaped on their now powerful younger brother. Since Joseph is one of the highest rulers in Egypt, his brothers fear for their lives. They seek to protect themselves by telling Joseph that Jacob wished for him to "forgive" them (vv. 16-17). Interestingly, the text does not indicate whether this is true or not. Regardless, lasting forgiveness is necessary because Joseph cannot get even with his brothers without endangering the promises made to his family. The hope of redemption in the promise to Abraham comes through forgiveness.

Forgiveness, in fact, is exactly what Joseph offers his brothers. Ultimately, he is able to offer forgiveness because he sees the situation from an eternal perspective, not an earthly one. This is why he asks, "Am I in the place of God?" (v. 19). The forgiveness Joseph extends does not make light of his brothers' actions or make them less evil. In fact, he calls them that. Moreover, Joseph certainly isn't telling the men they were justified in their actions because it led to their salvation through his current position. Instead, he reminds them that they "planned evil" against him. He does not act as if everything is now okay. Forgiveness requires that we identify evil for what it is. But it doesn't stop there.

Joseph then puts the evil into the larger context of God's plan: "You planned evil against me; God planned it for good to bring about the present result—the survival of many people" (v. 20). Indeed, God can use even wickedness to bring about his providential purposes, as the apostle Paul declares in his letter to the Romans (Rom 8:28). He doesn't tell his readers to grin and bear it. Paul tells them to recognize that the evil and wicked parts of the story do not fall outside of the plan of God. God will ultimately use *every* circumstance to accomplish his plans and help conform his people into the image of Christ. Though born before the time of the cross, Joseph sees the bigger picture of redemption and forgives his brothers in light of his similar, if less developed, understanding.

But Joseph does more than forgive his brothers; he comforts them and is kind to them, too. He promises to "take care of" them and their "children" (Gen 50:21). So, in spite of what they did to him in the past, he will protect them. Thus Joseph, the one who they feared would do them harm, is the one who will ensure their safety. Beyond forgiveness, he is gracious and gives them far more than they deserve. They never dreamed the one they mistreated would rise to be the second most powerful person in Egypt, much less their personal protector.

Joseph's Instructions and Death (50:22-26)

The book of Genesis ends with a somber scene. It does not end with the children of Israel making their way back to the land of promise but with Joseph's instructions concerning his body and bones. The Egyptian rulers believed they were gods and the children of gods. They believed they were above death. Joseph could have easily thought of himself as a master of death too, but clearly he does not.Though he has long ruled over Egypt by this point and successfully prevented the starvation of masses, Joseph knows he cannot stop death. In fact, his approaching passing brings to mind God's promise to Adam at the start of the book: "On the day that you eat from [the tree of knowledge of good and evil], you will certainly die" (2:17). As we've seen happen since he and his wife consumed the forbidden fruit, death has come calling for every person. (Well, except for Enoch, according to 5:24.) Joseph's power is no match for the curse. And Joseph recognizes that he will die.

Like his father, Joseph confronts this stark reality by making plans that honor God's promises and remain expectant of better things to come. He makes his family promise that they will take his bones with them when God takes them back to Canaan (50:24-25). These are not just funeral plans. According to the writer of Hebrews, this is an act of faith: "By faith Joseph, as he was nearing the end of his life, mentioned the exodus of the Israelites and gave instructions concerning his bones" (Heb 11:22; cf. Gen 50:24). Even on his deathbed, Joseph trusts that God is going to bring his people back to the land he promised to Abraham, Isaac, and Jacob. He is entrusting the transport of his remains to his brothers, and by extension the people of Israel, because he believes God is going to keep his promises. Thus like his father, Joseph dies in faith, awaiting the promise.

Genesis ends not with fulfillment but with waiting. Down to the death of the last key character mentioned within the book of Genesis, God's people are seen waiting. From Adam and Eve to Noah, from Abraham and Sarah to Isaac, from Jacob to Joseph, people die looking for the fulfillment of God's promises. But there is a reason Genesis does not end with the people in the land and a king on a throne. The author of Hebrews explains things this way:

> The [fallen] world was not worthy of them. . . . All these were approved through their faith, but they did not receive what was promised, since God had provided something better for us, so that they would not be made perfect without us. (Heb 11:38-40)

Thus, the faith of Joseph that expects his bones to enter the promised land is the same faith that looks forward to Jesus Christ through whom all the promises of the kingdom ultimately come.

Perhaps the most difficult reality for them and for us is to understand that the promises come through death. Jesus is the means through whom all the promises come. But in order for all of God's plan to happen, the True Israel, the Lion of Judah, a man whose life mirrors Joseph's in many ways, would have to die (John 12:23-24). After all, John the Baptist didn't understand this, nor did the apostles for a long time. But Jesus knew that fully receiving the promises made to Abraham requires the undoing of the curse of Adam and keeping the Genesis 3:15 promise to the serpent. And all of that would involve death: Christ's own (Gal 3:13-14). Nevertheless, just as the Spirit hovered over the waters at the beginning of creation, the Spirit of holiness would raise Jesus from the dead (Rom 1:4). And through his death and resurrection, Jesus would begin to undo the curse and usher in the promises. The end of the story, described in Revelation 21 and 22, in fact, looks much like the beginning. Jesus of Nazareth—the second Adam, the son of Abraham, the True Israel—stands in the presence of his people in a restored universe so that God will once again say that his creation is "very good" indeed (Gen 1:31). And it results in the blessing of all the nations of the world.

Without Genesis 1, we humans cannot understand who we are. Without Genesis 3, we cannot understand our plight. And without the rest of Genesis, we will fail to understand God's plan to restore all things through Christ. The present world is broken and full of evil, pain, and suffering. But just like the early people of Israel, we of the True Israel await a better future—one defined by promises God made to Abraham so many years ago. The patriarchs and matriarchs died in faith, looking and longing to see the promise fulfilled. They did not receive it. But in Christ, we have received it. Jesus is the promised seed, and through his death he will make all things new. The end looks like the beginning: the rule of a man, Jesus of Nazareth—the second Adam, the son of Abraham, the True Israel—standing in the presence of his people in a restored universe so that God will once again say that his creation is "very good indeed" (1:31).

Reflect and Discuss

1. How does the adoption of Ephraim and Manasseh impact the family of Jacob? What does the fact that these two boys of Egypt are now Hebrews suggest about identity and the promise?

2. The blessing of Ephraim over Manasseh continues the trend of God subverting human wisdom. What does this tell us about how God accomplishes his purposes?

3. Jacob's final moments anticipate his family's return to Canaan. What does the faith of Jacob in these last days reveal about the promises of God and his trust in God's faithfulness? Why should Christians continually meditate on God's promises, even at the end of their lives?

4. The tribes that come from these patriarchs are shown to be similar to their originators in the blessing Jacob gives. They share in the strengths and faults of their heads. How should the fact that Christ is the head of the church shape our identity? In what ways are we becoming more like Christ?

5. Judah would have been no one's expected choice for distinction. He is not the eldest or the favorite. However, through him comes the lineage of the Messiah. Why do you think God works through those who are unexpected (and unworthy) to accomplish his purposes?

6. Think about the four images Jacob uses to bless Judah. Which of these images do you find most helpful? How do they help you understand Jesus more clearly?

7. Jacob's death is not the end of the story of Israel. Why is Jesus's death not the end of the story for believers? What does the death of Jacob reveal about the future and hope that come from the promise made to Abraham?

8. Joseph's brothers are afraid of Joseph after Jacob dies. What does Joseph's reaction reveal about the true nature of forgiveness? What might it suggest about God's forgiveness?

9. Joseph's forgiveness of his brothers rests on the recognition that they intended evil but God used it for good. He does not ignore their malice and sin. Why must forgiveness always reckon with the reality of the hurt? How does Joseph give us a model for embracing the providence of God in our lives, even when things are hard?

10. Genesis ends with the promises unfulfilled. Even now, in fact, we are waiting for the ultimate consummation of these promises, which will occur at the return of Christ. What can we do to remain faithful and cling to the promises in the meantime?

CONCLUSION

The story of Genesis is part of the story of us all. All of us can relate to the sinful rebellion of Adam and Eve. All of us believers can relate to Abraham, who is sometimes faithful and sometimes cowardly. We also recognize in ourselves the tendencies of Jacob the trickster, who wrestles with God. However, we are not the central figure in the story. Neither are the patriarchs or the tribes of Israel. Abraham, Sarah, Isaac, Ishmael, Jacob, Esau, and all the rest are but supporting figures. The central figure in the story of redemption is Jesus Christ.

The story of Genesis may be our story in some ways, but the book is not about us. It is about the faithfulness of God to bring about his promised seed. As we read the stories of these flawed individuals, we should not look for ourselves but Christ. While he is never mentioned in the text, his earthly coming and role in human history are foreshadowed at many points. Noah, for instance, is a preserver of life and thus a type of Christ. Abraham trusts in God and is thus a type of Christ. Joseph brings salvation to his family and people and is thus a type of Christ. But though Christ is anticipated in Genesis and Psalms and Isaiah, we behold his presence in Luke and Romans and Revelation. He has come. And he will come again! Yes, as sure as God's Old Testament people eventually return to Canaan, Christ will return. And when he does, all will be made right and new.

Considering our spiritual ancestors should leave us feeling proud of their successes but also humbled by their glaring failures. We believers in Jesus are the descendants of these cowards, tricksters, and adulterers. Realizing that is enough to bow any head. But we are also coheirs with Jesus. That is enough to lift any head. We bow before the cross and lift our eyes to the Author of our faith.

Genesis is the story of our beginning. As it ends, the people of Israel are awaiting the fulfillment of the promises of God. We also are awaiting the fulfillment of the promises. We are sojourners and aliens in a world that is not our own. However, we have the promises of Jacob and Joseph to give us hope. They knew God is faithful to accomplish his will. They knew God would return them to Canaan. We also know God will be faithful to his people. Christ will return, and all will be made right and new.

We look to the past to understand the present and prepare for the future. The God who walked with Adam and Eve before the fall, saved Noah and his family, and called out to Abraham is the same God who raised Jesus from the dead and established his church. All of this was done for his glory and our good. So let us await his promises with the faith of Abraham, Jacob, and Joseph. We cannot see their fulfillment yet, but we know the character of the God in whose promises we are trusting. God is faithful to his promises even when we are unfaithful. As the twists throughout Genesis illustrate, he is capable of accomplishing what he has planned, despite our sinfulness and imperfect obedience.

The story of Genesis is the story of Christ. These may be our spiritual ancestors, but we are not constrained by heredity. We modern Christ followers are being made into the image of the one for whom those in the Old Testament era were looking. They looked for a Messiah. We are indwelt by his Spirit. This is the story of a God who enters history and works through the lives of people for the fulfillment of his promises. May we never forget that our Elder Brother is the King who crushes the head of the serpent. By the grace of God and the obedience of Christ, we are invited into a future where all the promises are fulfilled and the rule of the promised seed is never challenged.

WORKS CONSULTED

Alter, Robert. *Genesis.* New York: W. W. Norton, 1997.

Augustine. *Confessions.* Translated by Carolyn Hammond. Cambridge, MA: Harvard University Press, 2014.

Beale, G. K. *The Temple and the Church's Mission: A Biblical Theology of the Dwelling Place of God.* Edited by D. A. Carson. New Studies in Biblical Theology. Downer Groves, IL: IVP Academic, 2014.

————, and D. A. Carson, eds. *Commentary on the New Testament Use of the Old Testament.* Grand Rapids, MI: Baker Academic, 2007.

Brueggemann, Walter. *Genesis.* Interpretation: A Bible Commentary for Teaching and Preaching. Louisville, KY: Westminster John Knox, 2010.

Currid, John D. *Genesis: Chapters 1–25.* Welwyn Garden City, UK: Evangelical Press, 2003.

————. *Genesis: Chapters 25–50.* Welwyn Garden City, UK: Evangelical Press, 2003.

Dempster, Stephen. *Dominion and Dynasty: A Theology of the Hebrew Bible.* New Studies in Biblical Theology. Downer Groves, IL: IVP Academic, 2013.

DeRouchie, Jason. "The Blessing-Commission, the Promised Offspring, and the Toledot Structure of Genesis." JETS 56, no. 2 (2013): 219–47.

Duguid, Ian. *Living in the Gap between Promise and Reality: The Gospel according to Abraham.* The Gospel according to the Old Testament. Phillipsburg, NJ: P&R Publishing, 1999.

————. *Living in the Grip of Relentless Grace: The Gospel in the Lives of Isaac and Jacob.* The Gospel according to the Old Testament. Phillipsburg, NJ: P&R Publishing, 2002.

————, and M. P. Harmon. *Living in the Light of Inextinguishable Hope: The Gospel according to Joseph.* The Gospel according to the Old Testament. Phillipsburg, NJ: P&R Publishing, 2013.

Gentry, Peter, and Stephen Wellum. *Kingdom through Covenant: A Biblical-Theological Understanding of the Covenants*. Wheaton, IL: Crossway, 2012.

Goldingay, John, and Bill T. Arnold. *Genesis*. Baker Commentary on the Old Testament: Pentateuch. Grand Rapids, MI: Baker Academic, 2020.

Greidanus, Sidney. *Preaching Christ from Genesis: Foundations for Expository Sermons*. Grand Rapids, MI: Eerdmans, 2007.

Hamilton, James M. *God's Glory in Salvation through Judgment: A Biblical Theology*. Wheaton, IL: Crossway, 2010.

Hamilton, Victor. *The Book of Genesis, Chapters 1–17*. New International Commentary on the Old Testament. Grand Rapids, MI: Eerdmans, 1990.

———. *The Book of Genesis, Chapters 18–50*. New International Commentary on the Old Testament. Grand Rapids, MI: Eerdmans, 1995.

Kass, Leon. *The Beginning of Wisdom: Reading Genesis*. New York: Simon and Schuster, 2003.

Keller, Timothy J. "The Girl Nobody Wanted: Genesis 29:15-35." Pages 53–72 in *Heralds of the King: Christ-Centered Sermons in the Tradition of Edmund P. Clowney*. Edited by Dennis E. Johnson. Wheaton, IL: Crossway, 2009, 70.

Lloyd-Jones, Martin. *The Gospel in Genesis: From Fig Leaves to Faith*. Wheaton, IL: Crossway, 2009.

Longman, Tremper, III. *Genesis*. The Story of God Bible Commentary. Grand Rapids, MI: Zondervan Academic, 2016.

———. *How to Read Genesis*. How to Read Series. Downer Groves, IL: IVP Academic, 2009.

Mathews, Kenneth. *Genesis 1–11*. New American Commentary 1A. Nashville, TN: B&H Publishing, 1996.

———. *Genesis 11:27–50:26*. New American Commentary 1B. Nashville, TN: B&H Publishing, 2005.

Rosner, Brian, D. A. Carson, Graeme Goldsworthy, and T. Desmond Alexander, eds. *New Dictionary of Biblical Theology: Exploring the Unity Diversity of Scripture*. Downer Groves, IL: IVP Academic, 2000.

Waltke, B. K., and C. J. Fredricks. *Genesis: A Commentary*. Grand Rapids, MI: Zondervan Academic, 2016.

SCRIPTURE INDEX